D1546889

The Desert Frontier of Arabia

AL-JAWF

Through the Ages

The Desert Frontier of Arabia

AL-JAWF
Through the Ages

Amīr ʻAbd al-Raḥmān bin Aḥmad al-Sudairī
Governor of al-Jawf Province, Saʻūdī Arabia, 1943-1990

Translated into English and revised and enlarged under the supervision
of the ʻAbd al-Raḥmān al-Sudairī Foundation

STACEY INTERNATIONAL
LONDON

The Desert Frontier of Arabia: al-Jawf Through the Ages by Amīr ʻAbd al-Raḥmān bin Aḥmad al-Sudairī

Published by Stacey International, 128 Kensington Church Street, London W8 4BH

British Library Cataloguing-in-Publication Data
A catalogue record for this book is available from the British Library

ISBN 0 905743 75 X (Paperback edition)
ISBN 0 905743 86 5 (Cased edition)

Set in 11/13 Bembo by SX Composing Ltd, Rayleigh, Essex

Printed and bound by Tien Wah Press, Singapore

CONTENTS

PART SIX
WESTERN TRAVELLERS TO AL-JAWF REGION

PART SEVEN
THE PEOPLE OF AL-JAWF PROVINCE

APPENDICES

Preface to the English Edition

In the course of developing the special collection of Dār al-Jawf lil-'Ulūm, the public library established by the 'Abd al-Raḥmān al-Sudairī Foundation at Sakākā, al-Jawf, the Foundation concluded that this collection, which is intended to cover comprehensively al-Jawf and northern Arabia, would be enhanced and made more useful and accessible if items that were only available in a foreign language were translated. The Foundation, therefore, started working on a programme of translations. Given that the main users of the Library are Arabic speaking, the focus of the programme was translations into the Arabic language. The Foundation, however, decided for a number of reasons to make an exception to this rule and undertake the translation of this work from Arabic to English as its first project.

The original Arabic edition of this book, published jointly by the 'Abd al-Raḥmān al-Sudairī Foundation and Macmillan Publishers Limited, appeared in 1985 under the title *al-Jawf: Wādi'l-Nafākh*. The idea and work on this Arabic edition were initiated by the author, the founder of the Foundation and former Governor of al-Jawf, in around 1963, the year in which he founded the original public library at Sakākā, which was the predecessor to the present Dār al-Jawf lil-'Ulūm and precursor to the Foundation. His objective was to prepare a comprehensive if not exhaustive reference work on the history of al-Jawf, and the final product became a corner-stone in the emerging special collection of Dār al-Jawf lil-'Ulūm. The reference quality of the book, its centrality in our special collection and the international growth of interest in the history and archaeology of al-Jawf made it imperative that we undertake this translation on a priority basis.

When this project was taken in hand, it was felt, firstly, that there was room for improvement in the text of the original Arabic edition and that some chapters required extensive rewriting (for at the time of the preparation of the Arabic edition some important sources for the history of the area could not be procured); secondly, that since we were going to bring out a translated version several years later, the chapter on the archaeology and archaeological monuments of al-Jawf was out of date due to the considerable amount of survey work which had been carried out in the meantime; and thirdly, that the chapter on recent development in al-Jawf needed to be updated. With the permission of the author it was decided that the present edition should allow for the necessary changes or additions to the original version. The major variations from the original are worth special notice. The chapter on recent development in al-Jawf, duly enlarged, now appears as an appendix. The chapter on archaeology and archaeological monuments of al-Jawf has been segmented, and each segment, after revision and enlargement, has been merged with the part of the book to which it relates or with which it has greater affinity. The contents of the book have been oriented towards a chronological order. The introductory chapter now includes notes on three important constituent geographical parts of al-Jawf – al-Jawba, al-Nafūd, and the Wādi'l-Sirḥān – as well as several extra additions. There are major additions in the chapters on the pre-Islamic history of al-Jawf. The chapters "The Coming of Islam to Dūmat al-Jandal" and "Dūmat al-Jandal in the Time of the First Caliph, Abū Bakr" have been redrafted and enlarged, relying mostly on primary sources. A new chapter on the history of al-Jawf during the mediaeval period (following the arbitration) has been added. The chapter on al-Jawf during the time of the first Sa'ūdī state has been enlarged. In the chapter on the Turkish occupation of al-Jawf, Charles M. Doughty's account of the episode as well as a critical analysis of the chronology of the events have been added. In the chapter on the Western travellers to al-Jawf, Lady Anne Blunt's account has been expanded, and the account of Baron Eduard Nolde, who visited al-Jawf in 1893, has been included. Lastly, in this edition the footnotes refer more frequently to the sources used and the bibliography has been revised and enlarged. The Arabic edition followed the pattern of giving, where useful, the Hijrī date first and then the date according to the Christian calendar. This pattern has been retained in the English edition, the Hijrī date now given in italics.

Many eminent scholars extended their cooperation, in large measure or small, in the improvement of this book or parts of it. I would specially like to mention Professor Dr A.R. al-Ansary, member of Majlis al-Shūrā (the Consultative Council) of the Kingdom of Sa'ūdī Arabia. Dr Ansary devoted a great amount of his time to go through the whole manuscript and gave immensely valuable suggestions about rearranging the contents and renaming some of the chapters or subchapters. In addition, he made an important contribution to the text of Part Two "The Prehistory of al-Jawf Region" and gave editorial comments on the whole manuscript. I would also like to mention Dr Geoffrey R.D. King, for his role in reviewing and commenting on a preliminary translation of the original text; Dr Sa'd al-Ṣuwayyān, for the final translation of the Arabic verses; Dr Khaleel I. al-Muaikel, for permitting us to use his doctoral dissertation on the archaeology and archaeological monuments of al-Jawf, and for his useful suggestions; Dr Sa'd al-Bāzi'ī and Dr Mus'ad al-Shamān, for extending significant help in the translation, respectively, of Arabic verses and Turkish documents; and Dr 'Abd al-Raḥmān al-Sharīf, for his efforts to identify some place names.

The people at the Foundation who are responsible for the completion of this enlarged English version and who deserve special mention and acknowledgement are many, but if one person had to be identified as being primarily responsible for completing this project, this would be Mushtāq Aḥmad, our librarian in charge of foreign languages. Aḥmad not only made valuable suggestions for changes and additions but also reworked a preliminary translation. Moreover, he systemized the romanization of Arabic names and words by using a standard transliteration scheme, expanded the bibliography, added footnotes, typed part of the manuscript, checked the galley proofs and attended to many other duties. We thank Aḥmad and admire his patience, perseverance and dedication.

Mushtāq Aḥmad, however, was not alone. ʻAlī al-Rāshid, the former Assistant Managing Director who oversaw the initiation of this project and continued to be involved with it until the end, was responsible for developing the strategy and framework for the work, and participated in reviewing and critiquing the final drafts. To Sālim al-Dhāhir, the present Assistant Managing Director, is due the credit for maintaining continuity and focus and for sorting out the many problems that arose. Nabīl al-Mongī M. Shabaka, the Head Librarian, collected from various quarters the data for the appendix on recent development in al-Jawf, checked the conversion of dates of the Muslim calendar to the Gregorian, verified the accuracy of the bibliographical entries, and helped in many ways, including translation of some passages; Manṣūr Yūsuf A. al-Shabūl assisted in resolving some of the problems in the translation and did much of the administrative work relating to the book; Eduardo Manuel typed part of the manuscript; Jun Raymundo and Ḥāmid al-Shaikh provided secretarial and adminstrative assistance; and Yāsir Muṣṭafā Jābir of the Jawf emirate office extended help and assistance in the translation work.

To those mentioned above and the many unnamed participants from within the Foundation and from without, including the many readers who sent us suggestions and criticisms after the publication of the original edition, we offer our gratitude and acknowledge our intellectual indebtedness. Each and every one of them has helped us complete a project that we hope will serve the cause of promoting knowledge in the best tradition of this Foundation.

I know I speak for every member of this Foundation when I say that we are only proud to be able to serve al-Jawf and pursue the goals of the Founder, who dedicated most of his life and much of his resources to public service and towards promoting progress in al-Jawf. It may be only illuminating, particularly to the foreign reader, to know that this man, who grew up in an isolated agrarian and bare-bone community in a small town in Najd and whose only formal education was at the *Kuttāb* (the traditional school for teaching the Qur'ān and basic reading and writing), was always at the forefront of every advance in this region – not merely accepting but typically advocating progress. There may be no evidence more telling of his recognition of the importance of education and learning and his passion for promoting it than the public library that he founded, especially when considering that there were no similar models in his immediate community to draw upon. The public library for women that he established was the first in Saʻūdī Arabia. And, to his credit, this initiative and drive were always offered under a sense of duty and with the humility of one who feels fortunate to have had the opportunity and means to be constructive. It has been his lifelong passion to see al-Jawf thrive and develop. We offer this not in the narrow sense of celebrating an individual, but in the more meaningful sense of highlighting a tradition of dedication to learning, public service and humility that is the heritage of this Foundation, and its guiding spirit. And at an even higher level, it may be only instructive for us here to reflect on the wisdom of a generation that embraced progress, accommodated change and managed prosperity with moderation, realism and a reasonable degree of tolerance, and in the process contributed to the emergence of a more peaceful and prosperous society.

Every book has its share of mistakes; I can only hope that this one does not have many. It is presented to the reader in the same spirit as was the Arabic edition: we do not claim that it is the last word on the history of al-Jawf, and we wish that it proves useful and opens the way for further research on an area where the spirit of history breathes all around.

Ziyād bin ʻAbd al-Raḥmān al-Sudairī
Managing Director
ʻAbd al-Raḥmān al-Sudairī Foundation

Preface to the Original Arabic Edition

In the Name of God, Most Gracious, Most Merciful

God blessed the children of Adam and let them inherit the earth, and they settled on it and started profiting from what God had given them of His bounties. Their progress sometimes waxed and sometimes waned during the ages, for such is the way of God with His creation. The man of today is the heir to the world of the man of yesterday, and at times he feels a yearning for a greater awareness of the world of yesterday. That is what inspired me to try to write this history of the Jawf region, the inhabitants of which – and I am one – have been expressing frequently their desire to know more about its past history, ancient as well as of recent times.

I have resided in this region for a period of forty-three years, living through its different stages in the march of events, adjusting to the demands of life in it, identifying completely with its society, and developing a great liking for its people. For me the compiling of its history has therefore been like the realization of a dream and the fulfilment of an obligation, and I deemed it to be an appropriate response to the questions of many about the history of the area, specially in the circumstances when there was no book available on the comprehensive history of the region, the only treatment of its history being in the form of a chapter or section in larger historical or other works or in the shape of brief articles or booklets.

The idea of starting work on this book has eluded me for many years, my vehement desire to see it materialize stimulating me to undertake it while my appreciation of the difficulties in collecting all the needed bits of information – on account of the non-availability of most of the required sources – deterring me from it. After a long period of hesitation, I determined to make a start when the circumstances became more favourable. I worked with a fine group including citizens from al-Jawf and residents working in this region, who participated in the various tasks towards the creation of a unified whole. We did our best to acquire the important source material from various Arab and Muslim countries as well as the Western world. The resulting history of al-Jawf is the product of what was available to us from information and research sources. This book, therefore, does not purport to present all or even half of what there is on the subject: it is the outcome of an effort to present an independent work on the history of al-Jawf. It follows that we wish to benefit fully from the opinions of the readers of this book and would welcome any information which throws light on what is obscure in it, or explains what is unduly brief, or complements what falls short, or corrects what needs to be corrected. This would enable us to eliminate the mistakes of the present edition when the publication of its revised edition is undertaken.

The title of this book means *al-Jawf, the Valley of Flatulence.* It is a reference to the well-known old nickname of the Jawf depression used by the bedouin of northern Arabia on account of the excessive hospitality of the people of al-Jawf and the extra care they take of their guest [by offering him the best food available and entreating him to keep on eating even when he wants to stop]. In view of the moving quality of this allusion to their tradition of generosity, there cannot be a more beautiful title for this book than this.

In conclusion, I wish to express my sincere thanks to all the people and institutions that contributed to the removal of obstacles faced by us in this endeavour, whatever the level or nature of their contribution. I want to thank particularly the staff and friends of the 'Abd al-Raḥmān al-Sudairī Foundation who have been directly involved in the preparation of this book. More prominent from among them are: Dr 'Ārif Mufaḍḍī al-Mis'ar, who devoted a great amount of his time and actively participated in the preparation of this book; Ṣāliḥ 'Alī al-Ṣāliḥ and Colonel Colin Paddock, who played their role by collecting sources from different places; and Yāsir Muṣṭafā Jābir, who has been continuously involved with this project from the beginning, at times translating, at others drafting. I also offer my thanks to those who joined this project at later stages: they are Dr Geoffrey R.D. King, Aḥmad Sālim al-Jumaid and *al-Shaikh* 'Abd al-Raḥmān Naṣr Allāh, whose review and suggestions had been very important and highly valuable; Muḥammad Yūnus al-Hudhail and Yūsuf Nāṣir al-Ḥamd al-Hashshāsh, who collected the information relating to the tribes and families inhabiting the Jawf region; and 'Alī al-Rāshid and Yūsuf Abū 'Awād, who compiled the statistical data contained in this book. I pray to Almighty God to grant success to all of them and to guide us to the right path.

'Abd al-Raḥmān bin Aḥmad al-Sudairī

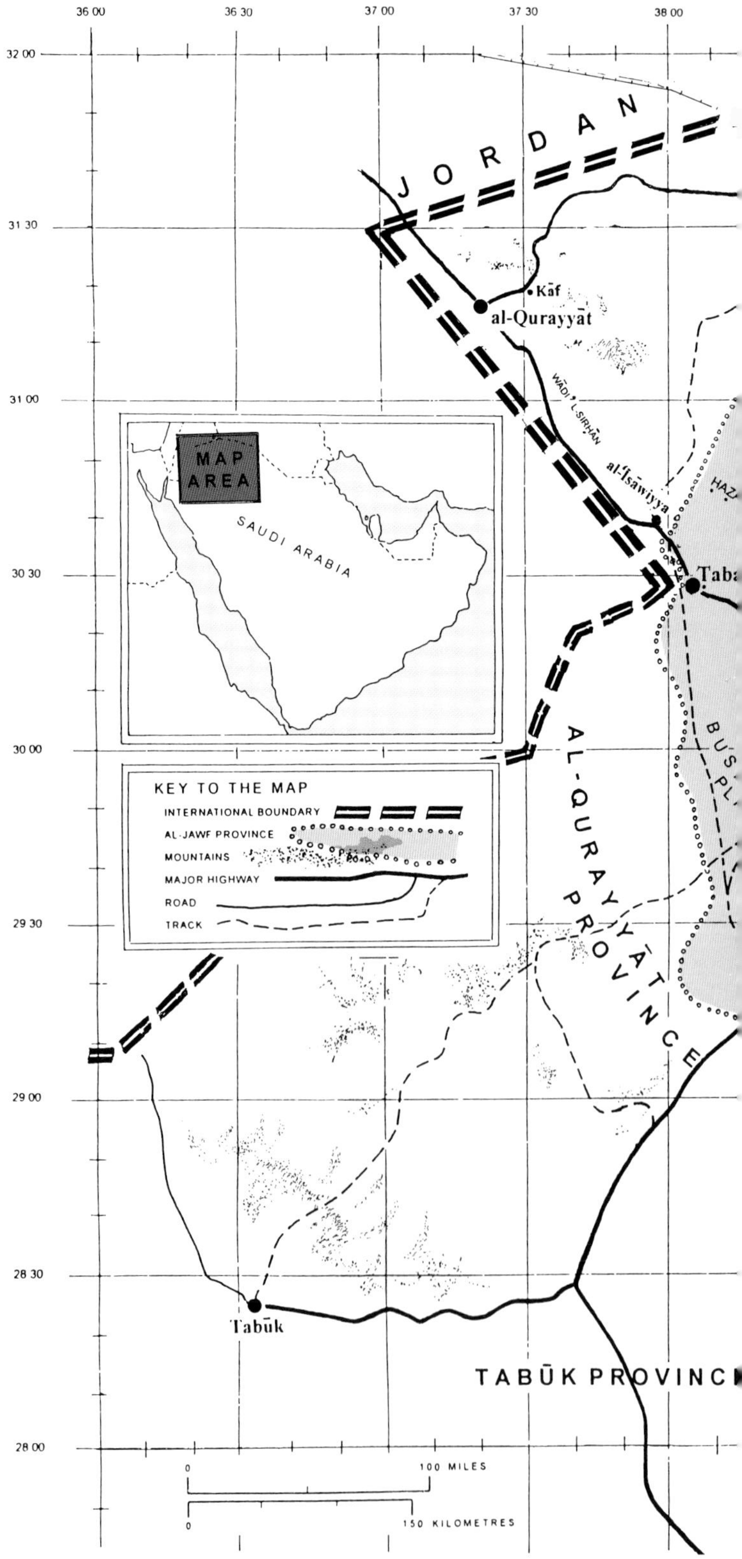
36 00
36 30
37 00
37 30
38 00
32 00
31 30
31 00
30 30
30 00
29 30
29 00
28 30
28 00
JORDAN
Kāf
al-Qurayyāt
WĀDĪ 'L-SIRHĀN
al-Īsāwiyya
Taba
MAP AREA
SAUDI ARABIA
KEY TO THE MAP
INTERNATIONAL BOUNDARY
AL-JAWF PROVINCE
MOUNTAINS
MAJOR HIGHWAY
ROAD
TRACK
AL-QURAYYĀT PROVINCE
Tabūk
TABŪK PROVINC
0
100 MILES
0
150 KILOMETRES

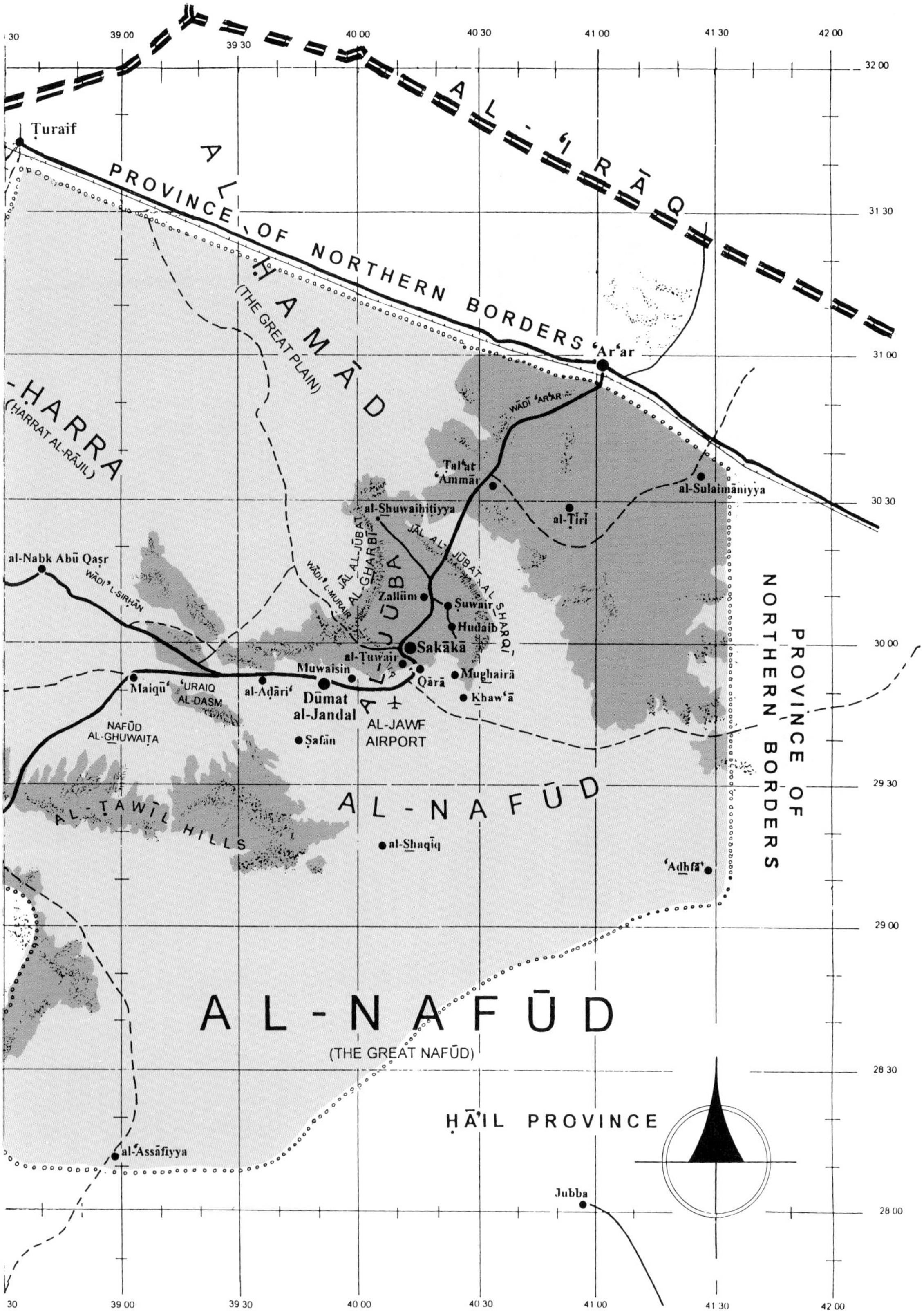
AL-ʻIRĀQ
PROVINCE OF NORTHERN BORDERS
Ṭuraif
AL-ḤAMĀD
(THE GREAT PLAIN)
AL-ḤARRA
(HARRAT AL-RĀJIL)
ʻArʻar
WĀDĪ ʻARʻAR
Talʻat ʻAmmār
al-Sulaimāniyya
al-Shuwaihitiyya
al-Ṭirī
JĀL AL-JŪBAT AL-GHARBĪ
JĀL AL-JŪBAT AL-SHARQĪ
al-Nabk Abū Qaṣr
WĀDĪ ʼL-SIRḤĀN
WĀDĪ ʼL-MURAIR
AL-JUBA
Zallūm
Ṣuwair
Hudaib
Sakākā
al-Ṭuwair
Muwaisin
Maiqūʻ
ʻURAIQ AL-DASM
al-Aḍāriʻ
Dūmat al-Jandal
Qārā
Mughairā
Khawʻā
AL-JAWF AIRPORT
NAFŪD AL-GHUWAIṬA
Ṣafān
AL-ṬAWĪL HILLS
AL-NAFŪD
al-Shaqīq
ʻAdhfāʼ
PROVINCE OF NORTHERN BORDERS
AL-NAFŪD
(THE GREAT NAFŪD)
ḤĀʼIL PROVINCE
al-ʻAssāfiyya
Jubba

In the Name of God, Most Gracious, Most Merciful

PART ONE

INTRODUCTION

1
Historical Background

The record of human occupation of al-Jawf, based on archaeological and written sources, goes back to very early times, and it is the intention of this book to give a survey of this history from ancient times down to the present. It is a particular feature of the records for the history of al-Jawf that, though a considerable amount of reliable material is available, there are gaps in the record. For instance, for the Assyrian period or the early Islamic period in the history of the area a great amount of detailed information is available to the researcher. On the other hand, due to the scarcity of written sources, very little, if anything, is known about the period prior to the rise of Assyria and the period from the 7th century BC to the coming of Islam. A similar situation arises after the *1st*/7th century, for, after the spotlight of history had shone on the area during the early Islamic period, abruptly the area ceased to be of any importance to the historians, who, for this long interval, made only a few passing references to al-Jawf. It is only with the expansion of the first Sa'ūdī state in the *12th*/18th century that al-Jawf appears once more in the accounts of the historians with clarity and detail.

To some extent, the problems faced by the researcher because of the gaps in the historical writings about al-Jawf can be overcome by studying the numerous archaeological monuments and sites in which al-Jawf fortunately abounds. It is a lucky accident that for the periods where the written sources are silent there are archaeological sites surviving to compensate for the gaps. There are a series of sites of human habitation which have left flint artifacts covering the timespan from the Palaeolithic period through to the Neolithic period, and at al-Rajājīl there is a remarkable group of standing stones dated to the Chalcolithic period. Similarly, for the centuries of near silence in the history of al-Jawf preceding the Islamic period, archaeological research carried out lately in the region has brought to light numerous Nabaṭaean inscriptions as well as evidence of Nabaṭaean pottery. This shows that al-Jawf was a settled area at the time the Nabaṭaeans dominated north-west Arabia from their capital at Petra in Jordan. Given the presence of water and the quality of the soil to support farming and a settled population, there is every possibility that al-Jawf had been a settled area throughout ancient times, engaging in trade with a network of important commercial towns that spread over the whole of Arabia and reached out to the rest of the Near East. This network extended from south-west Arabia and involved ancient towns including Makkat al-Mukarrama, al-Madīnat al-Munuwarra (or Yathrib, as it was called before Islam), Dīdān, Madā'in Ṣāliḥ, Taimā', Qaryat al Faw[1], and Gerrha (Arabic, al-Jarhā' and al-Jar'ā'). The advantage that al-Jawf enjoyed by virtue of its strategic location near the mouth of the Wādi'l-Sirḥān, on the threshold of Arabia, Syria and 'Irāq, perhaps made it inevitable that it should be an important participant in this pre-Islamic Arabian trade. Hence it is not surprising to find evidence of the presence of the Nabaṭaeans in al-Jawf, given their well-known monopoly, during their heyday, of commerce in the northern regions of the Peninsula.

After the dawn of Islam the historical records for the early Muslim period in the history of al-Jawf are abundant, one reason being that it was the area to which three Muslim expeditions were directed during the lifetime of Prophet Muḥammad (P.B.U.H.) and where a decisive victory was finally won during Abū Bakr's period by a Muslim army led by the famous commander Khālid bin al-Walīd. But suddenly al-Jawf faded from prominence following the fall of the Umayyad caliphate, with its capital in Damascus, in *132*/750. The 'Abbāsids, who had overthrown the Umayyads, transferred their capital to the newly-founded city of Baghdād in *145*/762. Once Baghdād gained pre-eminence, the entire system of roads and trade routes within Arabia underwent a momentous change. Rather than favouring the routes from the southern Arabian towns to the north, which had benefited al-Jawf in the past, the 'Abbāsids ensured that the main Arabian route ran from Kūfa in 'Irāq directly to the Holy Cities of Makkat al-Mukarrama and al-Madīnat al-Munuwarra in al-Ḥijāz. Many improvements were made in this great road to help the vast numbers of pilgrims who poured into the Holy Cities. This route is known still as Darb Zubaida, i.e. Zubaida Road.[2] Under the 'Abbāsids commerce, too, ran a different course, coming overland from the east and up the Arabian Gulf to 'Irāq and then went westwards to the Mediterranean and to Egypt. The effect was that al-Jawf was bypassed, and, as a result, it lost its significance as a commercial centre.

When the Arabian Peninsula began its modern revival in the *12th*/18th century, al-Jawf once again was endowed with importance because of its location in relation to the border between Arabia and Bilād al-Shām (Syria, Jordan and Lebanon). The first Sa'ūdī state rightly appreciated the significance of its strategic position and brought al-Jawf under its control in *1208*/1793. European travellers, too, began to visit it while following the routes from Jordan to other towns in north Arabia: indeed, the route to the heart of Arabia via al-Jawf was to become preferable, as the reports of the European travellers included in this volume indicate. The detailed accounts of the European travellers give us a clear picture of al-Jawf and its society over the past two centuries. For the period starting with the coming of the rule of the third Sa'ūdī state to the area in *1341*/1922, official and private records are abundantly available, though most of them need documentation. Historical information for the recent past is thus extensive, at times accompanied by photographs of al-Jawf and its inhabitants.

1. For an account of this, see A.R. al-Ansary, *Qaryat al-Fau: A Portrait of Pre-Islamic Civilisation in Saudi Arabia*, London, Croom Helm, 1982.
2. For an archaeological and historical account of this route, see Saad A. Al-Rashid, *Darb Zubaydah: The Pilgrim Road from Kufa to Mecca*, Riyadh, Riyadh University Libraries, 1980. The road was named after Zubaida, the favourite wife of the caliph Hārūn al-Rashīd, because she made an outstanding contribution towards improving the facilities, such as cisterns, dug wells, and rest houses, for the pilgrims and others travelling by this road.

2
The Geography of al-Jawf Region

THE MEANING OF THE NAME "AL-JAWF"

The dictionary meanings of the word *Jawf* have been given by a number of Arab lexicographers. The most celebrated of them, Ibn Manẓūr, gives a detailed discussion of the word and its derivatives,[1] of which the following are excerpts:

> [Noun] *jawf*: Low-lying land; the abdomen of a human being; the interior of the abdomen; [the part of the body] which is enclosed by the shoulders, upper arms, ribs, and flanks [i.e. the chest cavity and the abdominal cavity, together]. The plural is *ajwāf*.

It is in the first sense – low-lying land – that the word has been used as an appellation for al-Jawf.

Arab geographers have used the term "al-Jawf" to refer to various areas in the Arabian peninsula, including the plain between Makka and al-Madīna, the area between Najrān and Ḥaḍramawt, and a place in Yemen.[2] Yet another al-Jawf is Jawf Ḥimār – associated with Ḥimār bin Muwaili' (or Ṭuwaili'?) – about which Imru' al-Qais, the famous pre-Islamic Arab poet, says that it "is like the camel's abdomen, a wilderness I passed through." "Al-Jawf" also refers to an area, inhabited by Banū Sa'd, to the west of al-Aḥsā'. However, the Jawf[3] most frequently identified by the unqualified name of al-Jawf – the subject of this book – is the area situated near the southeastern end of Wādi'l-Sirḥān. It was formerly known as Jawf Āl 'Amr. (Āl 'Amr, a big branch of the Ṭayyi' tribe, used to live in the northern parts of the Nafūd desert and were the supreme power in the Jawf area for several centuries. Their name was used attributively.)[4] Some writers have mistakenly called al-Jawf by the name Jawf al-Sirḥān,[5] perhaps because of its proximity to the Wādi'l-Sirḥān.

It is important to note here that, at various times, the name al-Jawf has been used to refer to three geographical entities. Firstly, it has been used for the depression located in the centre of al-Jawf Province (described below). This depression has also been known in the past as al-Jawba or al-Jūba, and Jūbat al-Jawf. In the modern writings in English it is usually referred to as al-Jawf basin or depression and al-Jawf-Sakākā basin or depression. Secondly, the name is used for Dūmat al-Jandal, the ancient town located at the western edge of al-Jawf-Sakākā basin. Dūmat al-Jandal has traditionally been the capital of the region from the earliest times till the early 1930s. The older name of the town, i.e. Dūmat al-Jandal, has remained in use throughout and is at present again gaining more currency. Thirdly, the name al-Jawf is used for the administrative province of al-Jawf, a geographical entity much larger than al-Jawf-Sakākā depression. Al-Jawf Province, in upper north Arabia, is one of the fourteen administrative provinces of the Kingdom of Sa'ūdī Arabia. It is bounded on the north and east by the Province of the Northern Borders, on the west and north-west by the Province of al-Qurayyāt,[6] on the south and south-east by Ḥā'il Province, and on the south-west by Tabūk Province. The total area of the Jawf Province is about 58,425 square km.

The question arises: When was the name al-Jawf first used for these three entities? The administrative area of al-Jawf (later becoming the Province of al-Jawf) was constituted, immediately after the establishment of Sa'ūdī rule in the area, by incorporating the Jawf basin with the areas surrounding it on all sides – from the Ḥamād and adjoining areas, the Wādi'l-Sirḥān and its adjoining region, and the Nafūd desert. The administrative area was named at that time after the depression. So far as the town and the depression are concerned, it will be noted in the following chapters that for the ancient period and the early Islamic period it is the name Dūmat al-Jandal that we come across in historical and geographical literature. Even the prominent 13th century geographer Yāqūt al-Ḥamawī (d. *626*/1228-29) makes no mention of the name al-Jawf in his long article on Dūmat al-Jandal, but mentions the names of two other settlements of the area, Sakākā and al-Qārā, the latter by the name of Dhu'l-Qāra.[7] However there is one incidental reference from the early Islamic period to the name al-Jawf. This reference occurs in *al-Aghānī*, (Beirut, Dār al-Fikr lil-Jamī', *1390*/1970), vol. 2 p.122, of Abu'l-Faraj al-Aṣbahānī (d. *356*/966-67). Opinion has been expressed that this reference, made in connection with some battles that took place in al-Jawf between the Banū Sulaim and the Kalb tribe in the *1st century*, is beyond doubt a reference to the Jawf of this book.[8] So far as the first use of the name in the modern period is concerned, we find that the famous bibliographer Ḥājī Khalīfa (1609-1657) mentions al-Jawf in his book *Jihān numā'*.[9] It seems most likely that this is the first recorded application of the name to the area and the town in the modern era.

It follows from the above that for the period prior to the coming of the rule of the third Sa'ūdī state to the area, "al-Jawf", hereinafter, will mean the Jawf-Sakākā basin (unless the text expressly or implicitly indicates otherwise); where, on account of the demands of the text, the area constituting the present Province is intended to be connoted, phrases like "al-Jawf area" (or the area of al-Jawf) and "al-Jawf region" are employed. Dūmat al-Jandal is referred to as Dūmat al-Jandal or Dūma.

Considerable undulations of the terrain are a major topographical characteristic of the region, with depressions and high ground, *wādīs* – i.e. valleys or riverbeds – and plains. Sakākā, the principal town of the Province today, lies 30°N. and 40°E., and 580 m. above sea level. In general, the climate of the area is desert continental, cold in winter and hot and dry in summer. The maximum average summer temperature is 42°C., the hottest month being July. The average temperature in winter is 8.5°C., and the coldest month is January, when the temperature can fall to as low as −2° to −7°C.

Very short spring and autumn seasons divide summer from winter. The annual average rainfall for the years when it is plentiful – which recently have been few – is about 200 mm. It is recorded that the pastures of the area were covered with snow for two weeks in *1342*/1924. Annual mean humidity is 36.5 per cent.

A noteworthy feature of the climate of al-Jawf is the wind. In winter the prevailing wind is from the east, in spring from the west. It is the south-easterly winds that bring rain for the most part in winter, whereas in summer, they are hot and dry. The northerly and westerly winds, by contrast, are generally cold.

One may get the impression from the above that the climate of al-Jawf is characterized by extremes, but the weather is often quite pleasant, marked by fresh breezes. This frequent improvement is in part because of the agricultural areas, which are increasing in extent day by day on account of the excellence of the soil and the plentiful water, both near the surface and in the deeper aquifers.

The Province of al-Jawf is thus one of the most important areas for human settlement north of the great Nafūd desert. Among the factors contributing to this pre-eminence are, firstly, that its towns and villages have been favoured by God with two of the principal elements required to sustain life: the availability of sweet water and the suitability of the soil for agriculture. Secondly, al-Jawf enjoys a special place in antiquity as the most important crossing point between the Peninsula and the domains of the ancient empires of Syria, ʻIrāq and Persia, and the civilizations those empires represented – civilizations which had their roots in the distant past.

It is appropriate to give here a brief description of three important constituent parts of al-Jawf Province: al-Jawba or al-Jūba (the depression or pit), the Wādi'l-Sirḥān, or the Sirḥān depression, and al-Nafūd – also known as the Great Nafūd. Of these, al-Jawba is situated wholly within the Province – rather, it is the heart of the Province – whereas the Wādi'l-Sirḥān and al-Nafūd both extend far beyond the boundaries of al-Jawf Province, Wādi'l-Sirḥān north-north-west into al-Qurayyāt Province and Jordan, and al-Nafūd south and south-east into the Province of Ḥā'il and the Province of the Northern Borders.

The Western travellers visiting and passing through the area have recorded their views and experiences of these features. Some of their comments are given in Part Six.

Al-Jawba, or al-Jūba (the depression)

Al-Jawba or al-Jūba, the vast basin in the centre of the administrative Province of al-Jawf near the southern terminus of Wādi'l-Sirḥān, is about 100 km. in length and more than 25 km. in width. This depression is in reality a dissected part of the surrounding plateau, from 200 to 500 ft. below the plateau. It has often been spoken of as an ancient inland sea or lake.

The basin, lying between 39°42′ and 40°30′ E. long. and between 29°45′ and 30°30′ N. lat., is roughly triangular in shape. The southern base of this triangle runs along the northern fringe of al-Nafūd, and its northern apex is at al-S̲h̲uwaiḥiṭiyya. The depression is bounded on the east by Jāl al-Jawba al-S̲h̲arqī and on the west by Jāl al-Jawba al-Gharbī. Everywhere there are volcanic signs, including lava bombs, craters and lava flows.

Al-Jawba is one of the earliest sites of human occupation in western Asia. It is this basin that has, near al-Shuwaiḥiṭiyya, the earliest Stone Age site of human settlement so far discovered in Saʿūdī Arabia, to which an antiquity of over one million years has been attributed. Most of the major settlements of al-Jawf Province are located in this basin – including Sakākā and Dūmat al-Jandal – as are its archaeological monuments. It is, moreover, one of the main areas of agricultural activity in the Province.

Wādi'l-Sirḥān

Like al-Jawba, the Wādi'l-Sirḥān is a depression – it is not a *wādī* in the "river bed" sense of the word. Around 380 km. long and on average a 20 km. wide basin lying between 37°28′ and 39°00′ E. long. and between 29°50′ and 31°30′ N. lat., the canyon-like, jagged Wādi'l-Sirḥān is another example of the local enclosed drainage, a characteristic peculiar to the drainage system of the Arabian Peninsula. Running from south-south-east to north-north-west along Ḥarrat al-Rājil on its eastern side, this depression starts at a distance of around 30 km. from Dūmat al-Jandal and ends at al-Azraq in Jordan. Some geographers say that it extends to somewhere near ʿAmmān, implying a length of 480 km.[10]

The sandy area separating it and al-Jawba is known as ʿUraiq al-Dasm. Ḥamd al-Jāsir says that it appears that once the Wādi'l-Sirḥān depression and al-Jawba were one basin and that sand accumulated in the depression between them and partitioned them.[11] The lowest part appears to be in the neighbourhood of Ithra and Kāf, where the elevation is around 1,800 ft. above sea-level.

Though the Sirḥān depression receives drainage from both the eastern and western sides, the more important of the *wādīs* which empty their *sails* (floodwaters) into it are those on the western side starting from eastern Jordan. On the eastern side some shorter *wādīs*, coming from the neighbouring Ḥarra, are its tributaries.

Water is found in abundance in the Wādi'l-Sirḥān, at an almost uniform level of about 1,850 ft. The Wādi'l-Sirḥān was regarded in the past as the largest oasis area in the northern part of the Peninsula after Taimā'. It has numerous wells along its entire length and is at present an area of enormous agricultural activity in the Province and beyond.

Geologically the region is volcanic, and black basalt abounds as a result of past volcanic activity. Like al-Jawba, Wādi'l-Sirḥān also has been spoken of as an ancient sea or lake. There are considerable deposits of salt, which are well-known for their quality and the potential of their production. These deposits have been important for many centuries, and the significance placed on them by the Turks in the last century is evident from the documents recorded in the chapter on Turkish occupation of al-Jawf.

There are various interpretations of the name of this basin. It may be related to the Sirḥān tribe, which had been the strongest tribe of Ḥawrān on the modern Jordan-Syrian border until about *1060-1110*/1650-1700.[12] About this time, the

Sirḥān left Ḥawrān and settled in the area of al-Jawf; as a result, the *wādī* acquired the name "Wādi'l-Sirḥān", having formerly been known as Wādī Azraq. During mediaeval times the Wādi'l-Sirḥān was known to Arab geographers as *Baṭn al-Sirr* (the Depression of Mystery),[13] while in the Greek sources the Wādi'l-Sirḥān is referred to as *Syrmaion Pedion.*[14] An alternative explanation of the name Wādi'l-Sirḥān is derived from the fact that the word "Sirḥān" means "wolf", and it is suggested that wolves were found in the valley in great numbers.

There are a number of villages and settlements in the Wādi'l-Sirḥān. So far as al-Jawf is concerned, the main settlement is Ṭabarjal.

From the earliest times the Wādi'l-Sirḥān has served as a favourite route between the interior of the Peninsula and the Bilād al-Shām.

As mentioned above, the Wādi'l-Sirḥān and al-Jawba are both considered to have been inland seas or lakes in the distant past.[15] The theory is perhaps well founded and proof of this is apparent everywhere – seashells, corals, and fossilized remains of marine life are found in abundance in both depressions.

It would not be out of place to add here that in prehistoric times both al-Jawba and the Wādi'l-Sirḥān teemed with botanical life. Hundreds of thousands of pieces of petrified wood, large and small, are scattered throughout these areas. Occasionally, complete tree-trunks, though broken in large pieces, are found. The largest fossilized piece so far collected is 1.5 m. long, with a diameter of around 50 cm.

Al-Nafūd

The sand desert of al-Nafūd, or the Great Nafūd, situated approximately between 39°00′ and 43°00′ E. long, and between 27°00′ and 30°00′ N. lat., fills a vast irregular basin in north-western Sa'ūdī Arabia. With an estimated area of 26,000 square miles (67,300 sq. km.), it is the second largest sand body in the Arabian Peninsula after the Empty Quarter (al-Rub' al-Khālī) in the south-east, with which it is connected by the long arch of al-Dahnā' desert. Its level above the sea is not uniform: on the caravan route between al-Jawf and Ḥā'il the average altitude has been estimated to be around 3,000 ft. (914 m.). The topographic relief of dunes in the Nafūd may exceed 300 ft.

The most striking phenomenon of the Nafūd is its *falj*, a unique dune form. J.G. Lorimer has described it as follows:

> In shape it is semi-oval and resembles the print of a gigantic horse-hoof; the toe is the deepest part and points invariably to the north-west, while the floor of the hollow rises south-eastwards and reaches the ground level at the heel; the internal walls are inclined at an angle of 50 or 60 degrees to the horizon. The Falj is of all sizes, varying in area from 1 to 200 acres, but the average diameter is 300 to 400 yards and the ordinary depth from 150 to 250 feet. . . . Peculiar facts relating to these depressions are that, in spite of the instability of their sandy sides, they apparently remain constant in shape and size from year to year and even from generation to generation; that none of them retain water after rain; and that they lie in irregular courses or strings from west to east.[16]

The prevailing breezes in the Nafūd are from the west. Desert vegetation is abundant and the grazing excellent. The watering places nearest to Dūmat al-Jandal are Khaw'ā and al-Shaqīq.

The Nafūd has been a barrier to travel for ages. It has always held a spell for the natives as well as outsiders.

Mediaeval Arab geographers knew the Nafūd by the name Raml 'Ālij, and that is the name by which it was referred to by Prophet Muḥammad (P.B.U.H.). Later on it became known as "Ramlat Buḥtur" or Rimāl Buḥtur, because the tribe Banū Buḥtur from the Ṭayyi' dominated it at the time. Its present name is said to have originally been al-Nuhūd (plural of *Nahd*) – a reference to the shape of its dunes – from which it gradually changed to al-Nafūd.[17]

TOWNS AND VILLAGES OF AL-JAWF PROVINCE

There are about 200,000 inhabitants of the towns, villages and settlements situated in the administrative area of al-Jawf. The names of some of these places should be introduced here as they will be referred to frequently. With regard to population, the most important towns are Sakākā, Dūmat al-Jandal and Ṭabarjal. The villages include Qārā, al-Ṭuwair, Ṣuwair, al-Nabk Abū Qaṣr, Zallūm, Hudaib, al-Shuwaiḥiṭiyya, al-Aḍāri', Khaw'ā, al-Radīfa, al-Zabāra, al-Naẓāyim, Abū 'Ajram, al-'Ammāriyya, Maiqū', Ṣafān and Hadbān, among others.

Dūmat al-Jandal, Sakākā and Ṭabarjal: The Origin of Their Names

The Arab geographer Yāqūt al-Ḥamawī, writing in the *6th*/12th century, associates, on the authority of Ibn al-Kalbī and al-Zajjājī, the name of Dūmat al-Jandal with Prophet Ismā'īl's son, Dūmā'. According to Ibn al-Ḳalbī, as reported by Yāqūt, when the descendants of Ismā'īl had increased in number in the Tihāma coast of the Red Sea, Ismā'īl's son Dūmā' left the region and finally reached the present site of Dūmat al-Jandal. Here Dūmā' built a fortress for himself, which was subsequently named after him. Yāqūt states, on the authority of Abū Sa'd, that the epithet "Jandal" was added to the town's name because its fortress was built of stone.[18] Similarly, some Arab historians derive the name Dūma from Dūm, sometimes written Dūmān, or Dūmā, likewise deriving it from the name of Dūmā', the son of Ismā'īl, the son of Prophet Ibrāhīm. The word "Jandal" itself means a heap of stones. Alois Musil, on the other hand, is of the opinion that "the cognomen al-Ǧandal [al-Jandal] may be traced more readily to the reigning family than to the large stones, of which, in fact, merely the fort is built. Âl Ǧandal (Eben Ǧandal) is a very ancient family of Bedouins who camp in northern Arabia."[19] This solitary opinion is insignificant as against the long-standing authoritative opinion to the contrary.[20] Moreover, it carries little weight considering there is no indication whatsoever that Ibn Jandal ruled over the town at any time in its history.

From the Assyrian sources it is evident that the town was known to the Assyrians as Adummatu.[21]

The town is also referred to in Roman and Byzantine historical sources, which give it in various forms: Domata, Dumetha or Dumatha. However, although they mention the town, they do not elaborate on it nor do they indicate the meaning of the name.[22]

"Sakākā" derives from the root word "sakaka". Yāqūt al-Ḥamawī, on the authority of Abū Manṣūr, says that the words "Sukāk" and "Sukākā" – he spells the town's name as Sukākā – mean the region of the air between the earth and the sky.[23] On the other hand, if we consider the word Sakākā to have been derived from a different derivative, "sikka", of the same root word, then the most plausible meanings would be "meeting of the ways". In preference to these meanings, a modern local writer has tried to interpret the name afresh, arguing that the word either means "a group of straight wells of narrow opening" or has been derived from the saying "They built their houses in one line."[24] It should be added that in the saying the word "sikākan" has been used as an adverb and means "in one line".

Ṭabarjal is located at a place where several small *wādīs* (also called *Shu'bān* in Arabic; the singular form is *Shu'aib*) converge and end up in the Wādi'l-Sirḥān. To the west of the town is Shu'aib Ḥadraj. Shu'aib Abū Ḥawāyā ends up in the middle of the town. On the eastern side of the town is Shu'aib Ṭabarjal, which itself receives as tributaries a number of *wādīs*, including Shu'aib al-Ghuwail and Shu'aib Abu'l-Sulailiyyāt. The bedouin give the name of *al-rijla* to *wādīs* converging in a pattern like this. From *al-rijla* arose the name of the town Ṭabarjal – on account of its being the converging point of several *wādīs*.

The name Ṭabarjal appeared only after the beginning of settlement at the site of Ṭabarjal.[25]

---

1. Muḥammad bin Mukarram Ibn Manẓūr, *Lisān al-'Arab*, 15 vols., Beirut, Dār Ṣādir, 1955-56, vol. 9 pp.34-37.
2. See, e.g., Yāqūt al-Ḥamawī, *Mu'jam al-Buldān*, 5 vols., Beirut, Dār Ṣādir, 1955-57, vol. 2 pp.187-88; Ḥamd al-Jāsir, *al-Mu'jam al Jughrāfī li-Bilād al-'Arabiyyat al-Sa'ūdiyya: Shimāl al-Mamlaka*, 3 vols., Riyadh, Dār al-Yamāma, *1397*/1977, vol. 1 p.359.
3. For a discussion of the term Jawf and the name al-Jawf, see *Encyclopaedia of Islam*, New ed., s.v. "Djawf", by M. Quint, and s.v. "al-Djawf", by J. Mandaville.
4. Ḥamd al-Jāsir, *al-Mu'jam al-Jughrāfī*, vol. 1 p.359.
5. Niebuhr and Seetzen, according to Wallin, mention al-Jawf as Jawf al-Sirḥān. Georg Augustus Wallin, *Travels in Arabia (1845 and 1846)*, Cambridge, England, Falcon-Oleander, 1979, p.26; cf. *Encyclopaedia of Islam*, s.v. "Djawf", by M. Quint, who mentions Jawf al-Sirḥān as an entity different from al-Jawf (without elaborating on it in any way), most probably as an alternative name of the Wādi'l-Sirḥān.
6. By virtue of a Royal decree issued in *1414*/1993, al-Qurayyāt Province was merged with the Province of al-Jawf.
7. Yāqūt al-Ḥamawī, vol. 2 pp.487-89.
8. See, e.g., Ḥamd al-Jāsir, *al-Mu'jam al-Jughrāfī*, vol. 1 p.360.; see also Alois Musil, *Arabia Deserta: A Topographical Itinerary*, New York, American Geographical Society of New York, 1927, p.552.
9. Muṣṭafā bin 'Abd Allāh Kātib Chalabī Ḥājī Khalīfa, *Jihān numā'*, Istanbūl, *1145*/1732-33, p.530, cited by Musil, *Arabia Deserta*, p.553.
10. 'Abd al-Raḥmān Ṣādiq al-Sharīf, *Jughrāfiyyat al-Mamlakat al-'Arabiyyat al-Sa'ūdiyya*, 2 vols., Riyadh, Dār al-Marrīkh, *1404*/1984, vol. 1 p.90; Ḥusain Ḥamza Bindaqjī, *Jughrāfiyyat al-Mamlakat al-'Arabiyyat al-Sa'ūdiyya*, 3rd ed., Jeddah, The Author, *1401*/1981, pp.149-50; cf. Ḥamd al-Jāsir, *al-Mu'jam al-Jughrāfī*, vol. 3 pp.1336-39.
11. Ḥamd al-Jāsir, *al-Mu'jam al-Jughrāfī*, vol. 3 p.1339.

12. 'Umar Riḍā Kaḥḥāla, *Mu'jam Qabā'il al-'Arab*, 5 vols, Beirut, Mu'assasat al-Risāla, *1402*/1982, vol. 2 pp.507-08.
13. For description of the Baṭn al-Sirr route, that is Wādi'l-Sirḥān route, from 'Ammān to Taimā', see Muḥammad bin Aḥmad al-Maqdisī, *Aḥsan al-Taqāsīm fī Ma'rifat al-Aqālīm*, 2nd ed., edited by M.J. De Goeje, Leiden, E.J. Brill, 1906; reprint ed., Beirut, Maktabat Khayyāṭ, n.d., p.250.
14. Musil, *Arabia Deserta*, p.507.
15. See Lady Anne Blunt, *A Pilgrimage to Nejd, the Cradle of the Arab Race*, 2 vols., London, John Murray, 1881; reprint ed., London, Frank Cass, 1968, vol. 1 pp.88, 114; vol. 2 p.511; S.S. Butler, "Baghdad to Damascus viâ el Jauf, Northern Arabia", *The Geographical Journal* vol. 33, May 1909, pp.517-35 (524); cf. H. St.J. B. Philby, "Jauf and the North Arabian Desert", *The Geographical Journal* vol. 62, October 1923, pp.241-59 (251).
16. J.G. Lorimer, *Gazetteer of the Persian Gulf, Oman and Central Arabia*, 2 vols. in 6, Calcutta, India, Government Printing House, 1908; reprint ed., Farnborough, England, Gregg International, 1970, vol. 2B, pp.1295-96.
17. al-Sharīf, vol. 1 p.58; Ḥamd al-Jāsir, *al-Mu'jam al-Jughrāfī*, vol. 3 pp.872-75.
18. Yāqūt al-Ḥamawī, vol. 2 p.487.
19. Musil, *Arabia Deserta*, p.544.
20. For which see also p.38 below.
21. See F.V. Winnett and W.L. Reed, *Ancient Records from North Arabia*, Toronto, University of Toronto Press, 1970, p.71.
22. Musil, *Arabia Deserta*, pp.508, 532.
23. Yāqūt al-Ḥamawī, vol. 3 p.229.
24. 'Ārif Mufaḍḍī al-Mis'ar, "al-Jawba wa'l-Asmā' al-Mutarādifat al-Arba'a bain al-Lugha wa'l-Tārīkh wa'l-Shawāhid al-Shi'riyya", *al-Jawba: Malaff Thaqāfī Yuṣdar 'an Mu'assasat 'Abd al-Raḥmān al-Sudairī al-Khairiyya bi'l-Jawf*, no.5, May 1993, pp.40-41.
25. The process of settlement at this site started when *al-Shaikh* 'Āshiq bin Kāsib al-Laḥāwī wrote to the author a letter requesting the allotment of a piece of land in Shu'aib Ḥadraj with a view to settling there and cultivating it. The policy of the Government from the beginning was to encourage any proposal which contributed to the settlement of the bedouin in the Wādi'l-Sirḥān. The land, therefore, was granted to him. This step was taken in *Ṣafar 1376*/1956. It encouraged the elders and chiefs of the Sharārāt tribe to settle there. Gradually, Ṭabarjal became an important agricultural and commercial settlement. Among the first people to settle in the area, besides *al-Shaikh* 'Āshiq, were his brother Duḥailān, Samīr bin Ghāṣib al-Aṣwagh and Maqbūl bin Suwailim al-Laḥāwī as well as other groups from their tribe.

3
The Archaeological Importance of al-Jawf Region

Up to the mid-1970s no area of Sa'ūdī Arabia had been systematically surveyed to assess the country's archaeological resources. Archaeological knowledge of the Kingdom was in its infancy. Al-Jawf was no exception. Although in al-Jawf's case some information of variable quality existed in the writings of the Western travellers who had visited the area, almost the whole of this was restricted to the more obvious archaeological remains, such as the ancient structures or the inscriptions and rock drawings – only Winnett and Reed concerned themselves with pottery as well. Hence the travellers' accounts, for the most part, were helpful only in identifying some ancient sites.

In *1396*/1976 the Department of Antiquities and Museums embarked on an ambitious plan: that of "preparation of a comprehensive inventory of the archaeological resources of the Kingdom". A land area of more than 2,000,000 sq. km. was estimated to be involved. The whole country was divided into eight zones for the purpose of reconnoitring. Considering its archaeological importance, al-Jawf/Wādi'l-Sirḥān area was one of the first two areas – the second being the Eastern Province – selected for the first phase of this "Comprehensive Archaeological Survey Program". A team from the Department visited the region and carried out field-work during February, March and April 1976.[1] In 1977, the second phase of the survey of the northern region was completed.[2] The Wādi'l-Sirḥān was briefly surveyed again in *1400*/1980.[3]

After a lapse of five years, three teams from the Department of Antiquities and Museums visited the region in 1985: the first team to Dūmat al-Jandal to investigate the sites of Qaṣr Mārid and Masjid 'Umar, and other sites in the town,[4] the second to a site near al-S͟huwaiḥiṭiyya, to determine its age,[5] and the third to carry out a rock art and epigraphic survey of the northern region.[6]

In *1406*/1986 another expedition made further investigations at Dūmat al-Jandal in three different parts of the town.[7] During the same year some more field-work – including excavations at Dūmat al-Jandal, al-Ṭuwair and Muwaisin – was carried out by Khaleel Ibrahim al-Muaikel, with permission of the Department of Antiquities and Museums, as part of his studies for a doctoral degree from the University of Durham.[8]

Notwithstanding all this valuable work – which marks the archaeological importance of the region – the full story of the antiquities of al-Jawf, based on comprehensive investigation and extensive excavation, will take a great deal longer to unfold. Archaeologically, the Jawf region is regarded as one of the most important areas of the Peninsula, for various reasons. Firstly, it is important for Dūmat al-Jandal's role as one of the earliest recorded independent Arabian states, often enjoying dominion over the tribes of the region, and as a centre of ancient trade sited at the junction of routes linking Yemen with 'Irāq, and via Wādi'l-Sirḥān – the gateway to the Arabian Peninsula – with Syria and the Mediterranean.

Secondly, there exist in the Jawf region several important archaeological sites like the Mārid Castle, al-Rajājīl, and the ancient town of al-Ṭuwair.

Thirdly, the whole of the Jawf region is epigraphically one of the richest areas in the Peninsula. It abounds with ancient inscriptions and rock art.

Fourthly, as has been recently determined, of the earliest Stone Age sites so far discovered in the Kingdom of Sa'ūdī Arabia, the oldest is in al-Jawf, near al-Shuwaiḥiṭiyya, dating back more than one million years.[9]

Fifthly, the Wādi'l-Sirḥān had its own importance in antiquity. Archaeological and historical evidence lately accumulated testifies to its prominence as an area of ancient settlement as well as a trade route during the period of Nabaṭaean-Roman supremacy.[10] Archaeological sites abound in the valley.[11]

---

1. For a report of the team, see Robert McC. Adams et al., "Saudi Arabian Archaeological Reconnaissance, 1976: The Preliminary Report on the First Phase of the Comprehensive Archaeological Survey Program", *Atlal* vol. 1, *1397*/1977, pp.21-40 and plates 1-19.
2. For its report, see Peter J. Parr et al., "Preliminary Report on the Second Phase of the Northern Province Survey, *1397*/1977", *Atlal* vol. 2, *1398*/1978, pp.29-50 and plates 19-45.
3. See Michael Lloyd Ingraham et al., "Saudi Arabian Comprehensive Survey Program: c. Preliminary Report on a Reconnaissance Survey of the Northwestern Province (with a note on a Brief Survey of the Northern Province)", *Atlal* vol. 5, *1401*/1981, pp.59-84 and plates 65-97.
4. See Khaled Abdulaziz al-Dayel and Abdulaziz al-Shadukhi, "Excavations at Dumat al-Jandal, *1405*/1985", *Atlal* vol. 10, *1406*/1986, pp.64-79 and plates 73-85.
5. See Norman M. Whalen et al., "A Lower Pleistocene Site near Shuwaihitiyah in Northern Saudi Arabia", *Atlal* vol. 10, *1406*/1986, pp.94-101 and plates 94-100.
6. See Majeed Khan, Abdulrehman al-Kabawi, and Abdulrehman al-Zahrani, "Preliminary Report on the Second Phase of Comprehensive Rock Art and Epigraphic Survey of the Northern Province, *1405*/1985", *Atlal* vol. 10, *1406*/1986, pp.82-93 and plates 86-93.
7. For a report of the expedition, see Khaled Abdulaziz al-Dayel, "Excavations at Dumat al-Jandal, Second Season, *1406*/1986", *Atlal* vol. 11, *1409*/1988, pp.37-46 and plates 28-42.
8. See Khaleel Ibrahim al-Muaikel, "A Critical Study of the Archaeology of the Jawf region of Saudi Arabia with Additional Material on its History and Early Arabic Epigraphy", 2 vols. (Ph.D. dissertation, University of Durham, 1988).
9. Whalen, "A Lower Pleistocene Site Near Shuwaihitiyah", p.100.
10. See, e.g., G.W. Bowersock, *Roman Arabia*, Cambridge, Harvard University Press, 1983, pp.154-59.
11. Ingraham, p.80.

PART TWO

THE PREHISTORY OF AL-JAWF REGION

4
From Stone Age to Iron Age

The Arabian Peninsula lies on the boundaries of two areas of great prominence in the history of world civilizations. These are Mesopotamia and Bilād al-Shām on the one hand and Egypt on the other. Indigenous civilizations, too, have flourished in Arabia: for hundreds of thousands of years the Peninsula has been inhabited, and Man developed techniques to deal with the harsh local environment. The first tools of ancient Man in Arabia were of stone, bone or wood. Bone and wood being perishable, the only tools from very ancient periods that have survived the ravages of time are of stone. As examined by us in the last section of Part One, a number of archaeological surveys have been carried out by the Kingdom's Department of Antiquities and Museums in the Jawf region since *1396*/1976. This work has brought to light scores of archaeological sites, including those from which large numbers of stone tools pertaining to different periods were collected. Some of these sites are among the most important in the world in the story of ancient Man.

THE PALAEOLITHIC – NEOLITHIC PERIOD

Prior to the surveying work, our knowledge of the prehistory of the country was very meagre and sketchy. It was stated in 1952 that human settlement in South-West Asia has an age of around 100,000 years.[1] The opinion about ancient Man in Sa'ūdī Arabia was not dissimilar, and it was conjectured that "Saudi Arabia has been inhabited since Lower Paleolithic times [2.5 million years ago to c. 10,000 years ago], although the present evidence for the entire Stone Age is very limited and widely scattered."[2] In 1971 another authority wrote that archaeological evidence points to Man's existence in Arabia since the Pleistocene (the earliest epoch of the Quaternary period, starting some time around two million BP and ending c. 10,000 BP).[3] It would be noted that the opinion in both the cases was couched in terms of broad classification, without mentioning any specific time span.

After the start of the survey programme, the opinion was expressed, while introducing the first year's work, that "Arabia was indeed extensively exploited by human populations as early as pre-150,000 B.P."[4] This view was based mainly on the findings at the sites along the northern boundaries of the Nafūd desert, where the earliest settlements were recorded.[5] The next year, 1977, was to see further pushing of the date backwards. In the northern corner of al-Jawf-Sakākā basin a new site was discovered, ultimately to prove to be the oldest archaeological site in the Kingdom and "one of the very few Lower Pleistocene sites in Western Asia". From this site, which is situated on terraces bordering a tributary stream of the Wādi'l-Shuwaiḥiṭiyya, near the Shuwaiḥiṭiyya village, 97 artifacts were randomly collected, "57 of them quartzite cobbles and flakes having deep wide trimming scars and a heavy coating of patina". These were the earliest stone tools recorded in Sa'ūdī Arabia. The collection was unlike any other collection found in the country and was initially classified as "Lower Acheulean (or even pre-Acheulean)", that is belonging to the early part of the Palaeolithic period.[6]

On account of the interest aroused in archaeological circles by this site, the artifacts were examined more minutely three years later. Finding the results "highly interesting" but the sample so small that it "limited the credibility of the results", the Department sent another team in 1985 to investigate the site in depth for a period of two months. From 16 different localities, 1,884 artifacts were collected, among them heavy-duty tools (choppers, polyhedrons, spheroids, subspheroids and discoids), bifaces (including protobifaces, cleavers and picks), scrapers, small tools (notches, burins, borers and knives), and manufacturing tools (cores, nodules, chunks, flakes and hammerstones). One thousand, five hundred and seventeen of them were "very old", whereas 367 were "of more recent age". The material used was quartzite for the old artifacts and quartzite, chert or limestone for the more recent artifacts. The old artifacts were classified as "a facies of the Developed Oldowan; the recent artifacts were subsequent to that culture and time period". The conclusions reached were that the site "may be viewed as Developed Oldowan B with a time range between 1.3 and 1.0 million years ago", that it was "the oldest site . . . so far discovered in Saudi Arabia", and that it ranks among the oldest in Western Asia, demonstrating "the presence of early Homo erectus in Western Asia at a very early period of human prehistory". Another finding was that the area had been under occupation for a very long span of time, down to the Acheulean and post-Neolithic periods.[7]

Other sites belonging to the Lower Palaeolithic and the succeeding Middle Palaeolithic have been located in al-Jawf. The most important of them, representing both the Lower and the Middle Palaeolithic, was found in the southeast corner of al-Jawf-Sakākā basin near the northern edge of al-Nafūd. It covered an area of several square kilometres. The material employed was the chert from the neighbouring plateau. The bulk of the collection consists of cores and flakes.[8] The Mousterian tools of Middle Palaeolithic are also found abundantly in the region.[9]

The succeeding Upper Palaeolithic and Epi-Palaeolithic phases of occupation of al-Jawf region, like most other areas of the Arabian Peninsula, have left no definite evidence. "It may be assumed that this picture is related to the Late Glacial aridity (c. 15-13000 BP) of the Near Eastern desert region . . ."[10]

Sites attributable to the Neolithic period are very few in the northern parts of the country. From this period, signs of occupation were noted "on a limestone ridge in the Wādī ʻArʻar drainage system, northeast of Sakākā, where a surface collection of prismatic blades (backed and retouched), denticulates, burins, punches, bi-polar cores, and hoes was recovered." However, no Neolithic structures or remains were found at these sites. These sites are dated to the fourth millennium BC.[11]

THE CHALCOLITHIC – BRONZE AGE – IRON AGE

Neolithic occupation of the Jawf region in due course gave way to the Chalcolithic period until Bronze came to dominate in the fourth millennium BC, to be overtaken, in turn, by the Iron Age. Significant remains in the Jawf area from this period are stone circles, cairns, standing stones such as those at al-Rajājīl, and rock art (petroglyphs). Rock art, however, belongs partly to the period under review and partly to the Neolithic period; it is, therefore, discussed under a separate heading below.

Stone Circles

Stone circles of various sizes and shapes built by different techniques have been found throughout the Jawf region. They were probably meant for use as animal corrals, or they may be remains of enclosures of villages. They can be dated to the Chalcolithic period or Early Bronze Age, for the stone tools found parallel those of the Chalcolithic period already identified in Jordan and Palestine. In the Wādī ʻArʻar drainage system, in the northeast of Sakākā, these stone circles were found associated with flint assemblage dated to the fourth and early third millennium BC. One site there, typical of smaller complexes, "comprises a conglomeration of some sixteen structures". There are larger, more complex groupings as well, though they are not so common. Two such "veritable villages of stone enclosures" were found in the southern Wādi'l-Sirḥān. One of them, around 40 km. from Dūmat al-Jandal, covers an area of 150 x 100 m. on an isolated sandstone outcrop some 75 m. above the depression and has fifty or so structures, each in the region of 8-10 m. in diameter. The other, located around 25 km. from Dūma on three low limestone ridges at the edge of the valley, is larger and has over a hundred structures of complex "interlocking" type. On both the sites stone tools were abundant, the most interesting of them being retouched spear points with notched tangs. The "industry . . . belongs mainly to the Chalcolithic tradition of Palestine and Sinai. . . . A fourth millennium date is thus indicated, with the possibility of an extension into the third."[12]

Cairns

In addition to the stone circles, the region contains stone cairns in large numbers. These are usually sited on prominent ridges and sky-lines. Indications are that they belong to a number of different periods. In 1976 one cairn near Kāf in the northern Wādi'l-Sirḥān was excavated; it proved to cover an Iron Age grave of c. 7th century BC.[13]

Stone Pillars

Another very important cultural legacy of this period is the unique site of al-Rajājīl. It lies 10 km. southeast of Sakākā on the northern edge of al-Nafūd, its most prominent feature being the complex of standing stone pillars. Most of these pillars have fallen and broken. There are about fifty groups, each group comprising from two to nineteen columns. The height and width of the columns vary: some are as high as 3.5 m. and as wide as 75 cm. A somewhat less prominent feature of the site is that most of the pillar groups have behind them or attached to them a small oval, D-shaped or rectangular enclosure, the outline of which is clearly discernible.[14]

A less noticeable, but significant fact is that the columns were originally placed "in a straight line with the axis running through the pillars in a true north-south alignment. Thus the pillars faced east. . . ."[15] On excavation of one of the groups of pillars and the enclosure behind it, no traces of burials were found, nor any evidence of its use as a living structure. It was concluded that the structures do not seem to have served any "secular function" and that "the site could represent a communal gathering place for a number of disparate social groups to perform certain social or ethno-religious functions".[16]

There are various incised tribal marks (*Awsām*, plural of *wasm*) on a number of the columns. One group of marks is possibly a Thamūdic inscription.[17]

On the basis of the flint tools and pottery sherds found in the region of the pillars, this "fascinating and interesting archaeological site" has been dated to the middle of the fourth millennium BC (Chalcolithic period). It has rightly been regarded as "a unique cultural resource in the Kingdom of Saudi Arabia".[18]

Western visitors to the site will readily see a resemblance between al-Rajājīl and the massive remains at Stonehenge in England, which date from the third or second millennium BC.

No remains have so far been found which could definitely be declared to belong to the period between the dates assigned to the stone monuments mentioned above, that is late 4th to early 3rd millennium BC. In the words of the surveying team, "it is perhaps particularly disappointing that no Iron Age material was found in the Jawf region, despite a fairly extensive search. . . ."[19] Juris Zarins in a separate special article, describes as follows the seeming occupation gap, as far as settled population was concerned:

> Following the disappearance of the sedentary people of the Chalcolithic-Bronze Age, a large hiatus appears in the archaeological record [of al-Jawf]. It can be

Fossilized tree trunks from al-Jawf Province.

Al-Rajājīl sandstone pillars.

Another group of al-Rajāajīl standing stones, with mounds from other groups in the background.

Al-Rajājīl

Al-Rajājīl is one of the most important archaeological sites in Sa'ūdī Arabia. It is dated to the middle of the fourth millennium BC, and about 50 groups of sandstone pillars (most of them now fallen) are found here. There is little evidence of what purposes the pillars served, although it is thought that the site could have been a communal gathering place.

***Top*: Choppers – which would have been used as heavy-duty tools.**
***Bottom (left to right)*: Pointed chopper, biface.**

Al-Shuwaiḥiṭiyya

In 1985 the Kingdom's Department of Antiquities and Museums sent a survey team to investigate this site. Almost two thousand artifacts were recovered, a selection of which is shown on this page and on the following two pages. The team concluded that the site could be classified as Developed Oldowan B – between 1.3 and 1 million years old – and that it was the oldest recorded site in Sa'ūdī Arabia.

Polyhedrons.

All the photographs on this page are courtesy of *Atlal* journal.

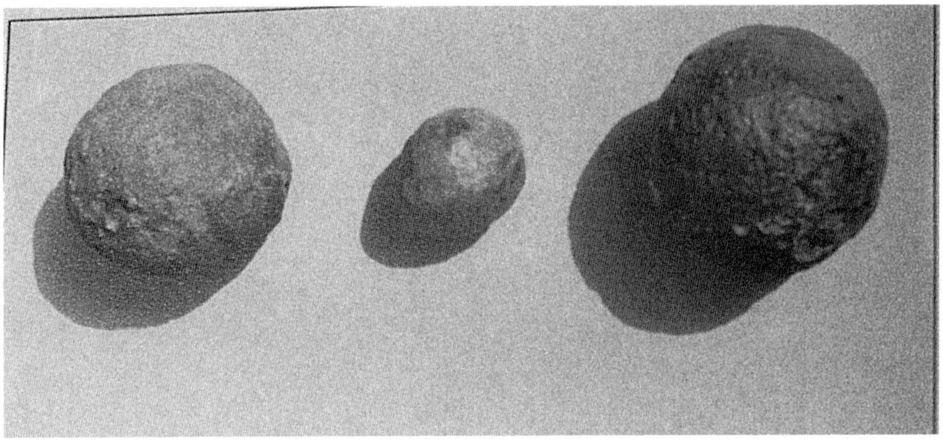

Spheroids.

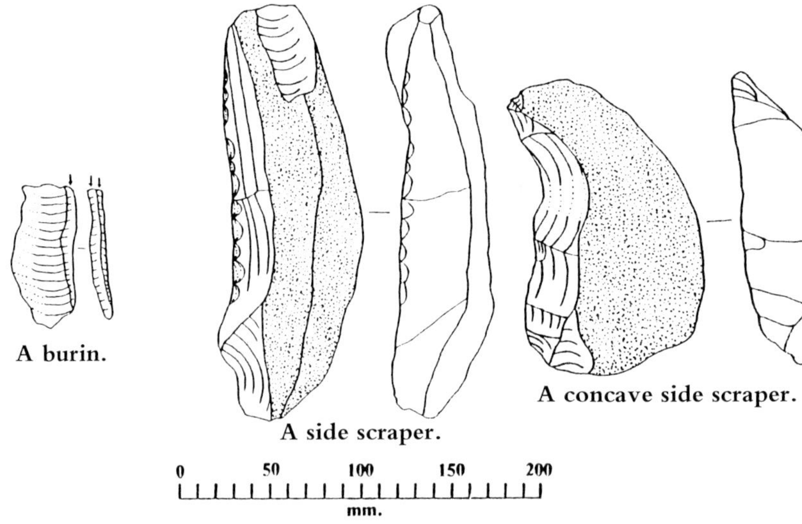

A burin.

A side scraper.

A concave side scraper.

Subspheroids.

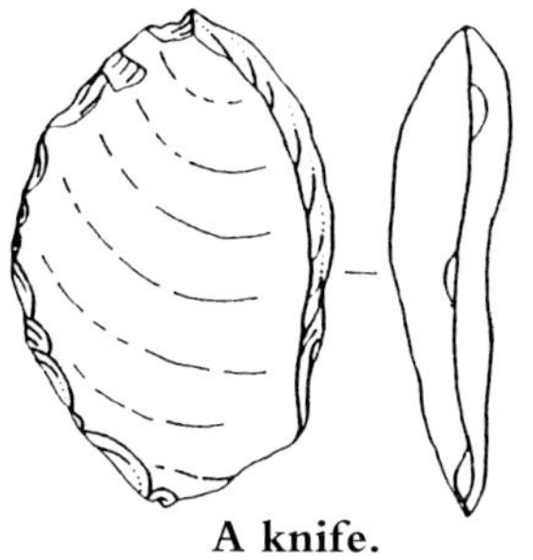

A knife.

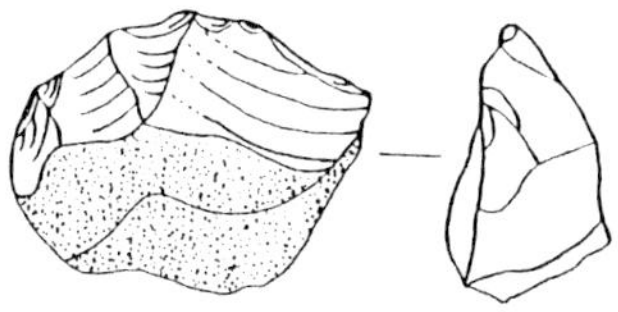

A transverse scraper.

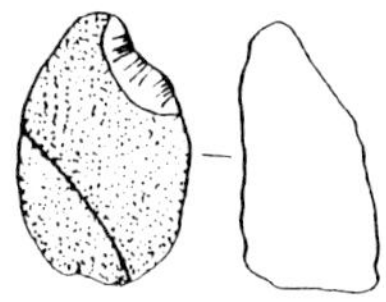

A notch.

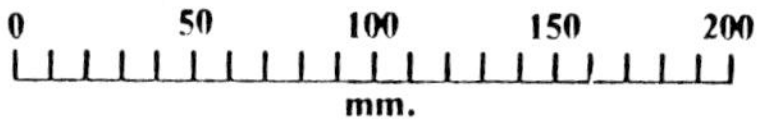

***Top (left to right)*: three burins, two borers.**
***Bottom (left to right)*: notches.**

All the photographs and line-drawings on this page and the page opposite are courtesy of *Atlal* journal.

> conjectured that during this period of the second millennium B.C. the domestic camel was introduced into the Jawf-Sakaka basin under increasing aridity, and the nomadic Bedouin make their first appearance.[20]

The subsequent occupation of al-Jawf in the 8th and 7th centuries BC is part of history and is very specifically dealt with by Assyrian sources, as we shall see in the next part of the book. However, further archaeological work at sites like Dūmat al-Jandal is needed to amplify the information given by the Assyrian texts. The span of time from the Hellenistic period down to the end of the Byzantine period is most promising for the archaeology of al-Jawf. Nabaṭaean, Roman and Byzantine artifacts have been discovered at Dūmat al-Jandal, evidencing its continuous occupation during these periods. Nabaṭaean presence in the Jawf region is well testified by the large numbers of Nabaṭaean inscriptions recorded in the area.

ROCK ART

Other important cultural remains in al-Jawf, belonging to the Stone Age as well as to the succeeding period, are inscriptions and rock art, both of which are found in abundance. The rock art and epigraphic survey team of the Department of Antiquities and Museums, which visited the area in *1405*/1985, located 10,374 different panels of rock art and inscriptions in the region, mostly in the area of al-Jawf-Sakākā basin. One thousand, four hundred and nine of these panels pertained to inscriptions – discussed in Part Three, Chapter 12 – and the rest to rock art.[21] The panels of Neolithic and Chalcolithic rock art numbered only four and seven respectively and are suggestive of the "scarcity of human occupation and human activity during the said cultural periods".[22] The Chalcolithic rock art is characterized by "the humans having comb-shaped headdresses and cattle with square and rectangular-shaped designs on bodies . . . and small horns".[23]

Rock art attributable to the Iron Age was also found to be widespread in the area. This, according to the epigraphists, is puzzling,[24] because the archaeological survey team had earlier found that the Bronze Age and Iron Age sites were rare in the area.[25]. The epigraphists expressed their inability to solve this enigma and remarked that they had "no evidence to trace how and when this [Iron Age] population settled in the area . . . [and from where it came]".[26]

From the differences between the rock art of the Jawf region and that of northwestern Arabia, that is the area of Tabūk, it was concluded that the people of al-Jawf were a culturally compact population with their own traditions and social and cultural values and that they had no contact with the people of northwestern Arabia.[27]

One interesting rock drawing found in the northwest of Sakākā, shows a couple of human figures in Roman dress and caps . . . "[These figures and] Nabataean inscriptions from the area suggest Nabataean influence on the local culture."[28]

The animals most frequently depicted in the rock art of the region are camel (both wild and domestic), ostrich, lion, ibex and horse. Cattle rarely appear. Hunting scenes are extremely rare,[29] except in the area south of al-Ṭuwair where a large number of ostrich-hunting scenes are depicted.[30] Also in the Ṭuwair area hundreds of fighting scenes, with horse riders holding long spears and attacking other riders, are depicted. *Awsām* (tribal marks) are also shown with the riders.[31]

Some sites of rock art and inscriptions in al-Jawf region are decribed in Part Three, Chapter 12.

---

1. Henry Field, *Ancient and Modern Man in Southwestern Asia*, Coral Gables, Florida, University of Miami Press, 1956, p.164.
2. Ibid., p.103.
3. Harold A. McClure, *The Arabian Peninsula and Prehistoric Populations*, Coconut Grove, Florida, Field Research Projects, 1971, p.72. The definition of "Pleistocene" is from *The Macmillan Dictionary of Archaeology*, London, 1983, p.397.
4. Abdullah H. Masry, "The Historic Legacy of Saudi Arabia", *Atlal* vol. 1, *1397*/1977, p.11.
5. Ibid., p.10.
6. See Parr, p.34; Whalen, "A Lower Pleistocene Site near Shuwayhitiyah", p.94.
7. Whalen, "A Lower Pleistocene Site near Shuwayhitiyah", pp.94-100.
8. Parr, pp.34-35.
9. Ibid., p.35.
10. Ibid., pp.35-36.
11. Ibid., p.36.
12. Ibid., pp.37-38.
13. Ibid., p.40.
14. Juris Zarins, "Rajājīl: A Unique Arabian Site from the Fourth Millennium B.C.", *Atlal* vol. 3, *1399*/1979, pp.73-74.
15. Ibid., p.74.
16. Ibid., pp.74, 76.
17. Ibid.; Winnett and Reed, p.12.
18. Zarins, "Rajājīl", pp.73, 75.
19. Parr, p.42.
20. Juris Zarins, "The Prehistory of the Jowf-Sakaka Area", 1977, Al-Sudairī Foundation MSS.
21. Khan, p.93.
22. Ibid., p.91.
23. Ibid., pp.91-92.
24. Ibid., p.92.
25. Ibid., p.88.
26. Ibid., p.92.
27. Ibid.
28. Ibid., p.84.
29. Ibid., p.89.
30. Ibid., p.83.
31. Ibid., pp.87-88.

PART THREE

THE PRE-ISLAMIC HISTORY OF AL-JAWF REGION

5

The Kingdom of Adummatu

The Jawf area first appears in written history at a time when the Assyrian Empire was the most powerful state of the Near East. The royal inscriptions of Assyria from the period of "the last and greatest phase of the Assyrian Empire [8th and 7th centuries BC]" provide us with a detailed picture of the political relationship of Dūmat al-Jandal, "the earliest recorded . . . independent Arabian state",[1] with Assyria and other neighbouring areas.

The part of the Arabian Peninsula that came into contact with the Assyrians was north Arabia, the area overlapping the desert that extends between Mesopotamia and Syria – now known as the Syrian desert or the Syro-Mesopotamian desert.[2] The Assyrian annals record a number of Assyrian military expeditions against this area. In these accounts the Assyrians refer to the area as "the land of Aribi". (Somewhat later, the Babylonians called the area Matu [land] A-Ra-bi or Matu Arabaai, thus giving it the same name; still later, the Persians referred to it as Arabaya.)[3] Dūmat al-Jandal was the central settlement in the "land of Aribi". One historian describes the position of Dūmat al-Jandal at that time and other geopolitical facts about the area as follows:

> In this period [9th to 7th centuries BC], Aribi is the northernmost part of Arabia between Syria and Mesopotamia, including the Palmyrene and Wādī Sirḥān. The Arabs are its nomadic and oasis inhabitants. The central oasis Adummatu is, according to Grohmann and Musil . . . Dūmat al-Djandal in the Djawf. The "kings" are chiefs partly of oasis settlements, partly of nomadic tribes.[4]

The first reference in the Assyrian records to a chief of Aribi is from the period of the Assyrian King Shalmaneser (or Salmanasar) III (r. 859-841 BC), occurring in the context of an event of considerable historical importance. It is not surprising that it is also the earliest recorded appearance of the word Arab, or, as Philip K. Hitti states, "the first unmistakable reference to the Arabians as such".[5] The annals show that an Arab chief, named Jindibu, joined forces with the Aramaeans (Syrians), Israelites, Cilicians, Egyptians, and Ammonites against the

Assyrians and participated, with one thousand camel troops, in a battle of the alliance against the Assyrian king in 853 BC at Qarqar on the Orontes river.[6] The Assyrian records boast of an overwhelming victory, which is doubted by some modern historians.[7] It has been pointed out by one authority that since the bedouin troops participating in the battle rode on camels, "we must look for the site of . . . [the] camp [of their chief] somewhere southeast of Damascus".[8]

The importance of this record for the history of upper north Arabia, apart from its primacy, lies in the fact that it shows the inhabitants of this area acting on the international political scene, forming alliances, and fighting for the sake of their liberty and the liberty of their allies.

Dūmat al-Jandal, at that time "the principal Arab settlement in upper North Arabia",[9] is referred to by the Assyrian annals as Adummatu, Adumu, and Adumat. In one source it is named as "Adumu, the fort of Aribi".[10] In another inscription the reference to the town or its fort is made as "the fort of Adumat, situated in the centre of an arid desert waste".[11] The records suggest that the oasis lay within the territory of the Arab tribe of Qedar [Kidri of the Assyrian records],[12] which held sway over north Arabia. "Palmyrena with the region southeast of Damascus was their habitat".[13] The camping areas of the individual clans of the Qedar and the clans of the other tribes subservient to the Qedar extended as far as the Nafūd desert. The settled people of Dūmat al-Jandal "were dependent upon the Ḳedar, because without the patronage of the latter trade caravans could not penetrate the desert."[14]

The annals of several Assyrian kings indicate that Dūmat al-Jandal was the capital city of a series of Arab queens. The texts name five different "queens of Aribi", mentioning Dūmat al-Jandal as their seat in the case of two of them (Queen Te'elkhunu or Telkhunu and Queen Tabu'a), while naming the rest (Queens Zabibē, Samsi [Arabic, Shams, Shamsa or Shamsiyya] and Yati'e or Iati'e) without giving the name of their capital city. Several authorities have expressed the view that most probably the three queens whose association with Dūmat al-Jandal is not specifically mentioned "resided there also".[15]

The sources show that Queen Te'elkhunu of Dūmat al-Jandal was the priestess of the deity Dilbat, which was worshipped by the people of Dūma under the name of 'Atarsamain and known elsewhere in the ancient Near East as Ishtar. Opinion has been expressed by scholars that in all likelihood the other queens also held the role of priestess to the deity.[16] Winnett and Reed, relying on Assyrian records, ascribe to these queens a political position that arose directly from their religious role as priestess:

> . . . [The queens] seem to have exercised more than religious powers . . . for both Tiglath-Pileser III (744-27 BC) and Sargon II (721-05) [kings of Assyria], in referring to the tribute received from foreign rulers, put Queen Samsi on a par with Pir'u of Musru ("Pharaoh of Egypt") and It'amar the Sabaean. The exalted position held by these North Arabian queens can only be accounted for by the assumption that the cult of Ishtar-'Atarsamain enjoyed tremendous prestige and popularity in North Arabia at that time. There can be no doubt that an important sanctuary of 'Atarsamain once existed in Adummatu/al-Jawf. Esarhaddon (680-69

> BC), in an attempt to win the goodwill of the Arabs, had a star of reddish gold, decorated with precious stones, made for the shrine. The star was no doubt a symbol of the goddess herself.[17]

The first north Arabian queen to appear in the Assyrian annals is Queen Zabibē. This occurs in the inscriptions of Tiglath-Pileser III, the founder of the second Assyrian Empire, and "the greatest of the Assyrian conquerors", who was the first Assyrian king to gain some measure of control over parts of north Arabia. His annals record that Queen Zabibē sent him tribute. According to some authorities this happened in approximately the third year of Tiglath-Pileser's reign,[18] whereas another historian gives the date as 738 BC[19] (which was the sixth year of his reign). As mentioned earlier, the records are silent about the capital city of the Queen, but several authorities say that it was most probably Dūmat al-Jandal. Grohmann writes that "she probably ruled the oasis of Adumu [Dūmat al-Jandal] and was high priestess of the Ḳedar tribe, to which the oasis paid tribute."[20]

The next queen mentioned in the records of the Assyrians is Queen Samsi, in c. 735 BC. Tiglath-Pileser III records that in the ninth year of his reign he subjugated Queen Samsi, who had broken an oath sworn by her by the great god Schamash that she would not cause the Assyrians trouble and would remain loyal to them. The King conquered two of her cities and encircled her camp, the Queen being left with no other course of action than surrendering and paying tribute of camels, both male and female.[21] It is thought that the cities conquered by the Assyrians "lie along the southeastern boundary of . . . [the domain of Damascus], possibly on the caravan road in the southern Ḥawrân. These cities, like all settlements on the line between the tilled fields and the desert, had been tributary to Queen Samsi."[22]

It is recorded in the Assyrian annals that the Queen suffered great losses in the battles: 1,100 men, 30,000 camels, and 20,000 sheep and goats, though these figures, according to one authority, "are no doubt highly inflated".[23]

A relief on the stele inscribed with the text relating the victory of the Assyrians shows two Assyrian horsemen pursuing a bedouin riding a camel. Trampled beneath them are the bodies of dead bedouin (with long hair thrown back) clad in loose clothes belted at the waist. A bedouin is also shown holding out his hands to the horsemen in supplication for mercy. Queen Samsi herself is shown barefoot, bearing a jar, her hair flowing. She had become weak with hunger and exhaustion and had apparently lost her senses.[24]

The Assyrians appointed a resident for her court to watch the conduct of the Queen and her subject tribes and report to his masters.[25]

What were the reasons for the Assyrian attack? It has been proposed that "perhaps Samsi had incurred . . . [the King's] wrath by aiding the hard-pressed King of Damascus" and that after the subjugation of Damascus the Assyrians turned their attention to the areas of the Queen.[26]

It has also been suggested that the Queen may not have been the only north Arabian ruler to side with the King of Damascus; probably other tribal chiefs also joined the coalition. The basis for this proposition is that the Assyrian annals record that in the same year in which the Assyrians overcame Queen Samsi, they also received tribute from "several Arab tribes, among them Mas'a, . . . Tema (Taymā'), Khayappa . . . , the Badana (southeast of the oasis of el-'Ela'-Daydan) and Sab'a (the Sabaeans)". Apparently, these tribes, too, were part of the alliance and were compelled to pay tribute to the Assyrians after having been subdued by them.[27]

Queen Samsi also appears in the annals of Sargon – alongside the Egyptian Pharaoh and It'amar the Sabaean – as a queen that paid tribute to the Assyrians in 715 BC. Sargon's annals also mention that

> [the tribute of Queen Samsi] . . . consisted of white female camels which the chiefs of the individual clans surrendered to the Assyrians in the name of their Queen. . . . [There is an inscription] which names four chiefs who, in the name of Queen Samsi, brought to the Great King 164 camels, specifically designated as "white".[28]

The names of the chiefs given in the inscription are: Jarapa, who was the leader of the group, Hataranu, Ganabu, and Tamranu.[29] According to an Arab historian, these are without doubt Arab names, though written in the Assyrian accent. Their original Arabic form, according to him, may have been Yarfa', Yarba' or Yarbū', Khāṭir or Khaṭar, Janāb or Janab, and Tamr or Tamār.[30]

King Sargon's annals also record, in the events of the same year (715 BC), the defeat of the Arabian tribes of Khayappa, Tamudi (Thamūd), Ibadidi, and the Marsimani at the hands of the Assyrians. Moreover, it is mentioned that the survivors of the battles were settled by the King in Samaria.[31]

The third queen of Aribi mentioned in the Assyrian annals is Queen Yati'e or Iati'e. This occurs in the annals of King Sennacherib (r. 715-681 BC) in the events of the years 703-02 BC. Queen Yati'e wanted to help the Babylonian King Marduk-apal-iddina against the Assyrians, and for this purpose she sent her brother Basqanu with troops. The annals record that Basqanu and most of his men were taken prisoner by Assyrian forces, following defeat at Kīsh.[32]

After Sennacherib had finally conquered Babylon in November 689 BC, he was able to turn his attention to north Arabia. Up to this point in the history of north Arabia, the Assyrians had campaigned against the chiefs, kings, and queens of Aribi but had not tried to strike at their base Dūmat al-Jandal, the central oasis of the land of Aribi. Sennacherib attacked Dūmat al-Jandal in about 688 BC, as recorded by the royal Assyrian annals. This campaign against Dūma is the first recorded attack on the oasis.

At this time the oasis and its surrounding desert was ruled by Queen Te'elkhunu – the fourth queen of Aribi appearing in the Assyrian records – her base mentioned as Adumu and Adumat, i.e. Dūmat al-Jandal. "The settlers of this large oasis were dependent upon the Ḳedar tribe which had control over Northern Arabia (the Palmyrene)."[33] The king or chief of the Qedar was Khaza'il or Ḥaza'il, and he had allied himself with the Queen. Assyrian annals record that:

> [in around 688 BC] Sennacherib undertook an expedition against Telḫunu, the Queen of the Arabs, defeated her in the desert (*madbari*), and captured many camels. The Queen, forsaking her tents, fled with Ḥazâel into the fort of Adumat, situated in the centre of an arid desert waste.[34]

It appears that when the Assyrian forces approached them, Queen Te'elkhunu and her supporters were camping in the desert somewhere near the western border region of Babylon, from which side the attack was most probably launched. Seeing the menacing arrival of the Assyrians, she and Khaza'il, who in all probability was acting as her military commander, fled to their fortified base in Dūmat al-Jandal. It has been suggested that at the time of the Assyrian attack "the influence of Queen Telḫunu must have extended up to the Babylonian frontier, since it was from Babylonia that trade caravans brought grain, cloth, and other articles necessary to the dwellers in the city of Adumu."[35]

It is recorded by another authority that King Sennacherib's annals also mention that the King's armies marched towards Dūmat al-Jandal and defeated the Arabs and the Qedar forces.[36] The annals of King Esarhaddon (r. 680-69 BC) and King Assurbanipal (r. 668-27BC) record that Queen Te'elkhunu, who was the priestess to the deity Dilbat, betrayed Khaza'il and defected to the Assyrians, and that Sennacherib took to Nineveh all the idols of Dūma and the Queen Te'elkhunu herself, together with her daughter, Princess Tabu'a (the fifth Queen of Aribi), who was to be brought up in a manner approved by the Assyrians and to be given an appropriate political training, preparing her to be a queen of the Arabs who was loyal to the Assyrians.[37] In regard to the relations of the Queen with the Qedar's chief, Khaza'il, it has been suggested that although Te'elkhunu exercised power as queen, Khaza'il was perhaps commander of the army and responsible for military operations. The Queen's anger may have been roused by Khaza'il's poor military leadership, or a result of the siege of Dūmat al-Jandal and the manner of its defence.[38] In any case, Queen Te'elkhunu made peace with the Assyrians, and the army of Sennacherib took over Dūma.[39]

As for Khaza'il, he was able to escape from the Assyrian siege of Dūma and to withdraw with his followers into the desert, where Sennacherib was unable to pursue them or to inflict further losses on them. Khaza'il remained there throughout the lifetime of Sennacherib, and it was only with the death of Sennacherib and the succession of his son Esarhaddon that the reasons for hostility vanished. Khaza'il went to Nineveh to meet the new King and took numerous gifts with him. Esarhaddon received Khaza'il favourably, accepted the gifts, and returned to him the captured idols of Adummatu – Dilbat, Daja, Nuhaia, Ebirillu and Atar Kurumaia.[40] (Although Dilbat [or 'Atarsamain] was the chief diety of Dūmat al-Jandal, and perhaps of the whole of the northern part of the Peninsula, the other deities also had a following, and worship of at least some of them continued after the Assyrian period.[41]) Some of the idols had been damaged when they were carried to Assyria. Esarhaddon ordered their repair before handing them over to Khaza'il. At the same time he ordered that a statement be inscribed on the idols to the effect that the Assyrian deities were superior to them. The King also directed that his name, too, be inscribed over them.[42] It was Esarhaddon's wish to appoint Tabu'a as Queen of the Arabs: as we have seen, she had been given Assyrian education in order to ensure that she should be a vehicle of Assyrian dominance over the Arabs. She was installed as Queen, but this arrangement was not long-lasting, for the enmity between the Assyrians and the Arabs by this stage was so deep that it could not be overcome simply by granting a crown and appointing a king or a queen.[43] At the same time, Esarhaddon recognized K͟haza'il as king of the tribe of Qedar in return for an increased tribute of 65 camels.[44] When K͟haza'il died in c. 675 BC, Esarhaddon appointed Uaite', K͟haza'il's son, as king in his place, in return for a large tribute which included 1,000 *minae* of gold, in addition to 1,000 precious stones and fifty camels. Uaite' agreed heedlessly to these excessive conditions in order to gain the crown.[45]

However, events turned out not as Uaite' had anticipated, for his people rebelled against him, refusing to acknowledge a king who had been forced to accept harsh conditions. The leader of the rebellion against him and against the Assyrians was a certain Wahb (whose name is given in various forms – Awb, Awbu, Uabo, Uaabo, Wahbu). The Assyrians were naturally greatly angered and despatched an army to quell the rebellion. The expedition was successful and Wahb was taken as a captive to Nineveh. However, this was not the end of the Qedar uprising, for Uaite' led yet another rebellion against the Assyrians, raiding the frontier of their empire from the desert vastnesses. The Assyrian annals record that Uaite' "has forgotten the treaty, he has forgotten the good deeds shown him" and that Esarhaddon suppressed a rebellion headed by Uaite'. As a consequence, the idols of the Arabs were seized for the second time and taken, along with the prisoners, to Assyria. Uaite', however, fled alone to distant regions difficult for the Assyrians to penetrate and capture him.[46] It is not known whether on this occasion Esarhaddon himself came to Arabia. It has been suggested that "the Assyrian army did not enter Adumu . . . , for Tabûa, its mistress, remained faithful."[47]

In the fifth year of his reign (676-75 BC) Esarhaddon undertook a campaign against the Arab tribes inhabiting the areas of "Bāzu" and "K͟hazu", the location of which scholars have not been able to determine conclusively. Different suggested locations range from the Wādi'l-Sirḥān in the Jawf Province to the al-Aḥsā' region (in the Eastern Province of Sa'ūdi Arabia) on the Arabian Gulf.[48]

Esarhaddon died in 669 BC. Seeing that his best course was to reconcile with the Assyrians, Uaite' went to the new Assyrian king, Esarhaddon's son Assurbanipal, and sought his goodwill. Assurbanipal pardoned and reinstated him and returned the idols of his tribe.[49]

After the death of Esarhaddon, Assurbanipal's brother Shamash-shum-ukin was installed as King of Babylonia (in 668 BC) in accordance with the succession arrangements made by Esarhaddon. When bad blood developed between the two brothers, the north Arabians again sided with the Babylonians. When Shamash-shum-ukin formed, in 656 BC, a secret alliance with other peoples in order to prepare himself for his planned revolt against Assurbanipal, the Arabs were an integral part of the league. Shamash-shum-ukin made a premature attack against Assyria in 652 BC, without waiting for the assistance that had been promised by Egypt. The rebellion lasted for four years.[50] The Qedar helped the Babylonians on two fronts: they conducted raids on the Assyrian borders adjoining their lands and, making a more meaningful contribution to the uprising, sent reinforcements to Shamash-shum-ukin in Babylonia.

Qedar tribesmen, under their king, Uaite', "plundered . . . the western borders of the desert from Edom in the south to Ḥama' in the north". Assurbanipal directed his Syrian garrisons to meet this challenge. After various encounters between the two sides in which the Arabs faced reverses, the Qedar retreated to their desert areas. Uaite' took refuge with Natnu, the King of the Nabaitai.[51] In the absence of Uaite', the Qedar tribe chose Ammulati as their new chief. Ammulati, however, made incursions into the territory of Moab, where he and Uaite''s wife Adiya, who had placed herself under Ammulati's protection, were captured by Kamaskhalta', the King of Moab, and sent to the Assyrian capital.[52] This occurred in 648 BC, but before this, Ammulati had assisted Shamash-shum-ukin in his revolt and had raided the land of Amurru, which was at the time under Assyrian control. Assurbanipal was, therefore, pleased to receive the news of the victory of Kamaskhalta'. The scene of the capture of Ammulati and Adiya is drawn on the walls of a room of Assurbanipal's palace.[53]

To help Shamash-shum-ukin in his revolt, Uaite' sent camel troops under the command of Abiate and Aimu, the sons of a certain Te'ri. The alliance started losing the war, and by 650 BC Babylon itself came under siege. Abiate, with his Qedar reinforcements, had also retreated to Babylon. "When later the . . . garrison began to suffer hunger, he cut his way through the besieging Assyrian army and regained his freedom with the loss of most of his soldiers. With the remainder he appeared at Nineveh and appealed for mercy." He was pardoned and appointed King of the Qedar under the usual conditions of payment of "tribute in gold, precious stones, eyebrow dyes, camels, and donkeys".[54]

After the fall of Babylon towards the end of 648 BC, Natnu, the King of the Nabaṭaeans, too, decided that it was time to pay homage to Assurbanipal. For that purpose, "he delivered into the hands of the Assyrians Uaite', the Ḳedar King, who had sought refuge with him."[55] It is mentioned in the annals of Assurbanipal that Uaite' was put in a cage and displayed at one of the city gates.[56]

However, peace between the north Arabians and the Assyrians was not to last long. The last encounter between them reported in the Assyrian annals occurred about seven years later. When, in 641-40 BC, Assurbanipal was at war with the King of Elam, the Qedar tribe under the leadership of Uaite' II (a nephew of the earlier King Uaite' and son of Bir Dadda, acknowledged as their head chief by the Qedar) and Abiate, son of Te'ri (who either had not been able to assume the kingship of the Qedar after he was designated as such by Assurbanipal or had subsequently been replaced by Uaite'), again revolted against the Assyrians and attacked the Assyrian regions bordering the Arab lands. When Assurbanipal sent a large force against them, the Qedar requested help from Natnu, the Nabaṭaean king, who decided to come to their rescue. Two other tribes, Isamme' and 'Atarsamain, also joined forces with them. In the ensuing battles that took place between the Arab tribes and Assyrians at various places around Tadmor (Palmyra, modern Tadmur or Tudmur), the Assyrians won resounding victories, and their soldiers "drove the men, women, donkeys, camels, cows, and sheep in great numbers to Assyria". The idols of the Qedar, and Uaite''s mother and wife were also captured. Uaite' saved himself by fleeing. Abiate and his brother Aimu were captured in another battle near Khukhurina.[57]

What were the motives of the Assyrians behind the periodic raids on north Arabia? The broader situation was that Egypt and Babylonia were hostile to Assyria. The Arabs followed a pro-Babylonian policy on account of their long-standing political and cultural relations with Babylonia. The bedouins, "a thorn in the side of the Assyrian Empire", used to harass the Assyrian provinces in Syria and obstruct the smooth flow of commercial traffic passing through Syria on the Assyrian trade routes to the Mediterranean. In their ventures the bedouins were aided by Egypt and Babylonia. According to one view, the purpose of these campaigns against Aribi was "to chastise the unconquerable Bedouins".[58] The raids "served the general purpose of securing the Assyrian borderlands and lines of communication" and "were clearly not wars of conquest but punitive expeditions intended to recall the erring nomads to their duties as Assyrian vassals."[59]

The successive Assyrian campaigns against Dūmat al-Jandal and the neighbouring Arab tribes were followed by the campaigns of the kings of the Chaldaean (Neo-Babylonian) dynasty (626-539 BC) of Babylonia, heirs to the Assyrian Empire (which disappeared from history in 609 BC). Nebuchadrezzar II, the greatest king of this dynasty (r. 605-562 BC), launched an attack in 599 BC on the Arab tribes. Babylonian records indicate that he sent a force against the Arabs inhabiting the desert and that the Babylonians plundered the possessions of the Arabs, including livestock and idols, before returning.[60] The desert and the tribes inhabiting it are not named, nor is the route followed by the Chaldaean force mentioned. Scholars suggest that the Qedar tribe was leading the other tribes in this encounter.[61]

In about 552 BC, Nabonidus (r. 556-539 BC) left his son Bel-shar-ushur in control of Babylonia and attacked Dūmat al-Jandal. (Historians speculate that he followed the route which passes through Bilād al-Shām and east Jordan, the later Ḥajj route from Syria to Makkat al-Mukarrama.)[62] Then he marched with his army onward to Taimā' – around 300 km. to the south-south-west of Dūma – which he conquered and where he subsequently built a great castle, named *Ablaq*, like his palace in Babylon. Nabonidus remained in Taimā' until he was obliged to return to Babylonia on the menacing arrival of the Persians, who threatened his 'Irāqī possessions and ultimately overthrew him and his dynasty in 539 BC.[63] "The precise dates of his self-imposed exile are not known. In his inscriptions Nabonidus claimed to have been among the Arabs for 10 years."[64]

"After the Persian capture of Babylon . . . a short-lived satrapy called Arabaya was created in Northern Arabia."[65] The founder of the new Persian Empire (Achaemenid Empire), Cyrus the Great, is reported to have received the assistance of some Arab camel troops in his attack on Babylonia,[66] but there is no evidence to suggest that he or his successors ever tried to subjugate Arabia on a larger scale. While writing about the third Achaemenid Emperor, Darius the Great (r. 522-486 BC), the 5th century BC Greek historian Herodotus says that:

> . . . [The dominion of Darius] extended over the whole of Asia, with the exception of Arabia. The Arabs had never been reduced to subjugation by the Persians, but friendly relations had continued between the two countries ever since the Arabs let Cambyses [the son and successor of Cyrus] pass through their territory on his Egyptian campaign [in 525 BC].[67]

Winnett and Reed speculate that Dūmat al-Jandal may have come under Persian rule, but concede that there is no evidence to support this.[68]

The Greek Empire displaced the Persian Empire in south-west Asia. There are reports that its founder, Alexander the Great (356-323 BC), while he was at Babylon immediately before his death, decided to send a fleet downriver, as well as an army, to conquer some parts of Arabia. His plan seemingly was to strike overland from Kuwait to the Gulf of 'Aqaba – Dūmat al-Jandal is directly on this planned route of march. However, three days before the date on which the forces were to set out, Alexander fell ill and died ten days later.[69] His successors did not care to pursue his plan.

The next people to leave a mark on the historical canvas of al-Jawf region were the Nabaṭaeans, "originally a nomadic Arab group who had gradually settled to form a state" [70] towards the end of the fourth century BC, drawing their strength mainly from commerce. (Their prosperity rested on their role in the caravan trade between southern Arabia and "the classical cities of the Mediterranean".)[71] In the last century of the first millennium BC, their kingdom (Nabaṭaea), with its capital at Petra in present-day southern Jordan, supplanted the earlier successive states in northwestern Arabia, gaining control of al-Ḥijr (present Madā'in Ṣāliḥ), Dūmat al-Jandal, and the Wādi'l-Sirḥān.[72] They built up a group of strategically-placed cities throughout the region, and the Wādi'l-Sirḥān served as "the connecting lifeline between the two widely separated parts of the Nabataean kingdom".[73] The Nabaṭaeans have not left any written record of their domination of Dūmat al-Jandal and the Wādi'l-Sirḥān, but archaeology provides solid evidence of that (see Part Three, Chapters 11 and 12). The Greek geographer and historian Strabo (c. 64BC to 23) records in his *Geography* (XVI, 4:24) that at the time of the Arabian expedition of Aelius Gallus, the Roman prefect of Egypt, in 24BC, the Nabaṭaeans were in control of al-Ḥijr. The middle of the 1st century BC or a little earlier seems to be the most likely date for the Nabaṭaean takeover of al-Ḥijr[74] and, most probably, of Dūmat al-Jandal, which saw under them its most flourishing period during the ancient times.[75]

The Nabaṭaean Kingdom was annexed by the Romans in 106 during the time of Emperor Trajan. For the period following this, the geographical and historical sources "provide no guidance in the determination of Roman administrative boundaries".[76] Consequently, there is disagreement among scholars over the exact boundaries of the *Provincia Arabia*, the Roman province encompassing the newly-acquired territories. There would be no disagreement so far as the Roman control of the core of the former Nabaṭaean Kingdom is concerned, but problems arise when one comes to the control of "the edges, where the province bleeds into the desert . . ."[77] It is unlikely that the Romans and, later, the Byzantines had any clearly-defined "boundaries within the wastes of the great Syrian desert".[78] For an appraisal of the nature and scope of the Roman and Byzantine relations with al-Jawf region, we have relied for the most part on a special article by Dr Geoffrey King (see pp.54–58), though the reader will come across in the following chapters a few isolated glances into the contacts of the area with other regional powers at the time of the rise of Islam.

---

1. Abdullah H. Masry, op. cit., p.14.
2. See *Encyclopaedia of Islam*, new ed., s.v. "al-'Arab", by A. Grohmann; ibid. s.v. "Badw. II. (c) Bedouin Nomadism in Arabia", by H. von Wissmann; Jawād 'Alī, *al-Mufaṣṣal fī Tārīkh al-'Arab qabl al-Islām*, 10 vols., Beirut, Dār al-'Ilm lil-Malāyīn, 1976-78, vol. 1 pp.16, 18, 164, 165; Bernard Lewis, *The Arabs in History*, 5th ed., London, Hutchinson, 1977, p.11; cf. P. K. Hitti, *History of the Arabs*, 10 ed., London, Macmillan, 1970, p.39 and Musil, *Arabia Deserta*, p.479.
3. Jawād 'Alī, vol. 1 p.165.
4. *Encyclopaedia of Islam*, s.v. "Badw. II. (c) Bedouin Nomadism in Arabia," by H. von Wissmann.
5. Hitti, p.37.
6. For a translation of the original Assyrian text, see D.D. Luckenbill, *Ancient Records of Assyria and Babylonia*, 2 vols., Chicago, 1927, vol. 1 p.611, quoted in Hitti, p.37. See also Jawād 'Alī, vol. 1 pp.574-76. Musil, *Arabia Deserta*, p.477. Lewis, op.cit., p.11.
7. See, e.g., Arnold J. Toynbee, *A Study of History*, abridgement by D.C. Somervell, 2 vols., Oxford, Oxford University Press, 1987, vol. 1 p.339; William W. Hallo and William Kelly Simpson, *The Ancient Near East: A History*, New York, Harcourt Brace Jovanovich, 1971, pp.127-28.
8. Musil, *Arabia Deserta*, p.477.
9. Winnett and Reed, p.71.
10. George Smith, *History of Sennacherib*, London, 1878, p.138, quoted in Musil, *Arabia Deserta*, p.480.
11. V. Scheil, *Miscelles I. La campagne de Sennachérib contre les Arabes*, Orientalistische Literaturzeitung, vol. 7, Berlin, 1904, cols. 69-70, quoted in Musil, *Arabia Deserta*, p.480.
12. Winnett and Reed, p.71.
13. Hitti, p.42.
14. Musil, *Arabia Deserta*, p.481.
15. See, e.g., *Encyclopaedia of Islam*, s.v. "al-'Arab", by A. Grohmann; Musil, *Arabia Deserta*, p.477; Winnett and Reed, p.71.
16. See Winnett and Reed, p.72; Musil, *Arabia Deserta*, p.477.
17. Winnett and Reed, p.72.
18. A.T. Olmstead, *History of Assyria*, London, C. Scribner's Sons, 1923, p.189, cited by Jawād 'Alī, vol. 1 p.577.
19. Musil, *Arabia Deserta*, p.477, citing, among others, A.H. Layard, *Inscriptions in the Cuneiform Character from Assyrian Monuments*, London, 1882, plates 50 b, 67 a.
20. *Encyclopaedia of Islam*, s.v. "al-'Arab", by A. Grohmann.
21. Jawād 'Alī, vol. 1 pp.577-78, citing J.B. Pritchard, ed., *Ancient Near Eastern Texts*, Princeton, 1950, p.283 and Olmstead, op.cit., p.199.
22. Musil, *Arabia Deserta*, p.477.
23. Jawād 'Alī, vol. 1 p.578, citing Bruno Meissner, *Könige Babyloniens und Assyriens . . .*, Leipzig, 1926, plate 140.
24. Jawād 'Alī, vol. 1 pp.578-79, citing Olmstead, op.cit., p.199.
25. Musil, *Arabia Deserta*, p.477, citing, among others, Layard, op.cit., plate 66.
26. Ibid., p.477.

27. *Encyclopaedia of Islam*, s.v. "al-'Arab", by A. Grohmann; cf. Hitti, p.37 and Musil, *Arabia Deserta*, pp.477-79.
28. Musil, *Arabia Deserta*, p.480, citing, among others, Hugo Winckler, *Die Keilschrifttexte Sargon's nach den Papierabklatschen und Originaten neu herausgegeben*, 2 vols., Leipzig, 1889, vol. 2 plate 62.
29. Jawād 'Alī, vol. 1 p.579, citing, among others, Winckler, op.cit., vol. 2 plate 62.
30. Jawād 'Alī, vol. 1 p.579.
31. Musil, *Arabia Deserta*, p.479, citing, among others, Winckler, op.cit., vol. 2 plate 2, no.1.
32. Musil, *Arabia Deserta*, p.480, citing Sidney Smith, *The First Campaign of Sennacherib, King of Assyria, B.C. 705-681*, London, 1921, p.62; Jawād 'Alī, vol. 1 p.588, citing the same source; *Encyclopaedia of Islam*, s.v. "al-'Arab", by A. Grohmann.
33. *Encyclopaedia of Islam*, s.v. "al-'Arab", by A. Grohmann.
34. Musil, *Arabia Deserta*, p.480, citing, among others, Scheil, op.cit., cols. 69-70.
35. Musil, *Arabia Deserta*, p.480.
36. Jawād 'Alī, vol. 1 p.590, citing, among others, Olmstead, op.cit., p.310.
37. See Musil, *Arabia Deserta*, p.480, citing, among others, Smith, op.cit., p.138, and London, British Museum, Tablets K 3087 and K 3405; Jawād 'Alī, vol. 1 p.592 citing the same British Museum tablets.
38. Jawād 'Alī, vol. 1 p.592.
39. Ibid.
40. Ibid., pp.592-93, citing Pritchard, op.cit., p.291 and D.J. Wixman, *The Vassal-Treaties of Esarhaddon*, London, 1958, p.4.
41. Winnett and Reed, p.72.
42. Jawād 'Alī, vol. 1 p.593, citing Pritchard, op.cit., p.291.
43. Ibid.
44. Musil, *Arabia Deserta*, p.482, citing A.H. Rawlinson, *Cuneiform Inscriptions of Western Asia*, 5 vols., London, 1861-84, vol. 1 plates 45-47.
45. Ibid.; see also Jawād 'Alī, vol. 1 p.593, citing A. Grohmann, *Arabien*, Munich, 1963, plate 22.
46. See Jawād 'Alī, vol. 1 pp.593-94, citing, among others, Luckenbill, op.cit., vol. 2 p.916; Musil, *Arabia Deserta*, p.482, citing, among others, Maximilian Streck, *Assurbanipal und die letzen assyrischen Könige*, 3 vols. Vorderasiatische Bibliothek, no.7, Leipzig, 1916, vol. 2 p.377. Cf. Hitti, p.38, citing Luckenbill, op.cit., vol. 2 p.946. Hitti gives the approximate date of the event as 676 BC, which seems to be wrong because the events relate to the period following Khaza'il's death, which, according to most authorities, occurred in 675 BC.
47. Musil, *Arabia Deserta*, p.482.
48. For a detailed discussion on this campaign, see Jawād 'Alī, vol. 1 pp.594-600 and Musil, *Arabia Deserta*, pp.482-85. Musil proposes that it is the Wādi'l-Sirḥān and its adjoining regions that are meant by these names.
49. Musil, *Arabia Deserta*, p.485, citing, among others, Rawlinson, op.cit., vol. 3 plates 33-34.
50. Michael Roaf, *Cultural Atlas of Mesopotamia and the Ancient Near East*, New York, Facts on File, 1990, p.191.
51. Musil, *Arabia Deserta*, p.485, citing, among others, Rawlinson, op.cit., vol. 3 plates 33-34. Musil says that the Nabaṭaeans (Nabaitai of the Assyrians), "according to . . . Assyrian records had their camping grounds in the southern half of the depression of Sirḥān." *Arabia Deserta*, p.478. At another place he writes that, "[according to Assyrian sources Natnu's tribe] camped far away and none of his forefathers had sent envoys to the court at Nineveh". Then he suggests that "we must seek the Nabaitai in the southwestern part of Arabia Deserta, west of Adumu (Dûma), because here only the Assyrian influence had not previously penetrated." Ibid., p.486. Another historian, G.W. Bowersock, however, is of he opinion that "there is no secure basis for identifying . . . [the Nabaṭaeans] with the Nebaioth of the Old Testament or peoples of similar name in Assyrian documents." Bowersock, p.14.
52. Ibid., pp.485-86, citing among others, Rawlinson, op.cit., vol. 3 plates 34-36.
53. Jawād 'Alī, vol. 1 pp.601-02, citing London, British Museum, *A Guide to the Babylonian and Assyrian Antiquities*, London, 1992, p.184.
54. Musil, *Arabia Deserta*, p.486, citing, among others, Rawlinson, op.cit., vol. 5, pt.1, plates 9-10 and vol. 3 plates 35-36.
55. Ibid.
56. Jawād 'Alī, vol. 1 p.602, citing *Reallexikon der Assyriologie*, vol. 1 plate 126.
57. See Musil, *Arabia Deserta*, pp.486-89, citing, among others, Rawlinson, op.cit., vol. 3 plates 34-36 and vol. 5, pt.1, plates 9-10; Jawād 'Alī, vol. 1 p.603, citing Meissner, op.cit., plate 246.
58. Hitti, p.39; *Encyclopaedia of Islam*, s.v. "al-'Arab", by A. Grohmann.

59. Lewis, op.cit., p.11.
60. Jawād 'Alī, vol. 1 p.609, citing D.J. Wiseman, *Chronicles of Chaldaean Kings*, London, 1956, pp.31, 48, 71.
61. Jawād 'Alī, vol. 1 pp.609-10.
62. Ibid., vol. 1 p.611; see also Sidney Smith, *Babylonian Historical Texts Relating to the Capture and Downfall of Babylon*, London, 1924, p.84, cited by Alois Musil, *Northern Neğd: A Topographical Itinerary*, New York, American Geographical Society of New York, 1928, p.225.
63. Jawād 'Alī, vol. 1 pp.609-611.
64. Roaf, op.cit., p.201.
65. *Encyclopaedia of Islam*, s.v. "[Djazīrat] al-'Arab (vii) History I---Pre-Islamic", by G. Rentz.
66. Jawād 'Alī, vol. 1 pp.620-21, citing, among others, Grohmann, op.cit., plate 71.
67. Herodotus, *The Histories*, trans. Aubrey de Selincourt, rev. with an Introduction and Notes by A.R. Burn, Harmondsworth, England, Penguin Books, 1987, p.242.
68. Winnett and Reed, pp.72-73.
69. N.G.L. Hammond, *Alexander the Great: King, Commander and Statesman*, London, Chatto & Windus, 1981, pp.301, 306, 325.
70. John Healey, "The Nabataeans and Madā'in Ṣāliḥ", *Atlal* vol. 10, *1406*/1986, pp.108-16 (109).
71. Hitti, p.67.
72. See Masry, op.cit., p.15, and Daifullah Al-Talhi, Mohammad Al-Ibrahim and Jamal Mohammad Mursi, "Preliminary Report on al-Hijr Excavations during the First Season 1406/1986", *Atlal* vol. 11, *1409*/1988, pp.47-57 (48). On the basis of a statement of Pliny (*Natural History*, VI, 156) to the effect that the royal city of the Liḥyānites was Hegra (al-Ḥijr), and on the basis of some Nabaṭaean inscriptions in Madā'in Ṣāliḥ, written by a certian Mas'ūdu, who claims the credit for the overthrow of the Liḥyānite rule, scholars are of the same opinion that it was the state of the Liḥyānites at al-Ḥijr which "came to an end at the hands of the Nabataeans in the first century BC". See, e.g., Alois Musil, *The Northern Ḥeğâz: A Topographical Itinerary*, New York, American Geographical Society of New York, 1926, p.305, Healey, op.cit. , p.114, Al-Talhi, op.cit., pp.47-48, and Winnett and Reed, pp.120, 130.
73. Nelson Glueck, "Wadi Sirhan in North Arabia", *Bulletin of the American Schools of Oriental Research* vol. 96, 1944, pp.7-17 (7), quoted in Winnett and Reed, p.133.
74. Healey, op.cit., p.114.
75. al-Muaikel, vol.1, p.19.
76. Bowersock, pp.90-91.
77. Ibid., p.91.
78. Ibid., p.99.

6

The 3rd Century to the 5th Century

It is difficult to provide a clear synopsis of the history of a region which lacks adequate written records or archaeological evidence. This paucity of records makes itself felt recurrently in the history of al-Jawf. A hiatus in the record starts at the beginning of the Persian period in South West Asia, and it is only centuries later that al-Jawf re-emerges briefly into the light of history. Nevertheless, it is to be hoped that eventually archaeological research in the region, for which there is ample scope, will help to fill in some of these gaps.

Dūmat al-Jandal is mentioned in the 3rd century in the time of the famous Arab Queen Zenobia, who ruled Tadmor (Palmyra, modern Tadmur or Tudmur) from 267 to 272. It appears that she raided Dūma, but its fortress was too strong for her to overcome, and she returned unsuccessful. Her failure before the defences of Dūma made her utter the famous quip: "Mārid is rebellious and Ablaq is haughty." The Mārid in this saying is the Qaṣr Mārid in Dūmat al-Jandal, whereas Qaṣr al-Ablaq is the famous fortress of Taimā'.[1] It can be inferred from this brief report that in the period of Queen Zenobia's ascendancy, Dūmat al-Jandal and its fortress of Mārid had enough strength to resist Zenobia.

The city appears once again in the historical record in the 5th century when an Arab king, Imru' al-Qais, gained control of it. He originally resided in 'Irāq with his tribe at al-Ḥīra but subsequently migrated to Dūmat al-Jandal. His power in north Arabia increased to such an extent that he came to dominate the territory of what is now Jordan and managed to seize the Island of Tīrān (Iotabe), at the mouth of the Gulf of 'Aqaba, from the Byzantines.[2] It is interesting to note that another chieftain by the name of Imru' al-Qais was appointed by Muḥammad, the Prophet (P.B.U.H.), as leader of the tribes of Kalb and Quḍā'a two centuries later. This Imru' al-Qais had converted and given his allegiance to Islam. He was the son of al-Aṣbagh of the Kalb tribe, the dominant tribe around Dūma at the rise of Islam.

---

1. Aḥamd bin Muḥammad al-Nīsābūrī al-Maidānī, *Majma' al-Amthāl*, ed. Muḥammad Muḥyi'l-Dīn 'Abd al-Ḥamīd, 2 vols., Cairo, Dār al-Fikr, 1972, vol. 1 p.126; cf. 'Alī bin Ḥusain bin 'Alī al-Mas'ūdī, *Murūj al-Dhahab wa Ma'ādin al-Jawhar = Les Prairies d'Or*, ed. and trans. C. Barbier de Meynard and Pavet de Courteille, 9 vols., Paris, Société Asiatique, 1861-77, vol. 3 p.198.
2. See Musil, *The Northern Ḥeǧâz*, pp.306-09; Jawād 'Alī, vol. 2 pp.653-56; Ḥamd al-Jāsir, *Fī Shimāl Gharb al-Jazīra*, Riyadh, Dār al-Yamāma, *1390*/1970, pp.109-10.

7
The Kingdom of Ukaidir

At the time of the rise of Islam, Dūmat al-Jandal was ruled by al-Ukaidir bin 'Abd al-Malik of the Kinda tribe.[1] The first of the kings of Dūmat al-Jandal is said to have been Dujāja bin Qunāfa bin 'Adī bin Zuhair bin Junāb al-Kalbī. Of al-Ukaidir's Kindī origins it has been said that he was a descendant of the Kindī kings installed over the Kalb tribe by the Ḥimyarites.[2] The tribe of Kalb in this period was Christian. It dominated not only the territory around Dūmat al-Jandal but also the areas as far west as Tabūk in north-west Arabia.[3] Ḥamd al-Jāsir points out that the Kalb tribe, a branch of the Quḍā'a, which itself is of Qaḥṭānī origin, is mentioned in poetry as dominating the northern part of the Peninsula from the 'Ālij sands (now known as the great Nafūd). He says that at times its authority extended to the Nafūd region. As evidence of this he quotes the following verse of a poem of al-Akhnus bin Shihāb al-Taghlibī which refers to the lands held by the Kalb.[4]

Every tribe of Ma'add has its own marked land
  And designated quarters, in which it takes refuge.
The Lukaiz have Baḥrain and the seaside all to themselves.
  Should danger threaten them from India,
They fly on the backs of wild mounts,
  Swift as clouds that have poured out rain.
The Bakr have the land of 'Irāq. Should they wish,
  Yamāma's escarpment will fence them.
The Tamīm are located between the rugged hills and the soft sands;
  Their pastures will conceal them and sustain them.
And the Kalb extend from Khabt[5] and the sands of 'Ālij
  To the Ḥarrat al-Rajlā',[6] for which they would fight.[7]

F. Wüstenfeld mentions that the sub-tribe of the Kalb dominating this area was the Banū Kināna and that this territory had been allotted to them at a general assembly of the Kalb tribe.[8]

In Musil's opinion, al-Ukaidir's name was perhaps originally al-Akdar, a name by which he is known to poets, and that the form in which his name is written by the historians of the early Islamic period – al-Ukaidir – is a diminutive, invidiously given to him (a common practice among the Arabs whereby Ṭalḥa takes the diminutive form Ṭulaiḥa or the name Maslama becomes Musailima, for instance).[9] The name was also familiar in the early Islamic period, for the historian al-Mas'ūdī (d. *346*/957) mentions the killing in Egypt of a certain Ukaidir bin al-Ḥammām at the hands of Marwān bin al-Ḥakam bin Abī al-'Āṣ.[10] As for al-Ukaidir himself, he was highly regarded in his own day and his fame continued into later times. We find that al-Jāḥiẓ (d. *255*/869) included him in a list of the names of famous men from the ancient past. Al-Jāḥiẓ says that:

> Among the famous men known in former times for wisdom, leadership and eloquence were 'Ubaid bin Shariyya al-Jurhamī, Asquf Najrān, Ukaidir – lord of Dūmat al-Jandal – Ufai'ī Najrān, Dharib bin Hawṭ, 'Ulaim bin Janāb, 'Amr bin Rabī'a bin Ḥāritha bin 'Amr Muzīqiyā' and Judhaima bin Mālik bin Abrashī.[11]

There are various indications that Ukaidir and Dūmat al-Jandal had some sort of relationship with the great powers of Byzantium and Sassanian Iran. The close cooperation, at the time of the conquest of Dūmat al-Jandal in *12/633* at the hands of the Muslim commander Khālid bin al-Walīd, between Ukaidir on the one hand, and the Ghassānid King Ibn al-Aiham and the Ghassānid chieftain Jūdiyy bin Rabī'a on the other, suggests that Ukaidir was acting in accord with the Byzantines, with whom the Ghassānids were allied. It is recorded by al-Mas'ūdī that Ukaidir had accepted the Byzantine emperor, Heraclius, as his overlord. Al-Mas'ūdī even says that the first expedition of Prophet Muḥammad (P.B.U.H.) against Dūmat al-Jandal (which was governed at the time by Ukaidir) was the Prophet's first *ghazwa* against Rome.[12] This readily explains the Ghassānid cooperation with Ukaidir.

There is also evidence that Dūmat al-Jandal had contacts with al-Ḥīra, whose kings at some point had influence there.[13]

It is recounted that when Ukaidir went to al-Madīnat al-Munawwara, he brought with him a robe which had come to him from Chosroes, the Sassanian emperor, and which he intended to give to the Prophet (P.B.U.H.).[14] This indicates a relationship between Ukaidir and the Sassanians in the pre-Islamic period that had been close enough for their emperor to have sent a rich gift in the form of this robe to Ukaidir.

There is a legendary account of Ukaidir to the effect that he had lived as a youth in al-Ḥīra in southern 'Irāq, in a district of the town called Dūma, along with his brothers. They used to visit their uncles of the Kalb tribe in the desert. In the course of one of these expeditions, they came upon a ruined and deserted city of which nothing remained but a few walls built of boulders (*jandal*). According to the legend, they reconstructed the city and settled in it, planting olive trees and giving it the name Dūmat al-Jandal on account of its plentiful stones and after their district of Dūma in al-Ḥīra.[15] The account has been questioned by Musil on the grounds that Dūmat al-Jandal is more ancient than Dūmat al-Ḥīra and that there is no convincing evidence that Dūmat al-Jandal was ever abandoned.[16] Nevertheless, the story is interesting inasmuch as it associates the town of al-Ḥīra, allied to the Sassanians, with Ukaidir. It adds some weight to the view that Ukaidir had connections with al-Ḥīra, and not only with the Byzantines and their Ghassānid allies.

---

1. 'Alī bin Ḥusain bin 'Alī al-Mas'ūdī, *Kitāb al-Tanbīh wa'l-Ishrāf*, ed. M.J. De Goeje, Leiden, 1894; reprint ed., Beirut: Maktabat Khayyāṭ, 1965, p.248; Jawād 'Alī, vol. 4 p.233. Al-Ukaidir's full genealogy is given as follows: al-Ukaidir bin 'Abd al-Malik bin 'Abd al-Ḥayy bin A'yā bin al-Ḥārith bin Mu'āwiya bin Khilāda bin Abāma bin Salma bin Shukāma bin Shabīb bin al-Sukūn bin Ashras bin Shawr bin 'Afīr. Yāqūt al-Ḥamawī, vol. 2 p.487.
2. Ḥamd al-Jāsir, *Fī Shimāl Gharb al-Jazīra*, p.110.

3. Ibid.
4. Ibid.
5. The name Khabt (depression or basin or lowland) was usually employed poetically for the Jawf depression. Dūmat al-Jandal was often called by the Arabic poets Dūmat Khabt. See, e.g., Musil, *Arabia Deserta*, pp.65, 532, 535.
6. The Ḥarrat al-Rajlā' is the volcanic desert bordering the Wādi'l-Sirḥān on its east. At times it is referred to as al-Ḥarra (the volcanic desert).
7. al-Ḥasan bin Aḥmad Ibn al-Ḥā'ik al-Hamdānī, *Ṣifat Jazīrat al-'Arab*, ed. Muḥammad bin 'Alī al-Akwa' al-Ḥawālī, Riyadh, Dār al-Yamāma, *1394*/1974, pp.367-68.
8. Ferdinand Wüstenfeld, *Register zu den genealogischen tabellen der Arabischen stamme und familien . . .*, Osnabrück: Otto Zeller, 1853; reprint ed., 1966, s.v. "Kalb ben Wabara"; see also Yāqūt al-Ḥamawī, vol. 2 p.487 and Abū 'Ubaid 'Abd Allāh bin 'Abd al-'Azīz al-Bakrī al-Andalusī, *Mu'jam Mā Ista'jama min Asmā' al-Bilād wa'l-Mawāḍi'*, ed. Muṣṭafā al-Saqqā, 4 vols., Cairo, Lajnat al-Ta'līf wa'l-Tarjama wa'l- Nashr, *1364-71*/1945-51, vol. 1 pp.85-86.
9. Musil, *Arabia Deserta*, p.540.
10. al-Mas'ūdī, *Murūj al-Dhahab*, vol. 5 p.205.
11. 'Amr bin Baḥr al-Jāḥiẓ, *al-Bayān wa'l-Tabyīn*, ed. 'Abd al-Salām Hārūn, 4 vols. in 2, Cairo, Maktabat al-Khānjī, *1395*/1975, vol. 2 p.362.
12. al-Mas'ūdī, *al-Tanbīh*, p.248; Ḥamd al-Jāsir, *Fī Shimāl Gharb al-Jazīra*, p.111.
13. Ḥamd al-Jāsir, *Fī Shimāl Gharb al-Jazīra*, p.111; for an exhaustive discussion, see Musil, *Arabia Deserta*, pp.543-46.
14. Aḥmad bin 'Alī Ibn Ḥajar al-'Asqalānī, *al-Iṣāba fī Tamyīz al-Ṣaḥāba*, 4 vols., Cairo, Maṭba'at al-Sa'āda, *1328*/1910, vol. 1 p.126.
15. Aḥmad bin Yaḥyā al-Balādhurī, *Futūḥ al-Buldān*, ed. Ṣalāḥ al-Dīn al-Munajjid, 3 pts., Cairo, Maktabat al-Nahḍat al-Miṣriyya, 1956-57, vol. 1 p.75.
16. Musil, *Arabia Deserta*, pp.543-44.

8
The Market of Dūmat al-Jandal

In the pre-Islamic period, a series of markets were held in rotation at various places in the Arabian Peninsula. People would gather at these markets to buy, sell and barter. The market started on the first day of the third month (*Rabīʿ I*) of the lunisolar calendar of the bedouin [1] and lasted till the end of the year, its venue shifting every month. Among these markets, the month-long market of Dūmat al-Jandal was one of the oldest and regarded as one of the most important[2] since it was the first in the series and because of the geographical position of Dūma and the number of Arab tribes inhabiting the area. It was normal for the tribes to assemble in Dūmat al-Jandal every year on the first day of the month of *Rabīʿ I* and remain there till the end of the month with a view to engaging in trade.

We know something about the management of the market during the period immediately preceding the coming of Islam. According to the reports, Ukaidir, the lord of Dūmat al-Jandal, would supervise the people and exercise his authority over them on the opening day of the market. The market would then continue thus for half the month. Then perhaps the Banū Kalb used to take over the market, with some Kalb chieftain collecting a tithe on all sales and otherwise managing its affairs, and the market would then continue till the end of the month.[3] According to a rather different version, the market of Dūmat al-Jandal was managed either by al-Ukaidir or by Qunāfa al-Kalbī. The two leaders would participate in a contest and whoever got the better of his opponent in the riddle set for them was left to organize the market as he saw fit. Nobody from Syria or ʿIrāq could sell at the market without the permission of the lord of the market, nor could anyone buy or sell until the ruler had bought what he wanted.[4]

Those who controlled the Arab markets used tax collectors to collect a tithe on all sales from the merchants. At Dūmat al-Jandal, al-Ukaidir might have collected the tax, although it is possible that the Kalb chiefs, as we noted above, or someone from the G͟hassānids supervised the market and collected the tithe.[5]

Most of the numerous methods employed at the market for entering into the often intricate sale-purchase agreements had an element of gambling. For instance, one method used for the sale of garments was that the seller would invite the buyer to cast a pebble from some distance; whichever garment the pebble landed upon would be his for one dirham.[6] Another method involved touching one of the objects of purchase lying behind a curtain without looking at them. The outcome was binding. All trading practices that had an element of gambling in them were subsequently abolished by Islam.[7]

As the market of Dūmat al-Jandal was one of the largest markets of the Arabs, tribes from Syria, the Ḥijāz, and northern and western Najd, including the famous tribes of Kalb, G͟hassān and Ṭayyiʾ, would participate.[8] Historians have reported that while on their way to the market the Arabs faced great hardship on account of the danger and roughness of the route. Traders suffered the hardships of the journey only because of the profits. Among the participants in the market of Dūmat al-Jandal were the Quraish of Makka who, on their way to Dūmat al-Jandal, used to follow the route passing through a place called al-Ḥazan. (This territory was in the hands of the Muḍar tribe and, since the Quraish themselves were from the Muḍar, they enjoyed safe passage.)[9]

The market of Dūmat al-Jandal should be seen in the context of the trade routes of Arabia as a whole, as well as in the light of Dūmat al-Jandal's pre-eminence within Arabia during the ancient period. Dūmat al-Jandal lies on the routes from central and eastern Arabia to Syria and southern Palestine, where Gaza (Ghazza) was the chief port at which merchants would buy products from the countries of the Mediterranean. In the account of al-Ukaidir above, it has been mentioned that he appears to have had contact with al-Ḥīra in 'Irāq and commercial contacts with the Sassanian Empire in the east. It can thus be concluded that the trading relations of Dūmat al-Jandal extended well beyond Arabia itself into a more international sphere.

One important feature of these Arabian markets as a social institution was their connection with religious worship. It has been suggested that they were originally holy places where idols were established for the tribes to worship. The tribes would visit the idols during certain fixed pilgrimage seasons, and with the passage of time these seasons turned into the seasons of the markets.[10] In support of this proposition, several instances have been cited, among them those of the markets of Dūmat al-Jandal and 'Ukāẓ. The Banū Wabra used to come to Dūmat al-Jandal in order to worship the idol Wadd, whose guardianship was with the Banu'l-Farāfisa bin al-Aḥwas bin Kalb.[11] Similarly, about 'Ukāẓ, the site of the most famous pre-Islamic market of Arabia, it has been said that it was orginally a holy place where people used to go to perform pilgrimage and offer sacrifice of animals to the deities that had been established there.[12]

---

1. A lunar calendar, periodically adjusted by intercalations, to keep the months in step with the seasons.
2. See Aḥmad bin 'Alī al-Qalqashandī, *Ṣubḥ al-A'shā fī Ṣinā'at al-Inshā*, 14 vols., Cairo, al-Mu'assasat al-Miṣriyyat al-'Āmma li'l-Ta'līf wa'l-Tarjama wa'l-Ṭabā'a wa'l-Nashr, 1963, vol. 1 pp.410-11; Jawād 'Alī, vol. 7 pp.371, 387-88.
3. Jawād 'Alī, vol.7 p.371, citing, among others, Aḥmad bin Abī Ya'qūb Ibn Wāḍiḥ, known as al-Ya'qūbī, *Tārīkh al-Ya'qūbī*, ed. Muḥammad Ṣādiq Baḥr al-'Ulūm, 3 vols., Najaf, Maktabat al-Ḥaidariyya, 1964, vol. 1 p.226.
4. Jawād 'Alī, vol. 4 p.238, vol. 7 p.372, citing Muḥammad bin Ḥabīb al-Baghdādī, *Kitāb al-Muḥabbar*, ed. E. Lichtenstaedter, Hyderabad, India, 1942, pp.263f. and Abū 'Alī Aḥmad bin Muḥammad al-Marzūqī, *Kitāb al-Azmina wa'l-Amkina*, 2 vols., Hyderabad, India, 1914, vol. 2 pp.161f.
5. Jawād 'Alī, vol. 7 pp.478-79.
6. Muḥammad bin Abī Bakr Ibn Qayyim al-Jawziyya, *Zād al-Ma'ād fī Hady Khair al-'Ibād*, ed, Shu'aib al-Arna'ūṭ and 'Abd al-Qādir al-Arna'ūṭ, 5 vols., Beirut, Mu'assasat al-Risāla, 1979, vol. 5 p.817.
7. Ibid.; For a discussion of the various pre-Islamic trading practices, see Jawād 'Alī, vol. 7 pp.387-403.
8. Jawād 'Alī, vol. 7 p.372.
9. Jawād 'Alī, vol. 4 p.208, vol. 7 p.375, citing al-Marzūqī, op. cit., vol. 2 p.162.
10. Ibid., vol. 7 pp.382-83.
11. Jawād 'Alī, vol. 7 p.383; 'Alī bin Aḥmad Ibn Ḥazm, *Jamharat Ansāb al-'Arab*, ed. 'Abd al-Salām Muḥammad Hārūn, Cairo, Dār al-Ma'ārif, 1977, p.492.
12. See Jawād 'Alī, vol. 7 pp.382-83; al-Bakrī, op. cit., vol. 3 p.959.

9

The Cultural Significance of Dūmat al-Jandal

There is literary evidence that Dūmat al-Jandal in the pre-Islamic period contributed to the introduction of writing and also to the spread of poetry. There are very clear specific references to the effect that Dūmat al-Jandal had a role in the introduction of the Arabic script. We quote below the report of Aḥmad bin Yaḥyā al-Balādhurī (d. *279*/892-93), which he ascribes to 'Abbās bin Hishām bin Muḥammad bin al-Sā'ib al-Kalbī. The report says that the Arabic script was devised imitating the Syriac script and that it was introduced in Makka and other places during the period immediately before the coming of Islam.[1]

> Three persons from the Ṭayyi', Murāmir bin Murra, Aslam bin Sidra, and 'Āmir bin Jadara, got together at Baqqa and devised the script, making Arabic letters on the lines of the Syriac script. From them some people of al-Anbār learnt this script. Then the people of al-Ḥīra learnt it from the people of al-Anbār. Bishr bin 'Abd al-Malik, brother of Ukaidir . . ., the lord of Dūmat al-Jandal, used to go to al-Ḥīra and stay there for some time . . . He learnt the Arabic script from the people of al-Ḥīra. Some business then took him to Makka. Sufyān bin Umayya bin 'Abd Shams and Abū Qais bin 'Abd Manāf bin Zuhra bin Kilāb saw Bishr writing and asked him to teach them the script. He taught them the letters and demonstrated the script, and they started writing. Then Bishr, Sufyān and Abū Qais went to Ṭā'if for trading, and [there] Ghailān bin Salama al-Thaqafī . . . learnt the script from them . . .[2]

A poet of Dūmat al-Jandal recited the following lines, addressing them to the people of Makka for the favour done by the people of Dūmat al-Jandal to the Makkans in having taught them the art of writing:

> Don't deny the favours Bishr bestowed upon you:
> He had indeed a blessed and shining soul.
> He taught you the cursive script, so you could keep
> An account of your wealth that was scattered.
> You reckoned [your] riches that had been in disarray,
> And you brought an order to what was confused.
> You made your pens flow incessantly [till]
> You surpassed the scribes of Chosroes and Caesar.
> So you dispensed with the Musnad script[3] of the Ḥimyar tribe
> And with what the chiefs of the Ḥimyar had recorded in their books.[4]

Dūmat al-Jandal played a vital part in spreading the folk culture of pre-Islamic Arabia. According to "Abu'l-Mundhir Hishām Ibn al-Kalbī", as quoted by the author of al-'Iqd al-Farīd, "singing, without doubt, developed in the big towns of Arabia, that is, al-Madīna, al-Ṭā'if, Khaibar, Wādi'l-Qurā, Dūmat al-Jandal and al-Yamāma, all of which were gathering places for the fairs of Arabia".[5] From there it spread through the Peninsula.[6]

---

1. The archaic Arabic script used during the early Islamic state "obeys the same principles as Syriac". *Encyclopaedia of Islam*, s.v. "Khaṭṭ, (A.), Writing. i. – In the Arab World", by J. Sourdel-Thomine.
2. Al-Balādhurī, vol. 3 p.579. See also Ibn Ḥazm, p.429 and Jawād 'Alī, vol. 3 p.382, vol. 8 pp.111, 117-18, 158-74.
3. Epigraphic South Arabian script, as opposed to cursive Arabic script in use today.
4. 'Abd al-Raḥmān bin Abī Bakr Jalāl al-Dīn al-Suyūṭī, *al-Muzhir fī 'Ulūm al-Lugha wa Anwā'ihā*, ed. Muḥammad Aḥmad Jādd al-Mawlā, 'Alī Muḥammad al-Bajāwī, Muḥammad Abu'l-Faḍl Ibrāhīm, 2 vols., Cairo, Dār al-Turāth, n.d., vol. 2 p.347.
5. Aḥmad bin Muḥammad Ibn 'Abd Rabbih al-Andalusī, *Kitāb al-'Iqd al-Farīd*, ed. Aḥmad Amīn, Aḥmad al-Zain, Ibrāhīm al-Abyārī and 'Abd al-Salām Hārūn, 6 vols., Cairo, Lajnat al-Ta'līf wa'l-Tarjama wa'l-Nashr, 1940-50, vol. 6 p.27.
6. Jawād 'Alī, vol. 5 p.112.

10
Religion in Dūmat al-Jandal

Various idols had been worshipped in Dūmat al-Jandal since ancient times. But in the period immediately preceding the rise of Islam, Christianity and Juadism appear to have been practised there in conjuction with idolatry. Al-Balādhurī states that "[at the rise of Islam] the people of Dūmat al-Jandal belonged to the 'Ibād of Kūfa [sect of Christianity]",[1] meaning that they followed the East Syrian (later, Nestorian) church. Ibn Khaldūn, the celebrated historian of a later period, too, implies that the principal religion of the city and its surrounding areas at the rise of Islam was Christianity.[2] There is some indication that Jews also lived there at some time before the coming of Islam.[3] Jawād 'Alī draws the conclusion that the population of Dūmat al-Jandal was diverse in its religious following.[4] However, it seems that Christianity was the predominant religion by the 7th century. This view is substantiated by the circumstance that the Kalb tribe, which dominated the region surrounding the town, was, according to various reports, mostly Christian, having abandoned the worship of Wadd, a pagan deity, and also that the ruler of the town, al-Ukaidir, was a Christian.

Idolatry at its worst appears to have been practised in Dūma at some time in its history. J. Wellhausen quotes one Forphyrius as saying that the people of the town used to slaughter a human being every year at the foot of the idol (in Dūma) to gain its favour.[5]

The reports about idolatry in Dūmat al-Jandal in the period immediately before the coming of Islam relate mostly to the worship there of the idol Wadd, which was installed by one 'Awf bin 'Udhra from the Banū Wabra faction of the Quḍā'a tribe. The statue was given to him by 'Amr bin Luḥayy. 'Awf first carried the deity to Wādi'l-Qurā and then finally set it up at Dūmat al-Jandal. He named his son 'Abd Wadd (i.e. Wadd's slave).[6] Ibn Isḥāq (d. *151*/768-69), the famous biographer of the Prophet (P.B.U.H.), says that the Kalb bin Wabra bin Quḍā'a adopted Wadd as a deity at Dūma.[7]

Reference to the idol Wadd is made in the Holy Qur'ān (71: 23). Wadd is said to have been the deity of various other tribes in pre-Islamic Arabia, including the Thamūd, Liḥyān, Quraish – who called it Add – Tamīm, Ṭayyi', Khazraj, Hudhail and Lakhm. At the coming of Islam it was one of the largest statues in al-Ḥijāz.[8] Worship of idols was widespread among the Arabs before Islam, and idols are often mentioned in the context of their destruction by the Muslims in the early days of Islam. There were religious sanctuaries dedicated to various pagan idols in many parts of Arabia, besides Dūmat al-Jandal. Some of the religious sites of the Arabian tribes were more well-known, associated with the following deities: Suwā' (of the Banū Hudhail), Yaghūth (of the Banū Mudhḥij), Ya'ūq (of the Hamdān), Nasr (of the Ḥimyar), al-Lāt (of the Thaqīf in Ṭā'if), Manāt (of the Khazraj), al-'Uzzā (of the Quraish in the region of Makka) and

Āsāf and Nā'ila (at al-Ṣafā and al-Marwa in Makka itself). However, monotheism was not unknown to these people. There were men among them who used to call them to the worship of One God, notably, Quṣayy bin Kilāb bin Murra, the forefather of Prophet Muḥammad (P.B.U.H.), and Zaid bin 'Amr bin Nafīl. Zaid composed the following verses in order to incite others to embrace monotheism:

> Is it one Lord or a thousand lords
> I worship when things are sorted out?
> I left both al-Lāt and al-'Uzzā,
> As a man of insight would do.

The Banū 'Āmir al-Ajdār (Banu'l-Farāfiṣa bin al-Aḥwas from the Kalb) were the custodians of the idol Wadd in Dūmat al-Jandal. Al-Kalbī traces a report from Mālik bin Ḥāritha al-Ajdārī to the effect that he saw Wadd in his childhood when his father used to send him to the idol with milk to drink. Mālik says that he used to drink the milk himself and return, while his father thought that he had given it to Wadd. Mālik also gives a description of the idol:

> It was the statue of a huge man, as big as the largest of human-beings, covered with two robes, clothed with the one and cloaked with the other, carrying a sword on his waist and a bow on his shoulder, and between his hands were a lance to which was attached a standard, and a quiver full of arrows.[9]

It is clear from the reports of al-Kalbī that at the advent of Islam some Kalb factions used to practise idolatry, though, in view of the reports of al-Balādhurī and Ibn Khaldūn already cited, it may be said that most of the Kalb people had given up worshipping Wadd and turned to Christianity. In any case, the statue of Wadd in Dūmat al-Jandal was destroyed by Khālid bin al-Walīd in *9*/630 when he was sent by Prophet Muḥammad (P.B.U.H.) from Tabūk on a campaign against Ukaidir. When Khālid proceeded to destroy the idol, the Banū 'Abd Wadd and the Banū 'Āmir al-Ajdār tried to prevent him. Khālid had to fight with them before he could get the statue. Some members of the two families were killed and some injured. Among those killed were Qaṭan bin Shuraiḥ, from the 'Abd Wadd family, and Ḥassān bin Maṣād, a cousin of al-Ukaidir.[10]

---

1. al-Balādhurī, vol. 1 p.75.
2. 'Abd al-Raḥmān bin Muḥammad Ibn Khaldūn, *Tārīkh Ibn Khaldūn*, 7 vols., Būlāq, Egypt, *1284*/1867, vol. 2 p.82.
3. Yāqūt al-Ḥamawī, vol. 2 p.489.
4. Jawād 'Alī, vol. 6 p.600.
5. J. Wellhausen, *Reste Arabischen Heidentums*, Berlin, 1927, vol. 5 p.115, quoted in Jawād 'Alī, vol. 6 p.198.
6. Hishām bin Muḥammad bin al-Sā'ib al-Kalbī, *Kitāb al-Aṣnām*, ed. Aḥmad Zakī Bāshā, 2nd ed., Cairo, Dār al-Kutub al-Miṣriyya, 1925, p.34, cited by Jawād 'Alī, vol. 6 p.255.
7. 'Abd al-Malik Ibn Hishām, *al-Sīrat al-Nabawiyya*, ed. Muṣṭafā al-Saqqā, Ibrāhīm al-Abyārī and 'Abd al-Ḥafīẓ Shalabī, 2 vols, Cairo, Muṣṭafā al-Bābī al-Ḥalabī, 1955, vol. 1 p.78.
8. Jawād 'Alī, vol. 6 pp.256, 292-93.
9. al-Kalbī, pp.55-56, cited by Jawād 'Alī, vol. 6 p.256.
10. Ibid., p.55, cited by Jawād 'Alī, vol. 6 p.257.

11

The Ancient Towns of Dūmat al-Jandal and al-Ṭuwair, and Other Sites

Dūmat al-Jandal

The archaeological evidence demonstrates that Dūmat al-Jandal was a larger town in the ancient and mediaeval times than it was for most of the modern period. Very limited archaeological investigation has been carried out in the town so far. The earliest occupants attested by the archaeological findings are the Nabaṭaeans,[1] whose north-Arabian kingdom flourished during the last three centuries BC and the first century. Excavations have yielded numerous artifacts such as rings, pottery sherds, beads, ear-rings, nose-rings, pieces of vessels, figurines, and coins, most of them identifiable as Nabaṭaean, Roman, Byzantine and Hellenistic.[2] Little evidence has so far been found to shed light on the history of the town during the Assyrian and Babylonian periods.[3]

Dūmat al-Jandal is not rich in inscriptions and graffiti, as there are few rocky outcrops in the area to provide a surface. So far, one Minaean, one Latin and some Nabaṭaean inscriptions and a few fragments of Nabaṭaean graffiti, have been recorded from Dūmat al-Jandal for the ancient period.[4]

That Dūmat al-Jandal of the ancient period was much larger in size is proved by the evidence of the town wall. This town wall was mentioned by the mediaeval geographer Yāqūt al-Ḥamawī (d. *626*/1228-29) who recorded that "Dūma has a wall which fortifies it. Inside the walled area there is a formidable castle called Mārid . . ."[5] The 1976 reconnaissance team recorded the following:

> The most important structural remains of the [Roman-Nabaṭaean] period were found at al-Jawf [Dūmat al-Jandal]. . . . Here, to the west of the modern town, an area of the wadi bed at least 750 x 400 m. in size had been enclosed by a substantial wall of dry-stone masonry with a mudbrick superstructure . . . ; a portion of the sandstone ridge overlooking the wadi from the south had also been enclosed in a separate circuit of walling, while yet further lines of walls can be traced, though with difficulty, among the palm groves to the north of the modern town. The western area within the walls . . . has several wells and recent gardens, but the surface is littered with sherds which are consistently Roman-Nabataean, and there are some signs of buried masonry. There can be little doubt that this was an area of fields and perhaps houses in the Nabataean period, and the site would repay excavation.[6]

Khaleel al-Muaikel says that "a surprisingly large area was enclosed by the wall, not only the town itself but also the gardens encircling it."[7]

Parts of the wall in the western side of the town, in the Bāb al-Rawḍa area, were excavated in 1986 by the Department of Antiquities team. The wall there

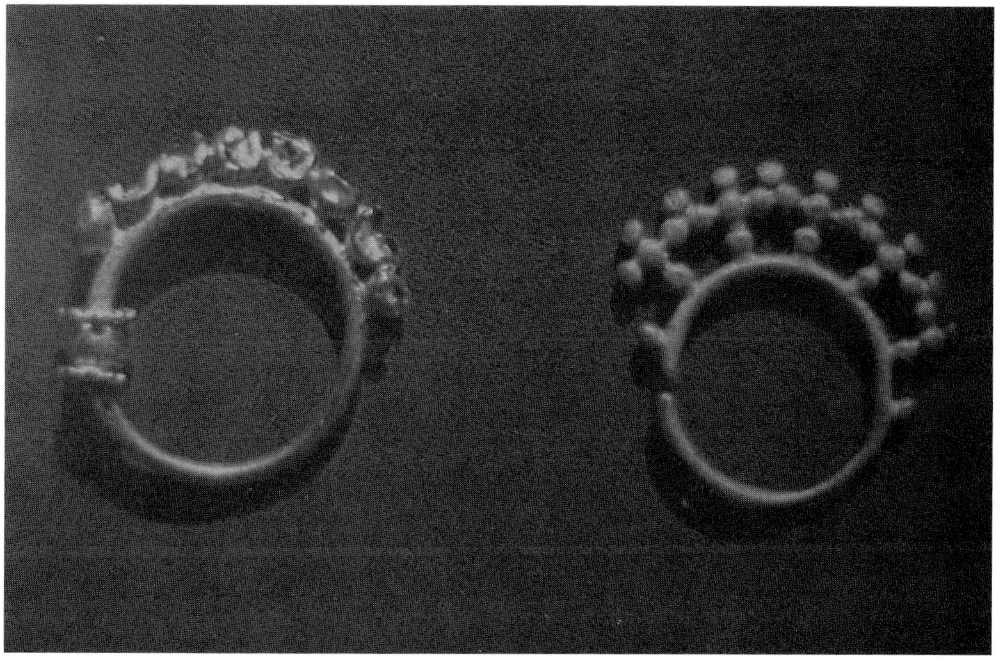

Two nose-rings from the Hellenistic period excavated from Dūmat al-Jandal (*Atlal* journal).

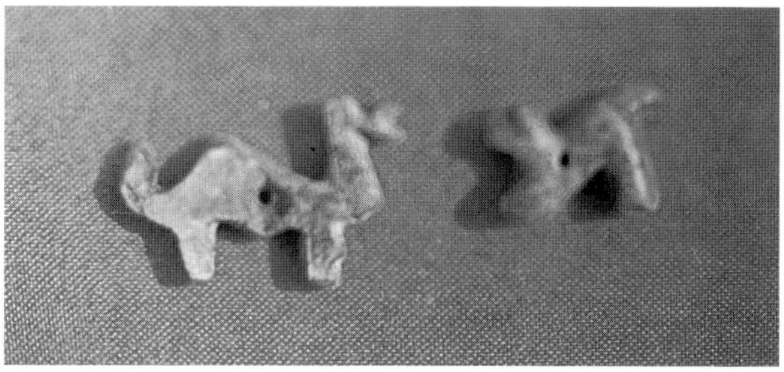

Bronze camel and dog figurines excavated from Dūmat al-Jandal (*Atlal* journal).

extended north and south and had buttresses located at specific distances, all interlocked with the structure of the wall. An ancient mount on the wall turned out to be a cube-shaped watch-tower, 5.8 m. long, 3.5 m. wide, and 5 m. high.[8]

There is a local tradition that entry to the town was possible through two gates, one named al-Nuqayyib and the other al-Burj. Over the wall hung a chain for visitors to pull; the guard at Qaṣr Mārid would then alert the guards of the gates to discover the identity of the newcomer.[9]

Al-Ṭuwair

This important site, a flat area of at least 500 x 200 m. covered by sand, with "signs of mudbrick walling, including what could well be a town wall", lies at a distance of about 8 km. to the south of Sakākā at the edge of al-Nafūd. It was discovered by the 1976 survey team. A large quantity of pottery sherds – tentatively dated to the first century BC – was found above and beneath the sand. Some of this high quality, wheel-made and fired pottery, which includes red, blue and green glazed ware, is Nabaṭaean.[10] Khaleel al-Muaikel suggests that this site "flourished between the 1st century BC and the 2nd century AD",[11] a view based upon a detailed study of its pottery, whose importance was highlighted by the 1977 survey team in the following words:

> . . . the al-Tuwayr ceramic assemblage provides an important, indeed unique, body of material linking the Syro-Palestinian (especially the Nabataean) and the Arabian Gulf-Parthian cultural spheres, suggesting that when excavated the site will be of major value for clarifying the chronology of these areas in the late 1st millennium BC and for illuminating the problems of regional interactions.[12]

Limited excavation work was carried out at the Ṭuwair site by the 1976-77 survey teams and Khaleel al-Muaikel, and the site requires a detailed survey and archaeological excavation. In view of its probable period, the site may be one of the ancient towns mentioned by Ptolemy of Alexandria (fl. 2nd century) in the region of Dūmat al-Jandal.[13]

Qaṣr Mārid (in Dūmat al-Jandal)

Qaṣr Mārid, or Ḥiṣn Mārid, as it was previously called, is "the most striking antiquity which al-Jawf has to offer . . . [and] is undoubtedly one of the most impressive structures to be seen in the whole of North Arabia."[14] It is a walled fortress overlooking the ancient town of Dūmat al-Jandal. It has been rebuilt to some extent though the greater part is original. The original building was rectangular but additions, including the conical towers, have been made. The lower parts of these towers are of stone, and the upper parts of mud brick.[15] Inside the *qaṣr* there is a deep well, still in a good state of preservation.

The building of a fortress at Dūmat al-Jandal by Dūmā', Prophet Ismā'īl's son, is mentioned in the reference to the founding of the town by him.[16] During the time of Prophet Muḥammad (P.B.U.H.) and the first Caliph, Abū Bakr, a fortress at Dūmat al-Jandal again appears in the historical records in the context of K͟hālid's expeditions.[17] Though the earliest chroniclers of Islamic history do not mention the name of that fortress, the geographer/historian Ibn K͟hurdād͟hbah (d.c.*280*/893), a contemporary of the historians al-Balād͟hurī, al-Ya'qūbī and al-Ṭabarī, mentions the fortress of Dūmat al-Jandal as being called Mārid[18] – without associating it with the expeditions of K͟hālid bin al-Walīd. Later, Yāqūt al-Ḥamawī, the geographer, names the fortress of Dūmat al-Jandal as "Ḥiṣn Mārid" and says that "it was the fortress of Ukaidir",[19] the ruler of the town at the time of K͟hālid bin Walīd's first expedition in *9*/630.

Literary references to the Mārid fortress by far predate the historical and geographical references. Mufaḍḍal bin Muḥammad al-Ḍabbī (d.c. *171*/787-88) was the first to record the famous proverb "Mārid is rebellious and Ablaq is haughty", adding by way of explanation that "this proverb is from Queen Zabba [Zenobia (r. 267-72)]. She marched on Mārid, the fortress of Dūmat al-Jandal, and al-Ablaq, the fortress of Taimā'; both the fortresses successfully resisted her attack. On this she spoke these words."[20] Ibn Manẓūr, the lexicographer, adds that the saying became a proverb for anything that is strong and formidable.[21]

The literary evidence is supported by recently-emerging scientific evidence. During the 1976 survey, "a sounding dug near Qasr Mārid produced, in its lowest layer, a homogeneous group of Roman-Nabataean pottery . . . of the 1st-2nd centuries AD."[22] In 1986, excavation by Khaleel Ibrahim al-Muaikel inside the *qaṣr* produced pottery sherds which constituted:

> . . . solid evidence of Nabataean occupation of Marid castle throughout the first century B.C. and the first century A.D., and perhaps in earlier periods. . . . It is believed that the construction of the castle was prior to the Nabataean occupation although it appears that the Nabataean era was its most prosperous period.[23]

Winnett and Reed have observed that "both the outer wall and the towers suffered considerable damage when in 1853 Talāl Ibn Rashīd of Ḥā'il bombarded the fortress with two old cannons."[24] The *qaṣr* remained under the control of the Rashīdīs till *1327*/1909, when Nawwāf Ibn Sha'lān retook it after a siege of 10 months. There is a local report that Nawwāf sent to Syria for the equipment needed to scale the walls.

The word "mārid" means "arrogant; disobedient; severe; transgressor". [25] Hence "Qaṣr Mārid" means "strongly-built castle". All indications are that this impressive structure was built to serve as a fortress and to defend the town against attacks, and, as we have seen above, it served that purpose throughout its long history.

Bi'r Saisār (or Bi'r Saisara)

This well, carved in a semi-conical shape in a low-lying hillock, is located 200 m. south-west of Qaṣr Za'bal (for a description of which, see Part Four, Chapter 18). It measures 9 m. by 8 m. at the mouth, and about 15 m. in depth. Hewn at the side of the well is a staircase leading down to the bottom. F.V. Winnett and

W.L. Reed, who visited the area in *1381*/1962, state that this well is similar to the one found at al-Jīb (ancient Gibeon) in Palestine.[26]

It is well known that some of the lower areas of Sakākā and the land to the east and south surrounding the well were once irrigated from Bi'r Saisār by means of underground and surface channels. These channels were buried under sand and have been discovered by chance.

Al-Mughairā

At al-Mughairā, 40 km. east of Sakākā, there are two carved water tanks, with stone-lined paths leading to them.

---

1. al-Muaikel, vol. 1 p.100.
2. See al-Dayel, "Excavations at Dumat al-Jandal, *1405*/1985", pp.64-79 and plates 73-85; al-Dayel, "Excavations at Dumat al-Jandal, Second Season, *1406*/1986", pp.37-46 and plates 28-42; al-Muaikel, vol. 1 pp.87-100.
3. al-Muaikel, vol. 1 p.100.
4. For a brief account of the Nabaṭaean and Minaean inscriptions see Winnett and Reed, p.73. A detailed discussion of the Latin inscription is given in the next chapter.
5. Yāqūt al-Ḥamawī, vol. 2 p.487.
6. Adams, p.38.
7. al-Muaikel, vol. 1 pp.328-29.
8. al-Dayel, "Excavations at Dumat al-Jandal, Second Season", pp.41-43.
9. See Ḥamd al-Jāsir, *Fī Shimāl Gharb al-Jazīra*, p.144; cf. Sa'd bin 'Abd Allāh bin Junaidal, *Bilād al-Jawf, aw, Dūmat al-Jandal*, Riyadh, Dār al-Yamāma, *1401*/1981, p.104.
10. Adams, pp.38-39; Parr, pp.42-43.
11. al-Muaikel, vol. 1 p.87.
12. Parr, p.44.
13. Adams, p.39.
14. Winnett and Reed, p.17.
15. Ibid.
16. Yāqūt al-Ḥamawī, vol.2 p.487.
17. For an account of these expeditions, see the first two chapters of Part Four.
18. 'Ubaid Allāh bin Aḥmad Khurdādhbah, *Kitāb al-Masālik wa'l-Mamālik*, ed. and trans. into French by M.J. De Goeje, Leiden, 1889, pp.128-29, quoted in al-Muaikel, vol. 1 p.37, and Musil, *Arabia Deserta*, p.532.
19. Yāqūt al-Ḥamawī, vol. 2 p.487.
20. al-Mufaḍḍal bin Muḥammad al-Ḍabbī, *Amthāl al-'Arab*, Istanbūl, al-Āstāna, *1300*/1884?, p.64, quoted in Abū 'Ubaid al-Qāsim bin Sallām, *Kitāb al-Amthāl*, ed. 'Abd al-Majīd al-Qaṭāmish, Dimashq, Dār al-Ma'mūn lil-Turāth, *1400*/1980, p.94; see also Ibn Manẓūr, op.cit., vol. 3 p.402.
21. Ibn Manẓūr, op.cit., vol.3 p.402.
22. Adams, p.38.
23. al-Muaikel, vol. 1 pp.92, 108-09.
24. Winnett and Reed, p.17.
25. See, e.g., Ibn Manẓūr, op.cit., vol.3 pp.400-02.
26. Winnett and Reed, p.11.

12
Inscriptions

A survey of the inscriptions in al-Jawf Province was carried out in *1405*/1985 by the rock art and epigraphic survey team of the Department of Antiquities and Museums, and it was noted that al-Jawf is one of the richest areas in the Kingdom in this respect. Of the 10,734 different panels of rock art and inscriptions in the region, mostly in the area of al-Jawba, 1409 contained inscriptions. Nine hundred and sixty seven of the inscriptions were Thamūdic (the Thamūd are first mentioned in the annals of the Assyrian king Sargon II [r. 721-705 BC]; they seem to have been more prominent from c.400 BC to 650), 116 Nabaṭaean (c. 300 BC – 106 CE), 325 Kūfic (early Islamic) and one Greek. [1] We give below a description of some of the sites in al-Jawf Province which have a concentration of inscriptions and rock art.

Qal'at al-Ṭuwair area

The area of Qal'at al-Ṭuwair (al-Ṭuwair castle) is adjacent to al-Ṭuwair village. The castle itself is of ancient origin and stands on an isolated sandstone hill, which is almost perpendicular on three sides. Some rooms have been partially hewn out of the rock on the sides and top of the mountain. The rocky area in the vicinity has a large number of inscriptions and drawings. Epigraphists who visited the area in 1985 described the site thus:

> The Qilat al-Tuwair area south of Sakkaka contains a high concentration of Thamudic inscriptions and petroglyphs. The ruins, well and some other structures associated with the old castle are dated to be pre-Islamic belonging to the Nabataean period (Parr, Zarins et al. 1976). Nabataean, Thamudic and Kufic inscriptions are located on the base rocks on which the castle is built. Also, rock art and [Thamūdic, Nabaṭaean and Kūfic] inscriptions are found on various rocks scattered around the old castle. Foot and hand prints are common. Large-sized camel figures, ostriches, donkeys and ibexes are depicted on the vertical surfaces of base rocks. The site is interesting as it represents various phases of human occupation.[2]

Jabal Burnus

Jabal Burnus is a sandstone hill close to Qaṣr Za'bal. Wind and rain have formed a smooth surface on the western face of the *Jabal* which has become blackened. Incised on this are a number of graffiti and rock drawings depicting female figures dancing with their arms raised. Nearby is an inscription in a mixture of Arabic and Nabaṭaean.[3]

The stone containing the Latin inscription.

Al-Qal'a

This is a group of rocks on the east of the road from Sakākā to 'Ar'ar at a distance of around 7 km. from Sakākā. The rocks are carved with Thamūdic and Nabaṭaean inscriptions, as well as a drawing showing seven ostriches.

We take up now one of the most important inscriptions coming to light from al-Jawf. This is a Latin inscription on a large-sized stone removed from Dūmat al-Jandal. When Dr Maḥmūd al-Ghūl, our late friend, visited the area in *1387*/1967 – he made this visit as a representative of the University of Riyadh (Arabic, al-Riyāḍ), now King Sa'ūd University, and during the course of his archaeological survey identified an ancient town-site 30 km. from 'Ar'ar – we showed him the inscription. Dr al-Ghūl's description of that is briefly as follows:

> This inscription was written by an individual named Flavius Dionysius, who describes himself as a centurion in the Third Cyrenaica Legion. He states in the inscription: "Asking for health for his two masters, the two Augusti, he fulfilled his vow to Great Jupiter and to holy Ṣalm." The two Augusti are the Emperors Septimius Severus and Caracalla, who shared the rule of the Roman Empire from 197 to 212.[4] The legion to which he belonged as a centurion had its base at Boṣrā,

the capital of the Roman Provincia Arabia. Cyrenaica (Arabic, Qūrna) is the present-day Barqa region in Libya, and Septimius Severus was originally from Libya. A similar find was made previously in Ḥawrān, which is not far from the Sa'ūdī Arabian border with Jordan, and researchers believe that the borders of Provincia Arabia reached to within only a few miles of the present border. The Dūmat al-Jandal inscription was found in a place where direct Roman rule was not suspected, at least until now, although a certain amount of Roman influence was known to exist beyond what were called the Outer *Limes*. This could indicate that the Romans, while at war with Persia in 'Irāq, sent down an army to Dūmat al-Jandal, out of concern that the Persians would use the route through Dūma to gain access to southern Palestine and Egypt. It could also have been that the campaigns of the Romans required the movement of a large force between Egypt and the war zone in 'Irāq.

The importance of Dūmat al-Jandal in terms of communications between 'Irāq, Syria and Egypt cannot be denied. It is sufficient to point out that the Muslims attached importance to ensuring their authority in Dūma before continuing to 'Irāq and Syria, and that Khālid bin al-Walīd came from al-Ḥīra to Yarmūk by way of Dūma, as the most reliable sources report.

The two deities mentioned in the inscription on the stone are Jupiter Ammon and Uranus Ammon, the Greek and Roman deities associated with the Egyptian Ammon. This would indicate Egyptian influence there and it has been suggested that some members of the Legion were from Egypt. The likelihood of this is increased by the Greek name of the centurion, Dionysius – Greece had a strong influence in Egypt at this period. As for "Holy Ṣalm", this is the deity Ṣalm known from other sources as the deity of the people of Taimā'. It appears that Ṣalm was also worshipped at Dūmat al-Jandal and was mentioned in the inscription in deference to the people of the town and the priestess of the temple, this being the usual custom in the days of polytheism.[5]

1. Khan, p.93.
2. Ibid., p.83.
3. Winnett and Reed, pp.8, 11.
4. An error on Dr al-Ghūl's part regarding the dates of their rule and of its sharing. Lucius Septimius Severus (146-211) was the Roman Emperor from 193 to 211, whereas his son Caracalla – nickname of Marcus Aurelius Antonius (188-217) – was the Emperor from 211 to 217. Caracalla, at the age of nine, was named as co-Emperor by his father in 197.
5. Maḥmūd al-Ghūl's personal letter to the author, dated *28 Shawwāl 1387*/19 January 1968. The inscription was made public by Dr al-Ghūl in 1972 at a conference on pre-Islamic Arabia at Harvard University. The inscribed stone itself was presented by the author to the King Sa'ūd University in Riyadh, where it is now kept in the Museum of the Department of Archaeology and Museology. This inscription has been discussed by a number of scholars, see, e.g., M. Speidel, "The Roman Army in Arabia", *Aufsteig und Niedergang der romischen Welt*, no. 2.8, 1977, pp.687-730; D.L. Kennedy, *Archaeological Explorations on the Roman Frontier in North-east Jordan*, Oxford, 1982, pp.188, 190; G.W. Bowersock, pp.98-99.

13

Dūmat al-Jandal, Northern Arabia and Bilād al-Shām, 1st century – *1st*/7th century[1]

At the beginning of this period, Dūmat al-Jandal lay within the territory of the Nabaṭaean Arabs, while at the end of the period, Dūma was part of the territory of the Muslim community that the Prophet Muḥammad had established in al-Madīna. In the intervening centuries between the annexation of the Nabaṭaean Kingdom in 106 by Rome and the coming of Islam in the *1st*/7th century, Dūma was outside the Roman and Byzantine frontiers in the Bilād al-Shām, and free of the successive Parthian and Sassanian states in the east. Yet in contrast to the earlier periods of Dūma's history, for which detailed information from Assyrian and Babylonian texts is available to us, we have very little historical or archaeological evidence on the Roman, Byzantine or early Islamic periods in the Dūma area.

Under the Nabaṭaeans, Dūma had been one of the major towns on the routes passing through their territory, which was spread over the area between Damascus in the north and Madā'in Ṣāliḥ in the south. With the annexation of the Nabaṭaean Kingdom by the Roman Emperor Trajan in 106, northern Arabia was to become isolated from the Mediterranean by the frontier defences (*limes*) that the Romans constructed: it was not until the Muslims overwhelmed the Byzantine successors of the Romans in *15*/636 at the Yarmūk that the frontier defences established by the Romans against the Arabs were finally breached, and as a consequence of the Muslim victories, Arabia and the Bilād al-Shām were reunited under the rule of the Rightly-Guided Caliphs and their successors.

The Roman frontier with Arabia was intimately related to the defence of the Via Nova Trajana, the great road linking Damascus, Boṣrā, 'Ammān and 'Aqaba, that the Emperor Trajan constructed between 106 and 117. To the east of this road, the Romans established a line of fortresses to form the *Limes Arabicus* between Roman territory in western Jordan, Palestine, and Syria, and the deserts of northern Arabia and central Syria. The defence system continued north where it was intended to protect the territory of Rome and its Byzantine successor from Parthian and Sassanian advances into north Syria from the Euphrates.

The Roman fortifications were overwhelmed in the 3rd century when the forces of Tadmor (Palmyra; Arabic, Tadmur) under Queen Zenobia brought the entire area from Asia Minor to Egypt under the Palmyrene Arabs. In the aftermath of the destruction of Palmyrene power by the Roman Emperor Aurelian in 272, the Romans reorganized their defensive system to ensure that the challenge to their control that the Palmyrenes had achieved could not be repeated. As a result, the Roman defensive system was improved. The concentration of Roman fortifications at the northern end of Wādi'l-Sirḥān around the oasis of Azraq underlines the importance that the Romans attributed to the Wādi'l-Sirḥān and the route from Dūma in the south. In Azraq itself the Roman *castellum* has an inscription dated 326–333. The *castellum* was the principal Roman centre of control in the desert of eastern Jordan, and its role as a control point over the northern Wādi'l-Sirḥān is emphasized by the presence of Qaṣr al-Usaikhin to the north-east of Azraq and, the south-west of Azraq, by a third *castellum*, Qaṣr al-'Uwainid (with an inscription of c. 198–211). This group of Roman fortresses is situated across the route out of central Arabia towards Ḥawrān slopes in the north, where yet other fortresses and settlements lay around the approaches to the provincial capital of Bostra (Boṣrā; Arabic, Buṣrā). The fortresses at the head of the Wādi'l-Sirḥān around Azraq straddled the route from the Wādī to the settled and cultivated areas to the west, on the edge of the desert.

The extent of Roman penetration of the deserts of eastern Jordan and Syria may well have been greater than is presently understood, and it has been suggested that certain Umayyad sites in the desert may have had Roman antecedents. In the south of Jordan, the wells at Bāyir show evidence of major occupation in the Nabaṭaean, Roman and early Byzantine periods, indicating concern to control access to these very important water sources, to which traffic from the south or from Dūma and the Wādi'l-Sirḥān in the south-east would naturally head.

Given this evidence of Roman concern to control access from the desert, it is hard to imagine that they did not pay some sort of attention to Dūma and the southern parts of the Wādi'l-Sirḥān. In view of this, a Latin inscription found at Dūmat al-Jandal is of particular importance (see pp.52–53). The text is in the name of a centurion, Flavius Dionysus, and was dated by the late Dr Maḥmūd al-Ghūl to 197–212; it is a firm indication of Roman contact of some sort with the south end of the Wādi'l-Sirḥān and with Dūma itself. Apart from the appreciation of the importance of the Wādi'l-Sirḥān and north Arabia that the disposition of their fortresses shows, there is evidence from elsewhere in the Ḥijāz that the Romans adopted a policy of advanced presence in the towns along the principal Arabian routes. A Greek and Nabaṭaean inscription dated between 166 and 169 has been found in a temple at Ruwāfa, south-west of Tabūk, in which the Roman Emperors Marcus Aurelius and Lucius Aurelius are mentioned.

The conversion of the Roman Empire to Christianity in the early 4th century led to a process of sustained penetration of the desert fringes of the Near East by monks establishing monasteries and retreats. Through political and other factors, the Byzantine successors of the Romans formed alliances with Arab frontier tribes that converted to Christianity as a result of their contact with the Byzantines. This process was most successful in the establishment of the Banū Ghassān frontier kingdom in the 6th century. In the course of the previous century, the defences of Byzantine Palestine had been invaded by Arab raiders on several occasions and the island of Tīrān (Iotabe) was actually lost to an Arab prince, Imru'al-Qais, along with its valuable customs post. In restoring their frontier defences after these incursions, the Byzantines concluded that better security could be achieved by supporting a native Arab principality; the system of appointing local Arab phylarchs from the Banū Ghassān, that was initiated in the early 6th century as a consequence of these difficulties, was to endure right up to the Muslim victory at the Yarmūk. A series of major Ghassānid archaeological sites reflect the sophistication of these Arab allies of Byzantium as well as the extent of their territorial control. At Ruṣāfa-Sergiopolis on the south side of the Euphrates in Syria is a major Ghassānid palace; further south at Qaṣr al-Ḥair al-Gharbī a monastery tower of the Ghassānids still survives, incorporated into the later Umayyad *qaṣr* of the Caliph Hishām bin 'Abd al-Malik. Other sites yet further south which have been associated to varying degrees with the Ghassānids include al-Jābiyya near Damascus, and al-Qasṭal in Jordan. It is clear from the accounts of the early Islamic period that Ghassānid power extended as far as Dūma when Khālid bin al-Walīd finally took the town for the Muslims in *13*/634.[2] It would appear that the Banū Ghassān still had authority over Dūma in the early 7th century, and although the town was ruled in the time of the Prophet Muḥammad by Ukaidir bin 'Abd al-Malik of Kinda, the military commander when Khālid bin al-Walīd finally took Dūma was al-Jūdiyy, of Ghassān. Al-Jūdiyy was defeated by Khālid, and his daughter was captured; subsequently, this Ghassānid princess was married by the Caliph Abū Bakr to his son 'Abd al-Raḥmān. Ukaidir is said to have acknowledged the authority of the Byzantine Emperor, Heraclius, and Islamic sources make it quite clear that Ukaidir was Christian. All this suggests that by the early *1st*/7th century, the Byzantines or their Ghassān allies had extended Byzantine influence and perhaps direct power as far as Dūma.

The Prophet sent expeditions against Dūma, and organized expeditions to Mu'ta and to Tabūk. At this time Byzantine and Ghassānid power in the north was only gradually reasserting itself following the Sassanian invasion and occupation of the Byzantine territiories of Syria, Palestine and Egypt between 611 and *6-7*/628: prior to these dates it would appear from archaeological work in Jordan that the Byzantines had already abandoned much of the more southerly part of the old Roman desert *limes* system, handing power to the Ghassān and other auxiliary troops drawn from allied Arab tribes. After the Sassanian invasion of Palestine in 614 and the disruption that followed, the system of Byzantine defences and Arab tribal alliances had to be re-established once the Emperor Heraclius had overcome and expelled the Sassanians (c. 7/628-9). Although Ghassānid power was no longer as great as it had been in the 6th century, they still played a major role in Byzantine forces concentrated in the Balqā' (in eastern Jordan) when the Prophet went north to Tabūk and, as mentioned above, at the final Muslim attack on Dūmat al-Jandal as well as at the ultimate defeat of the Byzantine forces at Yarmūk.

Thus, at the time of the Muslim expeditions into the southern frontier region of the Byzantine Empire in the days of the Prophet, the Byzantine defence system in that area had long been in the hands of Arab tribes allied to the Empire. The Byzantine Province of Palestine was divided into three parts:

Palaestina I, on the coast and in part of eastern Jordan; Palaestina II, consisting of the area around Lake Tiberias (Arabic, Ṭabariyya); and, from the end of the 4th century, Palaestina III Salutaris, extending from the Mediterranean coast at Gaza (Arabic, Ghazza) eastwards into the desert of eastern Jordan, beyond al-Karak in the north and ʻAqaba in the south. North of al-Karak up into the Ḥawrān lay Provincia Arabia, part of the old Nabaṭaean Kingdom. In the 5th century, the Byzantines' abandoning of the Roman fortifications mainly affected this southern desert area, Palaestina III, and in the 6th century defence here was transferred to the Ghassān, and to the Judhām, ʻĀmila, Bahrā', and the Baliyy tribes. It is these Arab tribes that appear allied to Heraclius at the time of the Prophet and during the Muslim conquests.

The Ghassān presence at Dūma in alliance with al-Ukaidir, himself the vassal of the Emperor Heraclius, therefore, is a part of a broad system that affected the Palaestina III region and probably other parts of north Arabia. The prominent position of Dūma as a market and its position on the routes from Arabia to the north and the east made it necessary for major states in the area to have some influence over it. It was for this reason that it became an important objective for the Muslim forces in the lifetime of the Prophet and thereafter. Yet with the subjugation of Dūma by Khālid bin al-Walīd, Dūma seems to fade from the attention of the chroniclers until it is mentioned again in the context of the arbitration between Muʻāwiya bin Abī Sufyān and ʻAlī bin Abī Ṭālib, and the events that followed.

Even though Dūma and the Wādi'l-Sirḥān received scant attention in the works of the Arab geographers and historians after this date, the fact remains that archaeological evidence from Jordan begs certain questions regarding the Umayyad period in the area and in the Wādi'l-Sirḥān and Dūma itself. Throughout the northern part of Jordan up into the Ḥawrān and beyond there are numerous sites which were occupied in the early Islamic and Umayyad period. The farmland of western Jordan and the Ḥawrān was clearly cultivated in this period, for the villages of the area have considerable quantities of early Islamic and Umayyad pottery indicating sustained and intensive use of these villages, many settled since Byzantine, Roman and earlier times. Furthermore, there are a number of palatial buildings in the Jordanian desert either built or expanded under the Umayyads. Between Azraq and ʻAmmān is a series of such major Umayyad sites, including Qaṣr ʻAmrā, Qaṣr al-Mushāsh and al-Muwaqqar; some were farms, or used for herding, but the intense distribution of these Umayyad sites towards Azraq and the Wādi'l-Sirḥān suggests that the Wādi'l-Sirḥān route may have been important and so too, in its turn, may have been Dūma. Unfortunately, archaeological research is too inadequate so far to draw any firm conclusions, but it may be premature to assume that Dūma and its region fade in importance when the literary references cease. Nevertheless, in Jordan as a whole, the coming of the ʻAbbāsids and the transfer of the centre of the Islamic caliphate to ʻIrāq in *132*/750 led to a decline of occupation at many sites. The absence of ʻAbbāsid pottery in much of the area suggests a change of routes through Arabia which followed the new prominence of ʻIrāq and the foundation of Baghdād. This in turn led to the abandonment or sharp decline of sites occupied in the Umayyad period in Jordan. This may well have affected Dūma, also bypassed by the routes through Arabia to the Holy Cities which were developed by the 'Abbāsids, most notably the Darb Zubaida from Baghdād to Makka. This route was greatly improved in the time of the Caliph Hārūn al-Rashīd by *Sitt* (lady) Zubaida, and its course, running far to the south of Dūma, reflects the degree to which Dūma, the Wādi'l-Sirḥān, and the Umayyad sites of Jordan were superseded as a result of the new political situation of the caliphate under the 'Abbāsids.[3]

Although the early 'Abbāsid period was one of decline in north-west Arabia and Jordan for the most part, a revival came in the aftermath of the victories of Ṣalāḥ al-Dīn al-Ayyūbī over the Crusaders in Palestine. Thereafter, signs of revitalization or re-occupation abound in the old settled areas of northern and western Jordan. Pottery finds ascribed to the Ayyūbid and the Mamlūk periods reflect the intensive development of these areas, and this same development extends up into Syria, and westwards into Palestine, continuing into Ottoman times. In the Jordan valley and at the south end of the Dead Sea, there is extensive archaeological evidence of the establishment of a sugar industry that supplied the demand created in the area during the Mamlūk period and later. The situation in the eastern desert area from the Ayyūbid period onwards is not yet clearly understood, although the old Roman fortress at Azraq was reconstructed in *634*/1257 by 'Izz al-Dīn Aibak for the Ayyūbids. Further north in the Ḥawrān villages and at Boṣrā, Ṣalkhad, and beyond at Damascus, Ayyūbid and, later, Mamlūk development of towns and villages was intensive. To the south at 'Aqaba, the Mamlūk Sulṭān Qānṣawh al-Ghawrī constructed a fortified *Khān* in *920*/1514-5. Further south, in the Ḥijāz, no archaeological work has been completed to elucidate these later Islamic periods, although an inscription on the *Qal'a* of Tabūk states that it was restored in *1064*/1653-54 by the Ottoman Sulṭān Muḥammad IV. That there was a general revitalization of the entire south of the Bilād al-Shām with the coming of the Ayyūbids is clear enough, not only in the great cities like Jerusalem and Damascus but in the smaller towns and oases as well, and this lasted into the Ottoman period. It is possible that this affected Dūma, for there is very meagre ceramic evidence showing that some Ayyūbid-Mamlūk pottery made its way to Dūma; it will be interesting to see to what extent future archaeological research in the area will indicate that Dūma participated in this efflorescence of Palestine, Syria and Jordan from the *6th*/12th century onwards.

---

1. From an article by Dr Geoffrey King, Department of Archaeology and Museology, King Saud University, Riyadh (*1403*/1983), with some changes in transliteration of names so that they conform to the system followed in this book.
2. According to al-Ṭabarī, whose chronology we have adopted for this event (see pp.73–74), the expedition occurred in *12*/633. *Editor*.
3. For a comprehensive study on this road, see Saad A. al-Rashid, Darb Zubaydah. A number of studies on it also appear in *Atlal*.

PART FOUR

HISTORY OF AL-JAWF REGION

AFTER THE RISE OF ISLAM UNTIL THE EMERGENCE OF THE FIRST SA'ŪDĪ STATE

14

The Coming of Islam to Dūmat al-Jandal

After the migration of the Prophet Muḥammad (P.B.U.H.) to al-Madīna in September 622, the Muslims there initially formed a religious community. After a short time this community felt the surge of a new national life and took shape as a state, which gained strength day by day. The early Islamic state, like any other, had to take steps for her own security, well-being and progress, with the tenets of Islam as the motivating force behind all its dealings. In these dealings it had to defend itself from hostile forces, wage war against enemies, enter into treaties, receive and send missions, and carry out other activities of this nature. The relations of the Islamic state with Dūmat al-Jandal were characterized by such dealings, as we shall see in this and the following chapter. In this chapter the course of events will be examined under three sub-headings, named after the three expeditions sent during the lifetime of the Prophet (P.B.U.H.) to Dūmat al-Jandal. Each of these expeditions had a different purpose. The first, led by the Prophet (P.B.U.H.) himself, was preventive and punitive in nature, the second had missionary motives, and the third was made with the aim of securing the frontiers and extending the influence of the Islamic state. The following chapter will include the discussion of the fourth campaign to Dūma, as a result of which the city state acceded to the Islamic state.

THE FIRST EXPEDITION

The circumstances under which the first expedition to Dūmat al-Jandal was undertaken have been explained by the early Muslim historians. Al-Wāqidī

(*130 – 210*/747-8 – 825-6) says that the Prophet (P.B.U.H.) was informed "that a large crowd of men had gathered at Dūmat al-Jandal and that they subjected the passing-by traders to oppression; that there was a large mart there, with its traders[1]; that to them had congregated a large number of men from the Arabs; and that they intended to make a hostile advance towards al-Madīna."[2] Al-Wāqidī also says that it was explained to the Prophet (P.B.U.H.) that a Muslim advance towards the area known as Adna'l-Shām (literally, the nearest Syria), which was one of the gateways of Syria, would have the effect of startling the Byzantine emperor.[3] It is not clear from the text whether the Prophet (P.B.U.H.), in undertaking the expedition, wanted to achieve this or whether he went ahead with his plan despite the risk. The more obvious purposes of the expedition were, firstly, to take a punitive action against the people of Dūma for their transgressions and, secondly, to preempt any possible hostile enemy move.

A somewhat later historian, al-Mas'ūdī (d.*346*/957-8), adds to the above the information that this expedition was the first of the Prophet's (P.B.U.H.) expeditions against Rome (Byzantium), that the ruler of Dūma at the time was Ukaidir bin 'Abd al-Malik al-Kindī, a Christian who had recognized Heraclius, the Roman Emperor, as his overlord, and that he used to obstruct traffic to al-Madīna and harass the Madīnese traders.[4]

Al-Wāqidī says that the expedition began on *25 Rabī' I 5*/24 August 626 and returned on *20 Rabī' II*/18 September.[5] This is substantiated in more general terms by Ibn Isḥāq (d.*151*/768-69), one of the earliest Muslim historians, who says that the Prophet (P.B.U.H.) set out on the expedition to Dūmat al-Jandal in *5* after passing the month of *Dhu'l-Ḥijja 4*/May 626 in al-Madīna.[6] Ibn Hishām (d.*213*/828-29), the renowned biographer of the Prophet (P.B.U.H.), specifies the month of the expedition as *Rabī' I (5)*, without mentioning its duration or giving any other details.[7]

On this occasion, according to al-Wāqidī, the Prophet (P.B.U.H.) appointed Sibā' bin 'Urfuṭa [al-Ghifārī] to act as governor of al-Madīna in his absence. The expedition set out with one thousand men, with a guide named Madhkūr from the Banū 'Udhra. Avoiding the regular route, they travelled by night and rested by day. When they were within one day's march from Dūma, the guide stopped them and went on a scouting mission. He came back after ascertaining where the camels and sheep of the enemy were, and the party then attacked the herds and herdsmen. The herdsmen sustained some losses and fled. When the news of this reached the people of Dūma, they scattered. The Prophet (P.B.U.H.) then camped at their deserted site. He sent out search parties, all of which returned after one day with some captured animals only – except Muḥammad bin Maslama, who brought in a single prisoner. The prisoner informed the Prophet (P.B.U.H.) that the people had fled the day before, on learning of the Muslim attack, and, on being offered Islam, became a Muslim. After staying there for some days, the expedition returned to al-Madīna.[8]

The early Muslim historians are not unanimous on the question of whether the Prophet (P.B.U.H.) came to Dūmat al-Jandal proper during the expedition. Al-Wāqidī's account gives the clear impression that he did. Ibn Sa'd (*168-230*/784-85

– 844-45) copies al-Wāqidī's account verbatim.[9] Al-Ṭabarī (*224-310*/838-39 – 922-23), who mentions al-Wāqidī as his sole source, and al-Mas'ūdī both clearly say that he reached Dūma.[10] On the other hand, Ibn Isḥāq says that the Prophet (P.B.U.H.) "returned before reaching it [i.e. Dūma]". He then adds that the Prophet (P.B.U.H.) did not have to go to battle during the expedition.[11]

The expedition was certainly not embarked upon with the intention of conquest and permanent garrisoning of Dūma. As we have seen above, the purpose was to deter aggression and punish the transgressors. However, the expedition clearly generated in the newly-emerging Islamic state at al-Madīna an interest in the strategically important oasis controlling trade routes from the south to Syria and 'Irāq.

Discussing the Prophet's (P.B.U.H.) expedition to Dūmat al-Jandal, Alois Musil asserts that it took place earlier in the year, in spring. In his view it would not have been possible to make the trip later in the year because of the lack of water in the wells and the aridity of the pastures for grazing the camels in the latter part of the summer, when the hijri months of *Rabī' I* and *Rabī' II* fell in *5*. The distance between Dūmat al-Jandal and al-Madīna is 700 km. and, in his view, it would have been difficult to cover 1,400 km. in 25 days, supposedly the total length of the Prophet's (P.B.U.H.) campaign.[12] Although there may be some basis for Musil's opinion that the expedition took place in the beginning of spring – due to ambiguity surrounding the evolution of the lunar calendar in the early Islamic period, the chronology of the events of the Prophet's (P.B.U.H.) time is not wholly settled[13] – we have to say that Musil, in arguing that the expedition could not have taken place in the heat of the late summer, ignores several important relevant factors such as the adaptation of the Arabs to the rigours of the desert life, the possibilities of travel by camels, and the morale and discipline in those who converted to the new faith.

It should be borne in mind that the Arabs were used to the harsh conditions of the desert life. Their adaptation to their environment was superb, giving them the ability to tap all the life-sustaining resources of the desert. They were accustomed to moving across desert tracts throughout the year according to the dictates of their circumstances, and the migrations that they had to make in winter and summer had become matters of mere routine for them. Also, let us view the matter in the light of the camel's capabilities. It is recorded by Douglas Carruthers in his introduction to the book of the Italian traveller Carlo Guarmani, who made a journey to Arabia in 1864, that Guarmani traversed 161 km. of the sand dunes of the Nafūd in 16 hours, that the German traveller Eduard Nolde's camel did 100 km. in seven hours, and that Lawrence of Arabia covered 145 km. in 22 hours. He also quotes Lawrence as saying that 80 miles (129 km.) a day is quite usual for raiding parties.[14] Another authority writes that "over long distances a riding camel is three times as quick as a horse. It can cover 300 km. in one day."[15] If three days are deducted from the duration of the Prophet's (P.B.U.H.) expedition on account of his stay in the area of Dūmat al-Jandal, the average daily rate of travel for the party comes to 64 km. Considering all the circumstances, there is no reason not to accept the idea that it was possible for the disciplined and highly-motivated hardy sons of the desert to cover this distance each day, even in late summer, by taking advantage of the cool of the desert night.

THE SECOND EXPEDITION

The second Muslim expedition to Dūmat al-Jandal took place in the month of *Sha'bān 6*/January-February 628.

To understand the motives behind this campaign, we need to set it in its historical setting. Nine months before this expedition the attack on al-Madīna by the Makkans and their Jewish and other allies – the Battle of the Trench, *Dhu'l-Qi'da 5*/March-April 627 – had ended in a victory for the Muslims. Immediately after that, the threat from the Jews of al-Madīna, who had violated their covenant with the Prophet (P.B.U.H.) during the Battle of the Trench, was removed. The power of the Hypocrites had also finally been broken. Arab tribes now gave due regard to the burgeoning Muslim power. At this juncture it was felt that the time had come for propagating Islam, for calling all men to faith in One God. It is towards this end that the second campaign to Dūmat al-Jandal seems to have been made. This is confirmed by al-Wāqidī, who records that the Prophet (P.B.U.H.) ordered 'Abd al-Raḥmān bin 'Awf, the leader of the campaign, to go to Dūmat al-Jandal and invite people to the Islamic faith.[16]

The story of the event, based on information from the accounts of the earliest Muslim historians, is that the Prophet (P.B.U.H.), when sending Ibn 'Awf to Dūmat al-Jandal, asked him to sit before him face-to-face, undid his turban and put on his head a black one, instructing him in its setting. The Prophet (P.B.U.H.) then ordered Bilāl bin Rabāḥ to give the flag to Ibn 'Awf, and said to Ibn 'Awf, "Take the expedition in the name of God in His path. Fight against those who deny God, in the matter of spoils do not breach your trust, do not act perfidiously, do not mutilate anybody and do not kill any child." Ibn 'Awf then set out for Dūma with seven hundred men. Arriving there, he invited people to join the Islamic faith. Three days later, after an initial hesitation, the Christian chief of the Kalb tribe, al-Aṣbagh bin 'Amr, along with a large number of men from his tribe, accepted Islam. Others (acknowledging the suzerainty of the Islamic state over the region) promised to pay the *jizya*.[17]

'Abd al-Raḥmān bin 'Awf sent a letter through one of his companions, Rāfi' bin Mukaith bin 'Amr al-Juhainī, to the Prophet (P.B.U.H.), giving him the good news and informing him that he intended to marry one of the women from the Kalb tribe. The Prophet (P.B.U.H.) wrote advising him to marry Tumāḍir, the daughter of al-Aṣbagh. Ibn 'Awf then married Tumāḍir – who was later to become the mother of his son Abū Salama – and returned to al-Madīna.[18]

One short account of the event, related by al-Wāqidī in addition to his principal account, varies a little from the preceding narrative, to the effect that the expedition was sent to the Kalb tribe (in the vicinity of Dūmat al-Jandal), that the Prophet (P.B.U.H.), at the time of Ibn 'Awf's departure, told him to marry the daughter of the king or chief of the Kalb tribe with their permission, and that Ibn 'Awf indeed married Tumāḍir, the daughter of their king, al-Aṣbagh bin 'Amr.[19] Al-Ṭabarī has restricted himself to copying this second account of al-Wāqidī.[20] Since both al-Wāqidī in his second account and al-Ṭabarī omit the name of Dūmat al-Jandal, it can be strongly argued that the expedition was aimed at the Kalb tribe camping in the vicinity of Dūma and not at the town itself. It has been pointed out that the title of "king" could not have been assumed by or ascribed to the chief of the Kalb tribe or a branch of the Kalb tribe because the Kalb had Ghassānians as their overlords, who would not have tolerated the use of such a title by their dependants.[21] This point is satisfactorily answered by the remarks of Jawād 'Alī given in a different but similar case – that of al-Ukaidir. He says that "it was a custom prevailing at the time among the chiefs of settlements to assume the title of *malik*", i.e. king, and that in reality the title was nothing more than the present-day title of "*shaikh*", i.e. head or chief.[22]

THE THIRD EXPEDITION

The third expedition to Dūmat al-Jandal was sent by the Prophet (P.B.U.H.) in *Rajab 9*/October-November 630. To understand the motives of the Prophet (P.B.U.H) in sending yet another expedition to the area, we have to look at the campaign undertaken by the Prophet (P.B.U.H.) to Tabūk, to which the campaign to Dūma was complementary. Ibn Sa'd writes that "the Prophet was informed that the Romans [Byzantines] had gathered in large numbers in Syria, that Heraclius [the Byzantine Emperor] had provided his troops with rations sufficient for one year, that with him had joined the tribes of Lakhm, Judhām, 'Āmila and Ghassān, and that the vanguards of their armies had advanced to al-Balqā'."[23] The Prophet (P.B.U.H.) decided to meet this impending menace and set out in October 630 on the last and greatest of the 27 expeditions in which he personally took part – that to Tabūk near the Gulf of 'Aqaba. On arriving in Tabūk with an army of 30,000 men, he learned that Heraclius at the time was either in Ḥimṣ or in Damascus, and that the Byzantine forces had withdrawn to the safety of their hinterland. After consulting his companions the Prophet (P.B.U.H.) decided not to advance any further. Instead, he went ahead with the task of impressing upon the people and city-states of the border regions the fact that their future lay with the Islamic state. He was successful in securing the submission of the Christian community of Aila ('Aqaba) and the Jewish communities of Jarbā', Adhruḥ and Maqnā, all of which agreed to pay *jizya* and were given covenants of security by him.[24] The northern frontiers of Arabia were thus secured through treaties of friendship – except for Dūmat al-Jandal, whose ruler, Ukaidir, did not come to pay homage. As the later events proved, the Prophet (P.B.U.H.) wanted to have a similar covenant of security with Ukaidir.

While examining the reasons for the two expeditions, let us see how a distinguished British historian interprets the massive Muslim drive towards the north. W. Montgomery Watt writes:

> The tribes along the road to Syria . . . had a long tradition of association with the Byzantine empire . . . [The Prophet] would realize that he had no chance of winning the tribes here until he showed that he could bring greater force to bear on this region than could Heraclius. The mounting of this huge expedition in October was a counterblast to what Heraclius had done in March [by defeating the Persians]. It was also, of course, a reconnaisance of the route to Syria, and an assertion that the Muslim sphere of influence extended over much of the ground traversed. Treaties concluded with small Christian and Jewish communities on and near the Gulf of Akaba, guaranteeing them protection in return for a payment of tribute, imply that this sphere of influence was intended to be permanent. A similar treaty with the ruler of the settled communities at Dūmat al-Jandal was concluded by Khālid ibn-al-Walīd in command of a force detached from the main body.[25]

The events of the expedition to Dūma, as narrated by Ibn Isḥāq, Ibn Sa'd and, in somewhat greater detail, al-Wāqidī, are as follows.

Before departing from Tabūk, the Prophet (P.B.U.H.) sent Khālid bin al-Walīd, who was accompanying him at the time, in command of 420 horsemen to Ukaidir of Dūmat al-Jandal.[26] Khālid expressed doubts about the success of his mission in view of the target being in the midst of the territory of the Kalb tribe and his force being small. The Prophet (P.B.U.H.) said, "You will find him hunting oryx; capture him then." Khālid then set out. They arrived within sight of Ukaidir's castle on a moonlit night. Ukaidir at the time was on the roof of the castle with his wife, al-Rabāb, daughter of Unaif bin'Āmir of Kinda, listening to his singing girl and drinking. Suddenly, there appeared some oryxes, which started rubbing their horns against the gate of the castle. Al-Rabāb noticed them and incited her husband to go after them. The Prince, accompanied by one of his brothers, Ḥassān, and others, rode out in pursuit of the animals. When they came near Khālid and his horsemen, waiting for them in complete silence, they were attacked. Ukaidir was captured, but Ḥassān resisted and was killed. Khālid told Ukaidir that his life could be spared till the time he was taken to the Prophet (P.B.U.H.), if he opened the oasis to him. Ukaidir agreed and was taken to the castle's gate. His brother, Muḍād, however, seeing Ukaidir under restraint, refused to open the gate. Ukaidir then gave Khālid his word that he would open the gate to him if he was set free and if Khālid promised to spare the lives of the occupants of the castle in exchange for mutually agreed compensation. An agreement was then reached between the two. Ukaidir promised to accompany Khālid, with Muḍād, to the Prophet (P.B.U.H.), whose decision he agreed to accept. Events transpired as agreed, and Khālid returned to al-Madīna with Ukaidir and his brother. The Prophet (P.B.U.H.) spared their lives and gave Ukaidir a covenant of protection in consideration for his agreeing to pay *jizya* to the Islamic state. Ukaidir then returned to Dūma.[27]

The Muslim historians relate that when Ukaidir came to the Prophet (P.B.U.H.), he appeared with a show of wealth and magnificence, wearing a golden cross and a conspicuous silken robe.[28] According to one version recorded by Ibn Ḥajar, he took out a robe with gold brocade which had been presented to him by Chosroes (Arabic, *Kisrā*, the Sassanian emperor) and said, "O Prophet of God, take this, for I give it to you." But the Prophet (P.B.U.H.) replied, "Take it back, for anyone who wears this in this world will be anathematized in the next." At this, Ukaidir returned to his own quarters, yet remained deeply discomfited that his gift had been rejected; he went back to the Prophet (P.B.U.H.) and said, "O Prophet of God, we people are of a family on which it is hard to have its gifts returned, so accept my present." Whereupon the Prophet (P.B.U.H.) said, "Give it to 'Umar [bin al-Khaṭṭāb, the future second Caliph]."[29] According to the account of the event by a different narrator, also recorded by Ibn Ḥajar, Ukaidir sent the Prophet (P.B.U.H.) a gown with gold embroidery and the Prophet (P.B.U.H.) wore it, and Ukaidir also presented a jar of *mann* (a type of sweet) to the Prophet (P.B.U.H.), who gave everyone a share.[30]

Agreement by Ukaidir to pay *jizya* implies that he did not convert to Islam on this occasion. However, there are reports to the contrary requiring attention and analysis. Both al-Wāqidī and Ibn Sa'd have included secondary reports, in addition to their main reports cited above, in which their narrator cites a letter from the Prophet (P.B.U.H.) to Ukaidir, which, among other things, states that Ukaidir accepted Islam in Dūma in the presence of Khālid.[31] The famous historian al-Balādhurī (d.*279*/892-93), too, says in his principal report that Ukaidir became a Muslim when brought to the Prophet (P.B.U.H.). He then gives a copy of the same letter with minor changes and omitting the name of Khālid bin al-Walīd.[32]

Al-Wāqidī's copy of the letter of the Prophet (P.B.U.H.) reads as follows:

> In the name of God, Most Gracious, Most Merciful. This is the letter from Muḥammad, the Prophet of God, to Ukaidir, since he accepted Islam and abjured the objects of worship and idols – in the presence of Khālid bin al-Walīd, the Sword of God – in Dūmat al-Jandal and its surrounding areas. To us [i.e. the Islamic state] belong the outskirts [i.e. areas outside the walled settlement of Dūma] where water is scanty; uncultivated lands, unbounded lands and wildernesses; chain-mail shirts; weapons; horses, mules and donkeys; and the fortress. For you is [the produce of] the palm-groves inside the walled settlement[33] and [that of] the land irrigated by free-flowing water, after a charge of one fifth [as tax]. [For the purposes of reckoning tax] your herds in the pastures shall not be gathered [to verify their numbers], nor will your single animals[34] be counted. Cultivation of vegetation is not forbidden you. No tithe shall be taken from you on your household goods. You shall offer prayer at its appointed time and pay *zakāt* [i.e. charity] as due.
>
> On you is the covenanted obligation to abide by this, and from us you will find its fulfilment with sincerity. God is our witness and those of the Muslims who are present.[35]

It is interesting to note that a similar covenant, for Dūmat al-Jandal, is recorded by Ibn Sa'd, under the heading "Delegation from Kalb". Most probably, the delegation visited the Prophet (P.B.U.H.) at al-Madīna in *10*/631-632, the year known as "the Year of Deputations", during which the people of Arabia sent their leaders in delegations to the Prophet (P.B.U.H.) and embraced Islam *en masse*. Ibn Sa'd relates that Ḥāritha bin Qaṭan bin 'Ulaim al-Kalbī and Ḥamal bin Sa'dāna bin 'Ulaim al-Kalbī came in a delegation to the Prophet (P.B.U.H.) and embraced Islam. The Prophet (P.B.U.H.) tied a standard for Ḥamal bin Sa'dāna – who later participated with that standard in the battle of Ṣiffīn on the side of Mu'āwiya. The Prophet (P.B.U.H.) wrote for Ḥāritha bin Qaṭan a document which reads as follows:

> This is the letter from Muḥammad, the Prophet of God, to those from the people of Dūmat al-Jandal and its surrounding areas who belong to the branches of the Kalb tribe under Ḥāritha bin Qaṭan. For us are the date palms in the outskirts, and for you are the palm-groves inside the walled settlement. A tithe will be charged on [the produce of] the land watered by free-flowing water, whereas half the tithe will be taken in the case of [the produce of] the land irrigated by water from wells. [For the purpose of reckoning tax] your herds in the pastures shall not be gathered [to verify their numbers], nor will your single animals be counted. You shall offer prayer at its appointed time and pay *zakāt* as due. Cultivation of vegetation is not forbidden you. No tithe shall be taken from you on your household goods.
>
> On you is the covenanted obligation to abide by this. From us you will get counsel and fulfilment [of the covenant] as well as protection of God and His Prophet.
>
> God is our witness and those of the Muslims who are present.[36]

Returning to the question of whether Ukaidir embraced Islam on this occasion, if we accept as genuine the Prophet's (P.B.U.H.) letter which says that he did so, then the accuracy of the earlier reports that the Prophet (P.B.U.H.) gave Ukaidir a covenant of protection in consideration of his agreeing to pay *jizya* becomes questionable, and *vice versa*. Three early Muslim historians, Ibn Isḥāq, Mūsā bin 'Uqba (d.*141*/758) and al-Wāqidī, are recognized as the main authorities on the life of the Prophet (P.B.U.H.).[37] As we have seen above, Ibn Isḥāq mentions only the effecting of an agreement on payment of *jizya* by Ukaidir. Al-Wāqidī also lays stress on the same fact and relegates the report regarding Ukaidir's becoming a Muslim to a secondary and minor position. The third authority, Mūsā bin 'Uqba, has been quoted by Ibn Qayyim al-Jawziyya as saying that when Ukaidir came to the Prophet (P.B.U.H.), the Prophet (P.B.U.H.) invited him to Islam, but he refused to convert and agreed on paying *jizya*.[38] Ibn Hishām, al-Ṭabarī and al-Mas'ūdī are silent on this point.[39] A famous later scholar ('Izz al-Dīn?) Ibn al-Athīr (*555-630*/1160-1233) has been quoted by Ibn Ḥajar as saying that "Ukaidir did not become a Muslim. This is something on which there is no disagreement among the biographers of the Prophet, and whosoever says that he accepted Islam is clearly in the wrong."[40] Thus we find that from among the early historians it is only al-Balādhurī who gives more prominence to his report concerning Ukaidir's embracing Islam than to that of his agreeing to pay *jizya*. If weight of scholarly opinion is any guide, then we can safely conclude that the authenticity of the reported letter of the Prophet (P.B.U.H.) to Ukaidir is doubtful and that Ukaidir remained and died a Christian.

This expedition to Dūmat al-Jandal, like the previous two, was not made with the intention of a permanent conquest of Dūma for the Muslim state. Therefore, garrisoning of the town was out of the question. After he left al-Madīna, Ukaidir had all the authority to manage the internal affairs of his domain as he wished, as had the rulers of other communities on the northern fringes of Arabia who had received the covenants of protection. A scrutiny of the circumstances of this campaign indicates that the Prophet (P.B.U.H.) wanted to minimize the chances of any possible threat from the direction of the Byzantine frontiers and to create a sphere of influence for the Islamic state. He succeeded in both these objectives.

---

1. A reference to the market of Dūma, discussed on pp.44-46 above.
2. Muḥammad bin 'Umar al-Wāqidī, *Kitāb al-Maghāzī*, ed. Marsden Jones, 3 vols, London, Oxford University Press, 1966, vol. 1 p.403.
3. Ibid.
4. al-Mas'ūdī, *al-Tanbīh*, p.248.
5. al-Wāqidī, vol. 1 p.402.
6. Ibn Hishām, vol. 2 p.213.
7. Ibid.
8. al-Wāqidī, vol. 1 pp.403-04.
9. Muḥammad Ibn Sa'd al-Zuhrī, *al-Ṭabaqāt al-Kubrā*, 9 vols., Beirut, Dār Ṣādir, 1957-58, vol. 2 pp.62-63.
10. Muḥammad Ibn Jarīr al-Ṭabarī, *Tārīkh al-Rusul wa'l-Mulūk*, ed. M.J. De Goeje and others, 4 vols. in 15, Leiden, 1879; reprint ed. Beirut, Maktabat al-Khayyāṭ, 1965, vol.1 pp.1462-63; al-Mas'ūdī, *al-Tanbīh*, pp.248-49.
11. Ibn Hishām, vol. 2 p.213.
12. Musil, *Arabia Deserta*, pp.535-36.
13. It is mentioned by the authorities on the Islamic calendar that there was in vogue in pre-Islamic Arabia a system of periodic intercalation (in the lunar year) of full lunar month or months after a certain number of years had gone by, the purpose being to bring the lunar year into line with the solar year at regular intervals. The reports about the number of months intercalated and the frequency of the action vary. Al-Bīrūnī [Abu'l-Raiḥān Muḥammad bin Aḥmad] and al-Maqrīzī [Aḥmad bin 'Alī al-Ḥusainī] say that nine months were added after every 24 lunar years [most probably in steps] whereas al-Mas'ūdī ['Alī bin Ḥusain bin 'Alī] says that one month used to be added after every three years. The experts holding the charge of the calendar affairs were from the Banū Kināna. It is recorded that this system was dispensed with by the Prophet (P.B.U.H.) in the 10th year of Hijra. The system of the Muslim Hijri calendar was introduced some years later by the 2nd Caliph, 'Umar bin al-Khaṭṭāb. 'Alī Ḥasan Mūsā, *al-Tawqīt wa'l-Taqwīm*, Beirut, Dār al-Fikr al- Mu'āṣir, *1410*/1990, pp.118-21. It is not clear whether or not, on the introduction of the new lunar calendar, the people converted to the new calendar the dates in their private documents and memoranda or the dates of particular events in their memories. The proposition that the first expedition to Dūmat al-Jandal took place in *Rabī' I* of the solar year of the bedouin, and not in that of the lunar year, is worthy of serious consideration in view of the fact that the expedition occurred before the practice of intercalation ceased and, further, that there is a mention by al-Wāqidī of the market of Dūmat al-Jandal being in progress before the Prophet (P.B.U.H.) set out on this journey. Al-Wāqidī, vol. 1 p.403. As seen in the chapter on the market of Dūma, the markets of Arabia were held according to the seasonal months, the month of the market of Dūma being *Rabī' I* – the beginning of spring season. However, until further research on the Islamic calendar and on the chronology of the events of the early Islamic period brings forth new facts, this remains uncertain.
14. Carlo Guarmani, *Northern Najd: A Journey from Jerusalem to Anaiza in Qasim*, trans. Lady Capel-Cure, with Introduction and Notes by Douglas Carruthers, London, Argonaut Press, 1938, pp.xxv-xxvi.
15. *Encyclopaedia of Islam*, New ed., s.v. "Badw II (c) Bedouin Nomadism in Arabia", by H. von Wissmann.
16. al-Wāqidī, vol. 2 p.560.
17. Ibid., pp.560-61; Ibn Hishām, vol. 2 p.632; Ibn Sa'd, vol. 2 p.89; vol. 3 p.129. *Jizya* was paid by those non-Muslim subjects of the Islamic state whose religion precluded them from serving in the army, in return for the protection secured for them by the arms of the Muslims. The tax was levied on able-bodied males, and not on women or children. The rate differed according to the financial status of the

subject, higher for the rich, lower for the poor.
18. al-Wāqidī, vol. 2 p.561; Ibn Sa'd, vol. 2 p.89.
19. al-Wāqidī, vol. 2 pp.561-62.
20. al-Ṭabarī, vol. 1 p.1556.
21. See, e.g., Musil, *Arabia Deserta*, p.538.
22. Jawād 'Alī, vol. 4 p.237.
23. Ibn Sa'd, vol. 2 p.165.
24. Ibid., vol. 1 pp.290-91; Ibn Hishām, vol. 2 pp.525-26; al-Mas'ūdī, *al-Tanbīh*, p.272; Muḥammad Ḥusayn Haykal, *The Life of Muḥammad*, trans. Ismā'īl Rāgī A. al-Fārūqī, n.p., North American Trust Publications, 1976, p.449.
25. W. Montgomery Watt, *Muḥammad: Prophet and Statesman*, New York, Oxford University Press, 1977, pp.218-19.
26. One divergent report quoted by Ibn Ḥajar is to the effect that on this occasion Abū Bakr, in command of a force of Muhājirūn, also accompanied Khālid and that they were given instructions not to kill Ukaidir but to capture him and to bring him to the Prophet (P.B.U.H.). See Ibn Ḥajar, vol. 1 p.126.
27. Ibn Hishām, vol. 2 p.526; Ibn Sa'd, vol. 2 p.166; al-Wāqidī, vol. 3 pp.1025-28.
28. al Wāqidī, vol. 3 pp.1029-30.
29. Ibn Ḥajar, vol. 1 p.126.
30. Ibid.
31. al-Wāqidī, vol. 3 p.1030; Ibn Sa'd, vol. 1 pp.288-89.
32. al-Balādhurī, vol. 1 p.73.
33. "The palm-groves inside the walled settlement" is a translation of "al-ḍāmina min al-nakhl", according to the interpretation of al-Balādhurī (see his *Futūḥ al-Buldān*, vol. 1 p.73). Al-Wāqidī, on the other hand, interprets the phrase to mean "date-palms that are deeply rooted in the earth".
34. al-Wāqidī adds here by way of commentary that up to 40 sheep are to be exempted for this purpose.
35. al-Wāqidī, vol. 3 p.1030.
36. Ibn Sa'd, vol. 1 pp.334-35.
37. See *Encyclopaedia of Islam*, New ed., s.v. "Ibn Isḥāḳ", by J.M.B. Jones.
38. Ibn Qayyim al-Jawziyya, vol. 3 p.539.
39. Ibn Hishām, vol. 2 pp.525-26; al-Ṭabarī, vol. 1 pp.2373-74; al-Mas'ūdī, *al-Tanbīh*, p.272.
40. Ibn Ḥajar, vol. 1 p.125. Full name of Ibn al-Athīr is not included by Ibn Ḥajar; most probably it is 'Izz al-Dīn 'Alī bin Muḥammad, the historian.

15
Dūmat al-Jandal in the time of the First Caliph, Abū Bakr

When the Prophet (P.B.U.H.) died in *Rabī' I 11*/June 632, and Abū Bakr succeeded him as head of the Islamic state, taking the title of "caliph", there occurred the revolt known in Islamic history as *ridda* or "apostasy". It affected most of the tribes outside al-Madīna, Makka and Ṭā'if. Some tribes completely broke away from Islam, following newly-risen false prophets and sooth-sayers; some remained Muslim but were not willing to recognize the authority of the Islamic state based at al-Madīna and refused to obey its agents and to pay *zakāt*.

Though Dūmat al-Jandal is not regarded as one of the major centres of revolt, there are reports that the tribes or, in certain cases, some factions of the tribes in Dūmat al-Jandal and its environs participated in the rebellion and that they were offering tough resistance long after allegiance to Islam and the Islamic state had been restored in most other areas. Al-Ṭabarī reports that to crush the rebellion Abū Bakr sent eleven different commanders to different tribes and areas. Two out of those commanders, 'Amr bin al-'Āṣ and Shuraḥbīl bin Ḥasana, were sent to the tribes around Dūma – specifically, the Quḍā'a and some factions of the Kalb – though Shuraḥbīl was ordered to fight first under the command of 'Ikrima bin Abī Jahl against the apostates of al-Yamāma and then to proceed to the region around Dūma.[1] But before the arrival of these commanders in the area, two other events occurred, influencing Dūmat al-Jandal profoundly. The first concerned Imru' al-Qais and the second was the campaign of Usāma bin Zaid bin Ḥāritha.

As noted in the last chapter, during Ibn 'Awf's expedition to Dūmat al-Jandal, al-Aṣbagh bin 'Amr and many of his fellow tribesmen from the Kalb accepted Islam. When the Prophet (P.B.U.H.) died, his designated overseer of the Quḍā'a and Kalb tribes was al-Aṣbagh's son, Imru' al-Qais. Imru' al-Qais was not influenced by the wave of apostasy and remained firm in his belief. But another leader of some factions of the Kalb tribe, Wadī'a, apostatized along with his followers. On learning of Wadī'a's apostasy, Abū Bakr directed Imru' al-Qais to take action against him. Imru' al-Qais advanced against Wadī'a,[2] who fled and took refuge in Dūmat al-Jandal.

The background of the second event, Usāma's campaign, is that during the Mu'ta campaign, sent by the Prophet (P.B.U.H.) in *Jumādā I 8*/September 629, under the command of Zaid bin Ḥāritha – Usāma's father – the Muslim army suffered a reversal at the hands of a huge Byzantine army supported by some Quḍā'a sub-tribes and the Lakhm and Judhām tribes. The Prophet (P.B.U.H.) wanted to punish the treacherous tribes and decided, a short time before his death, to send an army under Usāma's command towards that end. Usāma could not proceed on account of the Prophet's (P.B.U.H.) death. One of the first actions of Abū Bakr was to despatch Usāma on that expedition, instructing him to start with the territory of the Quḍā'a.[3]

On arriving in Quḍā'a territory, Usāma divided part of his cavalry into small raiding parties, which conducted punitive forays into enemy territory. Moreover, he besought those who had remained firm in their Islamic faith to fight against those who had apostatized. The apostates fled and sought refuge in Dūmat al-Jandal. There they joined the rebellious Kalb factions under Wadī'a. Usāma did not pursue them and concentrated instead on taking punitive action against some Judhām and Lakhm factions. After campaigning for around forty days, Usāma returned to al-Madīna with his army.[4]

Not much is recorded about the activities of 'Amr bin al-'Āṣ and Shuraḥbīl bin Ḥasana against the Quḍā'a and the factions of the Kalb under Wadi'a's influence. Shuraḥbīl was to join 'Amr after the victory of Khālid bin al-Walīd in the battle of al-Yamāma – 'Ikrima had failed to subdue the uprising there – in which Shuraḥbīl also participated.[5] He is reported departing from al-Madīna for Dūmat al-Jandal in the company of another commander, al Aqra' bin Ḥābis,[6] but it seems that al-Aqra' did not go directly to Dūma, for he is shown fighting alongside Khālid in his campaigns in 'Irāq prior to Khālid's coming to Dūma to the help of 'Iyāḍ bin Ghanm. Al-Aqra' accompanied Khālid to Dūma and took part in the battle at that time.[7] No activity of Shuraḥbīl in the Dūma region is recorded. However, it is mentioned that he was transferred to the Syrian front, though somewhat later. So far as 'Amr bin al-'Āṣ is concerned, it is reported that he was raiding the Baliyy, a sub-tribe of the Quḍā'a, and the Sa'd during the period the *ridda* battles were raging in other places.[8] That he was able to subdue the Quḍā'a is certain, for he and al-Walīd bin 'Uqba were holding the charge of the Quḍā'a before their departure to the front against the Byzantines opened in the beginning of *13*/March 634.[9] However, he did not make any advance against the oasis of Dūmat al-Jandal or Wadī'a and his followers from the Kalb, stationed there along with the apostates from the Quḍā'a and the enemies of the Islamic state from the town itself.

After the offensive against the main centres of the apostasy rebellion was successfully over near the end of *11*/March 633, al-Muthannā bin Ḥāritha, the leader of the Banū Shaibān, a sub-tribe of the Bakr bin Wā'il, domiciled on the Persian border in and around present-day Kuwait, started making successful raids on the border of 'Irāq near the delta of the Shaṭṭ al-'Arab and wrote to Abū Bakr asking for help.[10] After satisfying himself about al-Muthannā and his campaign, Abū Bakr gave to two generals the task of conquering 'Irāq: Khālid bin al-Walīd and 'Iyāḍ bin Ghanm. He directed Khālid to enter 'Irāq from the lower side – the Shaṭṭ al-'Arab side. 'Iyāḍ was ordered to effect his entry from the opposite direction and, for this purpose, to go to al-Muṣayyakh and start his campaign into upper 'Irāq from there. The target set for both was the famous old town of al-Ḥīra, located to the south-east of present-day Najaf.[11]

'Iyāḍ, at the time of receiving Abū Bakr's orders, was somewhere between al-Nabāj and al-Ḥijāz. His route to al-Muṣayyakh passed through the oasis of

Dūmat al-Jandal, where, as mentioned, a large number of apostates had taken refuge. The ruler of the town, al-Ukaidir, being bound in a treaty of peace with the Islamic state, was supposed not to be a party to the rebellion, but gave the apostates protection and help and allowed the oasis to become a stronghold of the opponents of Islam. Al-Balādhurī (see previous chapter) says that after the death of the Prophet (P.B.U.H.) Ukaidir refused to pay *zakāt* (like other apostates), and otherwise broke the terms of the treaty.[12] 'Iyāḍ, on arriving in the vicinity of Dūma, was confronted by the hostile forces gathered there. Involved in a prolonged show of strength, he could proceed no further on his assigned mission. As aptly put by al-Ṭabarī, "He was making the enemy unhappy, and the enemy was making him unhappy."[13]

Khālid bin al-Walīd, in the meantime, had joined with Muthannā in *Muḥarram 12*/March-April 633, assumed command of the combined forces, and started wresting 'Irāq from the Persians. Before the end of the third month of *12*, he had completed the conquest of al-Ḥīra, "the first apple to fall from the Persian tree". From 'Irāq, Khālid sent al-Walīd bin 'Uqba to Abū Bakr with spoils of war. The Caliph sent al-Walīd to Dūma with some reinforcements for the Muslim forces there. When al-Walīd arrived, 'Iyāḍ was engaged with the enemy in inconclusive skirmishes after the enemy had blocked his way. Al-Walīd advised him to request Khālid bin al-Walīd for help. 'Iyāḍ accepted his counsel and sent a letter to Khālid by messenger, who reached Khālid some days after his victory at 'Ain al-Tamr, a fortified place in the desert north-west of al-Kūfa. Khālid was glad to receive his request and wrote to him a very brief letter containing the following verses, renowned for their eloquence:

> Wait a little; competing horses will soon reach you,
> Carrying lions with bright swords,
> In battalion after battalion.[14]

Khālid left 'Uwaim bin al-Kāhil al-Aslamī behind and hastened to Dūmat al-Jandal, at a distance of around 500 kilometres, with the same forces with which he had taken 'Ain al-Tamr. News of his march reached the people of Dūma. Ḥamd al-Jāsir, relying mainly on al-Ṭabarī, gives the following account of the response of the people opposing 'Iyāḍ:

> When they heard he was coming, they called upon their allies of the Bahrā', Kalb, Ghassān, Tanūkh and Ḍajā'im. Wadī'a had earlier joined with them, along with the Kalb and Bahrā', supported by Ibn Wabra bin Rūmānas; al-Ḥidrajān came to them with the Ḍajā'im, and Ibn al-Aiham[15] came with contingents from the Ghassānids. At the time the news of Khālid's imminent arrival reached them, there were two leaders [of the forces in Dūmat al-Jandal], Ukaidir bin 'Abd al-Malik and al-Jūdiyy bin Rabī'a, and they disagreed [on whether to defend the town]. Ukaidir said, "I know Khālid better than anyone else does. No one has a luckier star than Khālid has and no one is sharper in battle than he is. There is no group of people, large or small, which ever faced Khālid in battle, and was not vanquished. Take heed of my advice and make peace with him." But they refused to do so. Ukaidir then departed, declaring, "I will not side with you in fighting

> against Khālid; it is your own affair." News of this reached Khālid, who sent 'Āṣim bin 'Amr to thwart Ukaidir's escape. 'Āṣim captured him and told him, "You will meet Amīr Khālid." When he was brought before Khālid, Khālid ordered his head to be cut off and his possessions to be seized.[16]

Al-Ṭabarī records the events that followed Khālid's arrival in the oasis:

> Khālid took Dūma between his forces and 'Iyāḍ's forces. The Arab allies of the people of Dūma who had come to their aid were camping around the [Mārid] castle, for the castle could not hold more. When Khālid had settled down, al-Jūdiyy and Wadī'a advanced towards him and were defeated. In the meantime, Ibn al-Ḥidrajān and Ibn al-Aiham attacked 'Iyāḍ's forces and were vanquished, too. Al-Jūdiyy and Wadī'a were captured by Khālid and al-Aqra' bin Ḥābis, respectively. The rest of their forces retreated to the citadel to seek refuge, but when the citadel became packed to the capacity, those who were inside closed the gate to their companions, leaving them outside. Some of the men left outside were from the Kalb tribe. Seeing them, 'Āṣim bin 'Amr said to his tribesmen, "O Banū Tamīm, the Kalb are your allies; console them[17] and protect them, for you would never get a chance like this." Hearing that, men from the Banū Tamīm took them under their protective custody.[18]

Al-Ṭabarī says that most of those left outside by their companions perished in the fighting, except those from the Kalb. Khālid then attended to the problem of forcing open the citadel's gate and at long last succeeded in bringing it down. In the ensuing fight inside the castle, the forces of Dūma met with disastrous defeat at the hands of Khālid and his army.[19] Thus ended the fourth and final Muslim expedition to the oasis of Dūmat al-Jandal, after which the town and the area remained firmly under Muslim control.

It is recorded by al-Ṭabarī that Khālid stayed in Dūma for a while before leaving for al-Ḥīra in 'Irāq, where he was given an enthusiastic welcome.[20]

As for the administration of the tribes in the region, we find that after the uprising of the apostates in the area was suppressed, the Caliph appointed 'Amr bin al-'Āṣ and al-Walīd bin 'Uqba as the overseers of the Quḍā'a tribe. This was a period of rapid development. After its initial successes on the front against the Persians, the Islamic state planned to open another front, that against the Byzantines. 'Amr bin al-'Āṣ was made commander of one of the three armies which were to campaign in Syria. Al-Walīd bin 'Uqba was detailed to the Jordan area. Both of them were directed to hand over their tribal duties to their assistants, which they did. 'Amr nominated a certain 'Amr of the 'Udhra tribe whereas al-Walīd nominated Imru' al-Qais bin al-Aṣbagh. Both of the new leaders commanded the respect of the tribes and obeyed the orders of the Caliph.[21] Nothing is reported about their activities thereafter expect that we find 'Amr al-'Udhrī fighting as a leader in the battle of al-Yarmūk in *Rajab 15*/August 636.[22]

Why did the Islamic state want to possess Dūmat al-Jandal? Or rather, what hastened the accession of Dūmat al-Jandal to the new state in al-Madīna? As the events were to prove, it was inevitable. One factor that quickened the pace of events was Dūmat al-Jandal's strategic location on the supply lines and trade routes in the region. To the east of Dūma Muslim armies were operating in 'Irāq, and to its north a new front (against the Byzantines) was soon to be opened by the Islamic state. Any hostile forces concentrated at a strategic point like Dūma could have posed a dangerous threat to the Muslim armies. Secondly, Dūma adopted a collision course. Its ruler, Ukaidir, in contravention of the treaty of peace he had entered into with the Prophet (P.B.U.H.), allowed the oasis to become a place of refuge for the enemies of Islam and the Islamic state and, in collusion with those enemies, was engaged in hostilities against the Muslim army. In short, Dūmat al-Jandal had become a dangerous pocket of resistance in the rear of the Muslim armies. No wise commander would have overlooked this threat.

Let us see what reasons Khālid bin al-Walīd gave for eliminating such pockets of resistance:

> I want to rid myself of the task of [subduing] the armed peoples who are in 'Iyāḍ's lot, so that we could settle Arabs in it [i.e. 'Irāq], so that the Muslim armies could be safe from an attack from their rear, and so that the Arabs could come to us peacefully without obstruction.[23]

Before concluding this chapter, let us add some comments on the chronology of the events.

Early Muslim historians have not mentioned the date of Khālid's campaign to Dūmat al-Jandal, but they have given dates for some isolated events in his 'Irāq campaigns, falling before and after the Dūma interlude, by which we can arrive at an approximate date. The dated event occurring before Khālid's march to Dūma is the signing of a treaty by Khālid with the people of al-Ḥīra – in *Rabī' I (3rd month) 12*.[24] After his departure from Dūma for al-Ḥīra, the dated event is his arrival at al-Firāḍ, situated on the bank of the Euphrates on the then 'Irāq-Syria border, in *Ramaḍān (9th month) 12*.[25] If we take careful note of the extent of Khālid's activities during the periods, first between his conquest of al-Ḥīra and Dūma, and secondly between his departure from Dūma for al-Ḥīra and his arrival at al-Firāḍ, we find that they are about equal. Thus we can conclude that the Dūma campaign fell somewhere in the middle of the time between the two dated events. That brings us to the 5th and 6th months of *12*/14 July to 10 September 633. It is most likely that the event occurred during this period.

Usāma departed from al-Madīna near the end of *Rabī' I 11*,[26] and so his action against the Quḍā'a must have taken place during *Rabī' II and Jumādā I 11*/July and August 632.

The apostasy rebellion started immediately after the Prophet's (P.B.U.H.) death. Hence Wadī'a's apostasy and the march of Imru' al-Qais against him seem to have occurred almost simultaneously with Usāma's expedition. As we have seen, on Usāma's punitive action, Quḍā'a apostates joined with Wadī'a in Dūmat al-Jandal.

The action of 'Amr bin al-'Āṣ against the Sa'd and Baliyy most probably occurred sometime at the beginning of the *ridda* campaigns, which were initiated by the Caliph Abū Bakr after Usāma's return, around the *5th or 6th month of 11*/August-September 632. We have already seen that he and al-Walīd bin 'Uqba held charge of the Quḍā'a before their departure to the Syrian front in the beginning of *13*/March 634. Al-Walīd bin 'Uqba must have assumed his duty after he brought reinforcements to 'Iyāḍ bin Ghanm, sometime in the 4th or 5th month of *12*/mid-June to mid-August 633.

'Iyāḍ bin Ghanm perhaps arrived on the scene in the first or second month of *12*/mid-March to mid-May 633, for he began his campaign at the same time Khālid bin al-Walīd went to southern 'Irāq.

---

1. al-Ṭabarī, vol. 1 pp.1880-81.
2. Ibid., p.1872.
3. Ibid., p.1851.
4. Ibid., pp.1872-73, 1851; 'Alī bin Muḥammad Ibn al-Athīr, *al-Kāmil fi'l-Tārīkh*, 10 vols., Beirut, Dār al-Fikr al-'Arabī, 1983, vol. 2 p.232.
5. al-Ṭabarī, vol. 1 pp.1930, 1937-38, 1963.
6. Ibid., p.1921.
7. Ibid., pp.2058-59, 2066-67.
8. Ibid., p.1963.
9. Ibid., pp.2083, 2078-79.
10. The raid on 'Irāq by al-Muthannā bin Ḥāritha, "though a minor affair in itself and undertaken possibly without the knowledge of the caliph, chronologically . . . stands at the commencement of the Moslem military enterprises." Hitti, p.148.
11. al-Ṭabarī, vol. 1 pp.2020-22.
12. al-Balādhurī, vol. 1 pp.73-74.
13. al-Ṭabarī, vol. 1 pp.2056, 2064-65.
14. Ibid. p.2064.
15. Though al-Ṭabarī does not mention the full name of the Ghassānid Ibn al-Aiham fighting at Dūmat al-Jandal against the Muslims, it is understood to be the last king of Ghassān, Jabala bin al-Aiham. (See *Encyclopaedia of Islam*, New ed., s.v. "Djabala bin al-Ayham", by Irfan Kawar). His presence at Dūma in its last act of defiance against the Islamic state, viewed in the light of the fact that the Ghassānids were allies of the Byzantines, implies some level of Byzantine involvement in the defence of Dūma. Conversely, Byzantine reliance upon their client Arab tribes for support against Muslim armies continued for some more years. We find that when, in *13*/634, a Muslim army, under the command of Khālid bin Sa'īd bin al-'Āṣī, assembled in Taimā', the Byzantines asked their Arab friends for help. Men from the tribes of Bahrā', Kalb, Salīḥ, Tanūkh, Lakhm, Judhām and Ghassān came to augment the Byzantine army, commanded by a patriarch named Bāhān. When the Byzantines attacked the advancing Muslim army near al-Qasṭal (in present-day Jordan), the Byzantines and their allies were badly defeated. Al-Ṭabarī, vol. 1: 2078-82. Similarly, the Ghassānids, under Ibn al-Aiham, and the Lakhm, Judhām and other tribes were in the vanguard of the Byzantine army in the battle of al-Yarmūk in *15*/636. Al-Balādhurī, vol. 1 pp.160-61.
16. Ḥamd al-Jāsir, *Fī Shimāl Gharb al-Jazīra*, pp.118-19. A different version of what became of Ukaidir in the period following the Prophet's (P.B.U.H.) death, recorded by Yāqūt al-Ḥamawī in his *Mu'jam al-Buldān*, vol. 2 pp.487-88, is that the second Caliph, 'Umar bin al-Khaṭṭāb, exiled him from Dūmat al-Jandal to al-Ḥīra, where he settled at a place near 'Ain al-Tamr and built a settlement called Dūma or Dūmā', and that the following verses were composed by a certain poet on the plight of his family:

    O he who saw the caravan leaving at dawn,
    [Caravan] of the folk of Āl Akdar [Āl Ukaidir], whose memory saddens me.

    They exchanged their secure settlements for wandering,
    Departing from a fortress that is the loftiest of fortresses.

    Historians do not give much credence to this version. See, e.g., Jawād 'Alī, vol. 4 p.235.
17. Some texts use here a different word which means, "Make them captives".

18. al-Ṭabarī, vol. 1 pp.2065-66.
19. Ibid., pp.2065-66.
20. Ibid., p.2067; some Arab historians say that after conquering Dūmat al-Jandal, Khālid marched onwards to Syria. See, e.g., al-Balādhurī, vol. 1 p.74.
21. al-Ṭabarī, vol. 1 p.2083.
22. Ibid., p.2094.
23. Ibid., p.2058.
24. Ibid., pp.2044-45; Ibn al-Athīr, vol. 2 p.267.
25. al-Ṭabarī, vol. 1 p.2073; Ibn al-Athīr, vol. 2 p.274.
26. al-Ṭabarī, vol. 1 p.1868.

16
The Arbitration between 'Alī bin Abī Ṭālib and Mu'āwiya bin Abī Sufyān

After the coming of Muslim rule to Dūmat al-Jandal, one of the most important events occurring there was the arbitration meeting between 'Alī bin Abī Ṭālib, the fourth Caliph, and Mu'āwiya bin Abī Sufyān, the governor of Syria. The dispute between the two sides had continued for some time and led to skirmishes and eventually to a major clash, the Battle of Ṣiffīn (*37*/657). The contenders for the caliphate agreed to arbitration by reference to the Qur'ān. Each side was to choose a representative, and the outcome of their discussions was to be decisive. It has been suggested that the arbitration was a strategem employed by Mu'āwiya in order to sow dissension among 'Alī's followers and thus gain respite for himself, for the fighting at Ṣiffīn seemed to be going against him. Al-Ṭabarī's account of the events surrounding the proposal for the arbitration is as follows:

> When 'Amr bin al-'Āṣ [the famous commander, who was Mu'āwiya's ally] saw that the position of the people of 'Irāq was growing stronger, he feared defeat and said to Mu'āwiya, "Would you like me to suggest to you a strategem which will create unity among us and disunity among them?" He replied, "Yes." 'Amr explained, "We will raise copies of the Holy Qur'ān and say, 'What is in the Qur'ān is the arbiter between us and you.' If some of them would refuse to accept that, there would be others who would say, 'Yes, we must accept.' So there would be dissension among them. And, on the other hand, if all of them accept the proposal, we would succeed in relieving ourselves of this fighting and of this war for the time being." They, therefore, hoisted copies of the Holy Qur'ān on their lances and said, "This book of Almighty God is [the source of judgement] between us. [If we keep fighting and dying like this] who will be there for [taking care of] the borders of the Syrians after the Syrians and of the 'Irāqīs after the 'Irāqīs?" When the people saw the Holy Qur'ān raised up, they said, "We respond to the Book of Almighty God and refer [the dispute] to it."[1]

It is narrated that 'Alī bin Abī Ṭālib saw through the ploy, but his followers did not support his view, and events transpired as 'Amr bin al-'Āṣ had anticipated. The 'Irāqī followers of 'Alī chose Abū Mūsā al-Ash'arī as their delegate, in spite of the opposition of 'Alī himself, while the Syrian supporters of Mu'āwiya bin Abī Sufyān chose 'Amr bin al-'Āṣ. It is said that 'Amr bin al-'Āṣ was wiser than Abū Mūsā. When the two met in Dūmat al-Jandal in *Ramaḍān 37*/February 658, they agreed that Mu'āwiya and 'Alī should both be deposed and that the matter be decided by the Muslims by consultation among themselves to choose a caliph of their liking.

According to Abū Mikhnaf, as reported by al-Ṭabarī:

> The two arbitrators joined up with the people who had gathered there. ['Amr bin al-'Āṣ] said, "Abū Mūsā, tell them that we have reached an agreement." Abū Mūsā said, "Amr and I have agreed on a solution; we pray that God, Exalted in Might, Full of Majesty, put in order the affair of this nation by means of that." 'Amr declared, "That is right and pious, Abū Mūsā! Come forward and speak." So Abū Mūsā came forward to speak. On this, Ibn 'Abbās said to him, "Woe to you. By God I think he has tricked you. If you have agreed on anything, let him speak about it before yourself, and you speak after him, because 'Amr is a treacherous man and I am not sure that there is a real agreement between you and him; if you stand up among the people [and announce something], he will oppose you." Abū Mūsā was a weak-minded person; he replied, "We have reached an agreement." Then he went forward, praised God and addressed the gathering: "O people, we have looked into the problem confronting this nation and found that there is nothing better and nothing more unifying for it in its present confusion than the solution on which 'Amr and I have agreed. That solution is that we remove both 'Alī and Mu'āwiya . . . So the problem is before you [now]. You choose someone whom you find fit as your ruler." Then he stepped aside and 'Amr bin al-'Āṣ came forward and praised God and said, "He has spoken and you have heard him depose his companion. I also depose his colleague, but I confirm my companion, Mu'āwiya. He is the [legal] next of kin of 'Uthmān bin 'Affān,[2] he is demanding revenge for his blood, and he is the most rightful person to take his place."
>
> On this, Abū Mūsā said, "May God frustrate you. You have betrayed me."[3]

There are mixed opinions about whether the site of the arbitration was Dūmat al-Jandal, for there is some indication that it took place at Adhruḥ in southern Jordan. However, there is a tendency among scholars to place the episode in Dūma, as far as the initial meeting between the representatives is concerned.[4] Yāqūt al-Ḥamawī says that most of the poets mention that the arbitration took place at Adhruḥ, and that only one, A'war al-Shanniyy, places the arbitration at Dūmat al-Jandal. A'war's verses are as follows:

> We accepted the rule of God in every land,
> [But] 'Amr and 'Abd Allāh are squabbling.
>
> The two blind *shaikhs* at Dūma, intent on intrigue,
> Will not lead the nation out of confusion.[5]

Interestingly, it is recorded by Abū Mūsā, on the authority of the Prophet (P.B.U.H.), that there had been a previous arbitration between the Jews at Dūmat al-Jandal by two unjust arbitrators.[6]

Ḥamd al-Jāsir quotes sources which show that the first choice for the meeting-place of the arbitrators was Dūmat al-Jandal and that Adhruḥ was the agreed alternative venue in case both or either of the arbitrators failed to reach Dūma, for the negotiations. Thus the convention dated *13 Ṣafar 37*/31 July 657 signed by 'Alī and Mu'āwiya – *Kitāb al-Qaḍiyya* – stated that 'Alī and Mu'āwiya would come to Dūmat al-Jandal in Ramaḍān [*37*/February-March 658], each having 400 companions with him; if they did not meet, they should meet the year after in Adhruḥ.[7] Ḥamd al-Jāsir quotes Ibn Khaldūn and Ibn al-Athīr, and the still earlier authority, al-Ṭabarī, to support the contention that the first contact was to take place in Dūmat al-Jandal and that Adhruḥ was the second choice as a meeting place. Ḥamd al-Jāsir also makes the following point:

> We add to this that Adhruḥ is in Syria [al-Shām] and not midway between the contending parties. 'Alī, as is well-known, was in Kūfa, while Mu'āwiya was in Damascus. Adhruḥ is near Damascus whereas Dūmat al-Jandal is at about the halfway point [between Damascus and Kūfa].[8]

Ḥamd al-Jāsir points out that the different accounts in al-Ṭabarī and the other historians arise from their varying interpretations of the *Kitāb al-Qaḍiyya* recording the terms and conditions of the arbitration. This document states that the arbitration should take place in Dūmat al-Jandal in the first year. If this were not to come about, then it should take place in Adhruḥ. It may be the case that Mu'āwiya proposed Adhruḥ rather than 'Alī, for the latter was determined upon having a meeting of the arbitrators in the first year. This is what actually happened,[9] that is, the meeting occurred, as we have seen, at Dūmat al-Jandal.

Ibn al-Athīr says that in *39*/659-60, Mu'āwiya sent Muslim bin 'Uqba al-Murrī to Dūmat al-Jandal, where the inhabitants had been refusing to offer allegiance to either 'Alī or Mu'āwiya. Muslim invited the people to obey Mu'āwiya and to declare their loyalty to him but they refused. News of this reached 'Alī, who sent Mālik bin Ka'b al-Ḥamdānī with a small force to Dūmat al-Jandal. On their arrival they fought with Muslim, who was taken by surprise. After a day's fighting, Muslim was defeated and he withdrew from Dūma. Mālik stayed on for a few days and invited the people to give their allegiance to 'Alī but they declined, saying that they would give their allegiance to no one until all agreed on an Imām. Mālik then left Dūma.[10]

---

1. al-Ṭabarī, vol. 1 p.3329.
2. 'Uthmān bin 'Affān was the third Caliph of Islam and was murdered by insurgents in al-Madīna in *35*/656.
3. al-Ṭabarī, vol. 1 pp.3358-59.
4. For a recent view supporting this, see *Encyclopaedia of Islam*, New ed., s.v. "'Alī b. Abī Ṭālib", by L. Veccia Vaglieri.
5. Yāqūt al-Ḥamawī, vol. 2 pp.488-89.
6. Ibid., p.489.
7. Ḥamd al-Jāsir, *Fī Shimāl Gharb al-Jazīra*, pp.120-21.
8. Ibid., p.121.
9. Ibid., pp.120-21.
10. Ibn al-Athīr, vol. 3 p.191.

17

Dūmat al-Jandal and al-Jawf Region from the Middle of the *1st*/7th Century to the End of the *12th*/18th Century

For the period from the arbitration between 'Alī bin Abī Ṭālib and Mu'āwiya bin Abī Sufyān in *37*/657-58 to the coming of the first Sa'ūdī state in the *12th*/18th century, there is scant evidence of the social and political history of Dūmat al-Jandal and the Jawf region. For this entire interlude there are only a few passing references to the town or the area in the writings of the geographers and historians. Even the epigraphic and archaeological records so far discovered are meagre. Furthermore, the local stories which are usually preserved by tradition are scarce. William Gifford Palgrave, the British traveller who came to al-Jawf in 1862, complaining of the deficiency of information about the history of the area for this period, remarked that "nowhere in Arabia have I met with scantier popular reminiscences and less of the old clannish feeling than in Djowf."[1]

This hiatus in the historical record can be attributed, for the most part, to the fact that after the coming of Islam, once the momentous events in the history of the area had come to pass, Dūmat al-Jandal declined in the prominence and prosperity it had enjoyed during the *Jāhiliyya*, that is the pre-Islamic period.[2] Before studying the causes of this decline, an assessment of the degree of the material decline undergone by Dūmat al-Jandal is in order. There is evidence from the archaeological remains of the town that the extent of the town and its orchards was much greater during the old days. The remains of the wall fortifying the town during the ancient times and for some centuries during the mediaeval period provide solid proof. This wall encircled a much larger area than the area the town comprised in its modern period,[3] and the agricultural domain of the town, too, was much larger than at the end of the period under discussion. The first European traveller to al-Jawf, Georg Augustus Wallin, who stayed at Dūmat al-Jandal for around four months in 1845, has the following to say about agricultural aspects of the town during what, according to him, was the pre-Islamic period. It should, however, be remembered that he did not have any very reliable means of determining the period of the civilization he is referring to:

> . . . the orchards and palm plantations spread over a larger part of the valley, there was a greater abundance of wells and springs, and the whole was enclosed by a common wall. In fact there are still many traces of a former cultivation more extended than in our days. From time to time there are discovered subterranean aqueducts, built of hewn square stones of a most careful and excellent workmanship, which in former times perhaps served the purpose of gathering the

> rain into the wells, or of carrying the water from springs and wells, which have now disappeared. During my sojourn here, an ancient aqueduct was laid open in Alsa'îdân, which was so spacious that a man could stand in it almost erect, and which seemed to lead to the only well, existing in that plantation. As it was quite filled up with sand, there was only a small part of it opened as yet, and neither its source nor its termination had been ascertained. Others have been discovered in the town itself, leading to places where at present no traces of cultivation are to be seen.[4]

Coming now to the causes of the decline in the fortunes of Dūmat al-Jandal and the Jawf region, we should at the outset say that they are quite complex. First, we have seen in the preceding pages that Dūmat al-Jandal had enjoyed the prestigious status of a city-state. Secondly, Dūma by no means thrived exclusively on the fruits of the oasis: among the people of the oasis were merchants who traded with other towns and regions. Thirdly, the town was the junction of two routes, the route from the Yemen and south-western Arabia north to Syria and Palestine (through the Wādi'l-Sirḥān) and the route from 'Irāq. Both these were busy caravan routes. Fourthly, the annual month-long market at Dūma attracted traders from the four corners of the Peninsula and from Syria and 'Irāq. Lastly, the town was a religious centre for the bedouin inhabiting or frequenting the surrounding desert. With its merger in the Islamic lands, Dūmat al-Jandal lost, or experienced a marked decrease in, all these advantages.

Some changes were immediate, others occurred during the next hundred years or so. Its status as a city-state came to an abrupt end. Also lost was the position of the town as a religious centre for the area. The annual markets of Arabia, too, fell into oblivion. Most importantly, the strategic position of Dūmat al-Jandal on the trade routes suffered a severe blow with the fall, in *132*/750, of the Umayyads, who ruled their Arab empire from Damascus. The 'Abbāsids, after overthrowing the Umayyad rule, moved the capital to the new city of Baghdād, and ensured that the principal Peninsular trade and caravan route ran from Kūfa in 'Irāq directly to the Holy Cities of Makkat al-Mukarrama and al-Madīnat al-Munawwara. Dūmat al-Jandal thus lost its position as a busy junction. The significance of the route from Yemen and south-western Arabia to Syria and southern Palestine passing through Dūmat al-Jandal was also eclipsed with the shifting of centre of power eastward. The adverse effects of these changes on the commercial life and trading community of the town can be well imagined.

In addition, another factor contributing to the decline of Dūmat al-Jandal during the Islamic period was perhaps the worsening of the environment: the victory of the desert over man. As pointed out by the archaeologists who surveyed the region in 1976, ". . . many sites in the al-Jawf basin are now being encroached upon by aeolian sand, and it is at least conceivable that the decline of the region [during the Islamic period] can be in part attributed to environmental changes."[5]

As we have noted, there are occasional isolated references to Dūmat al-Jandal and the Jawf region for the period under review. Most of these are of a geographical nature, stating the location of Dūmat al-Jandal and the distance (usually in terms of camel marches) between Dūmat al-Jandal and other important towns. References of another sort relate to the routes passing through Dūmat al-Jandal and the Wādi'l-Sirḥān, and their use by different people at different times – for instance, by the poet Mutanabbī, or by armed contingents like those of 'Alī bin Abī Ṭālib and Mu'āwiya bin Abī Sufyān during the period of hostilities between them, or those of the 'Abbāsids during the last days of the Umayyad period.[6] More importantly for our purpose, there are some references, of yet another category, which relate to the tribes in the area of al-Jawf and the Wādi'l-Sirḥān or to certain other conditions in the area. The first category of references has no relevance to the needs of the present times and the second has little historical value as far as this chapter is concerned. On the other hand, the references in the third category, albeit disjointed, can be of considerable value to those interested in the history of the area. We present below the story of the events in al-Jawf and the Wādi'l-Sirḥān as comprehensively as can be reconstructed from those references. We have not restricted ourselves to the classic authorities: modern writers who have attempted to throw light on the period under review have been included.

As we saw in the chapters on the Islamic expeditions to al-Jawf, the tribe dominating the area of al-Jawf was the Kalb. Our narrative unfolds with the history of the hostilities between the Kalb, a Qaḥṭānī tribe, and the Banū Sulaim of the Qais, an 'Adnānī tribe. (Qaḥṭān and 'Adnān are the two main branches to which most of the tribes of the Arabian Peninsula trace their origins. They were traditionally hostile to each other.) Abu'l-Faraj al-Aṣbahānī (d. *356*/966-67) writes:

> Ziyād bin Yazīd bin 'Umair bin al-Ḥubāb relates, on the authority of the elders of his tribe [Banū Sulaim], that 'Umair bin al-Ḥubāb raided on Kalb. He met a group of them comprising 600 or 700 men in al-Iklīl and killed a large number of them. . . .
>
> The Kalb again formed a group and 'Umair killed or wounded them. After that 'Umair raided again and met a group of them in al-Jawf and killed them. Then he made a raid on them in al-Samāwa and killed a very large number of them.[7]

Abu'l-Faraj then continues relating the attacks of the Qais on the Kalb in their areas and intermixes his narrative with verses on the subject from different poets.[8]

Al-Iklīl has not been positively identified. Musil, after considering al-Bakrī's placement of it in his *Mu'jam Mā Ista'jama*,[9] is of the view that "we should look for al-Iklīl in the vicinity of Dūma".[10] Al-Samāwa, also known as Samāwat Kalb, were the grazing grounds of the Kalb in the steppe between Syria and 'Irāq. According to al-Iṣṭakhrī, Samāwa is the name of the desert between Dūmat al-Jandal and 'Ain al-Tamr.[11] Musil comments that Dūmat al-Jandal marked the southern and 'Ain al-Tamr the eastern boundary of the desert of al-Samāwa and says that "the early Arabians called Arabia Deserta the desert as-Samâwa."[12] J.W. Fück observes that in al-Samāwa the centres of the Kalb were "the oases in the low-lying valley (al-khabt) formed by the Djawf and the Wādī Sirḥān . . ."[13] Al-Samāwa was also the name of a watering place within the desert of al-Samāwa.[14] It seems that it is the watering place that is intended by Abu'l-Faraj. Regarding al-Jawf, Ḥamd al-Jāsir says that "the Jawf here is this Jawf [Jawf Āl 'Amr] since it was one of the areas of the Kalb tribe".[15]

The bloody battles mentioned by Abu'l-Faraj had started with an attack of the Qais on a settlement of the Kalb in Qarqīsiyya. The Kalb retaliated by killing some men of the Qais living among them in Tadmur. The Qaisī attack on the Kalb in al-Iklīl then followed. The feud occurred during the time of the Umayyad caliph 'Abd al-Malik bin Marwān (r. *65-86*/685-705) and was the result of the antagonism of the two tribes arising out of many factors, chief among them being the influence of the Kalb at the Umayyad court. The rivalry between them had become more intense since the battle of Marj Rāhiṭ (July 684) in which the two tribal groups had taken opposite sides. The Kalb, whose chief, Ḥassān bin Mālik bin Baḥdal, had been instrumental in the succession of Marwān bin al-Ḥakam as caliph, were forming the nucleus of the whole army fighting on the Umayyad side. They had as their allies the Ghassān, Sakūn and Saksak, Tanūkh, Ṭayyi', and Qain. Fighting for the rival claimant to the caliphate, 'Abd Allāh bin Zubair, were Banū Sulaim of Qais supported by the 'Āmir of Hawāzin and the Dhubyān of Ghaṭafān. The battle was decided for the Umayyads, the Qais suffering a crushing defeat which they never forgot. Enduring hatred arose between the Kalb and the Qais, and the blood feuds that soon ensued weakened the Kalb to such an extent that they had to forgo their dominance of the Samāwa and even migrate for a while to Palestine.[16]

During the struggle for power between the 'Abbāsids and the Umayyads, the Kalb sent two thousand men to help the Umayyad governor of Baṣra, but the contingent defected on arrival there and fought on the 'Abbāsid side. However, immediately after the 'Abbāsid take-over of power, the Kalb participated in an unsuccessful revolt against the new rulers.[17]

In the latter part of the 'Abbāsid rule, the Kalbite bedouin groups mounted attacks on the central authorities. For instance, they revolted and killed the governor of Ḥimṣ in Syria in *250*/864. On another occasion, in *294*/906, in cooperation with other tribes, they defeated the governor of Moṣul (Arabic, al-Mawṣil) in 'Irāq, though later in that year a combined bedouin group of Kalb and Ṭayyi' was defeated in a battle by the 'Abbāsid arms.[18]

During the Carmathian (Arabic, Qarmaṭī) movement (from c.*261*/874-75 to *470*/1077-78) some of the Kalb factions, specially Banu'l-'Ulais bin Damdam, Banu'l-Aṣbagh,[19] and Banū Ziyād, were won over by the propagandists of that movement. From time to time the Kalbites joined the Carmathian campaigns, particularly those which were directed towards the north. After their attack on Ṭabariyya, in which they killed the deputy governor of Jordan, the 'Abbāsid caliph al-Muktafī (r. 902-08) sent a strong army against them. To save themselves from the wrath of the 'Abbāsids, the Kalb killed the Carmathian leader and took his head to Baghdād to demonstrate their loyalty to the Caliph, who decided not to take any action against them.[20]

The tribal 'neighbours' of the Kalb in their north were the Ṭayyi', a Qaḥṭānī tribe. The Kalb and the Ṭayyi' had strong friendly relations and were the strongest among the tribes inhabiting the northern regions of the Peninsula. On the western side, the Kalb had the 'Adnānī tribe 'Anaza as their neighbours. On the south-eastern side, their neighbours were the Ghaṭafān, also an 'Adnānī tribe.[21]

The Kalb began to weaken in the *4th*/10th century, because of their inclination towards sedentariness and settlement and the participation of some of their factions in the Carmathian movement.[22] The Kalb settled in many places in al-Jawf and the Wādi'l-Sirḥān. Some of their elements came under the patronage of other tribes. Those who had maintained their bedouin status kept a low profile in their old places or migrated in their weakened position towards the north.[23]

In the *4th*/10th century the dominance over the Nafūd desert passed to the Ṭayyi' tribe. The areas under their control kept expanding, to include al-Jawf, which became known as Jawf Āl 'Amr, after the Āl 'Amr, a branch of the Āl Faḍl, who are a subtribe of the Ṭayyi'.[24] Aḥmad bin Yaḥyā bin Faḍl Allāh al-'Umarī (*700-749*/1301-1349) writes that "the Āl 'Amr are [dominant] in al-Jawf".[25] He makes these remarks while enumerating the branches of the Āl Faḍl and their allies and the areas under their control. The Āl 'Amr had taken to living in al-Jawf before the *7th*/13th century. The influence of the Āl Faḍl kept increasing in north Arabia after the weakening of the Kalb, till the Āl Faḍl and their parent tribe, the Ṭayyi', dominated the areas extending from Syria to the Wādi'l-Sirḥān and al-Jawf. Their supremacy continued from the *7th* to the *9th century*/13th to the 15th century.[26] In al-Jawf, however, the Āl 'Amr probably remained dominant till the beginning of the *13th century*/end of the 18th century.[27] On the other hand, we find that a Kalb sub-tribe named al-Sirḥān was dominant in the Wādi'l-Sirḥān in the *12th*/18th century. The valley, according to Muṣṭafā al-Dabbāgh, was named after this sub-tribe, which later on migrated northwards to Jordan and Palestine, with some of its factions settling there.[28]

At the same time, with the weakening of the Kalb, the 'Anaza and the Ghaṭafān, too, had been making gradual inroads into the areas of the Kalb in the Wādi'l-Sirḥān and al-Jawf; for al-Ḥasan bin Aḥmad al-Hamdānī (d. *334*/945), in his book *Ṣifat Jazīrat al-'Arab*, says that in the Wādi'l-Sirḥān, which he names as Bayāḍ Qarqara, lived the Dhubyān (a branch of the Ghaṭafān).[29] Once there, some branches of the Ghaṭafān and other tribes of 'Adnānī origin started intermingling with the 'Anaza. The 'Anaza also started intermixing with a faction of the Ṭayyi', and some Kalb elements, too, joined them. Thus there emerged a new tribe with elements from both the Qaḥṭān and the 'Adnān, though the 'Adnānī elements ultimately dominated. This new tribe was Ruwala, identified as an 'Anaza sub-tribe. The Ruwala began to have an increasing and significant presence in the area after the fall of the first Sa'ūdī state in *1233*/1818.[30]

In addition to the history of the tribes in the area of al-Jawf and Wādi'l-Sirḥān, we have references about the practice of Islam by the people of Dūmat al-Jandal before the coming of the first Sa'ūdī state. They indicate that the people, like those of most other parts of the Arabian Peninsula, had introduced heretical innovations into Islam and had undermined the true spirit of Islam by practising semi-paganism and following the cult of saints.

Georg Augustus Wallin, writing about the religious practices in al-Jawf, relates that "in the early times of the Wahhâbies, one of the generals of Ibnu Sa'ood entered the town with an army, and destroyed an old tomb in the quarter of Alder', which was adorned by a cupola, and respected by the inhabitants as the sepulchre of Dhoo Alkarnein."[31]

An earlier writer, the famous bibliographer Ḥājī Khalīfa (1609-1657), confirms the existence of this tomb in the town. He says that ". . . in al-Jawf there springs a stream from under an enormous marble boulder above which the Ḥimyar Dhu'l-Qarnain had built a dome. In the year 1513 a great silver treasure was discovered nearby."[32]

The third author referring to the religious aspects of Dūmat al-Jandal before the Sa'ūdī take-over is William Gifford Palgrave, the British traveller who visited al-Jawf in the summer of 1862. We quote him in the full context of his writing, which is based, like that of Wallin before him, on the oral tradition of the people of the town:

> The inhabitants have not much to say regarding their origin or the date of their settlement here, nor do they possess any records of historical value on such topics . . . [After once having embraced Islam] at a later period, like the inhabitants of Arabia in general, they relapsed into semi-paganism, and the worship of local genii, or Djann, as they call them, till the sword of the Wahhabee conqueror revived their Islam. . . . In pedigree they lay claim to be descended from the great clan of Ṭā'i [Ṭayyi'], celebrated in old Arab history . . .[33]

---

1. William Gifford Palgrave, *Narrative of a Year's Journey through Central and Eastern Arabia (1862-63)*, 3rd. ed., 2 vols., London, Macmillan, 1866, vol. 1 p.62.
2. See, e.g., Musil, *Arabia Deserta*, p.552.
3. See, e.g., al-Muaikel, vol.1 pp.328-29; Wallin, p.31.
4. Wallin, p.31.
5. Adams, p.39.
6. For a brief account of the routes passing through Dūmat al-Jandal and their use, see Musil, *Arabia Deserta*, pp.520-23.
7. Abu'l-Faraj 'Alī bin al-Ḥusain al-Aṣbahānī, *al-Aghānī*, 20 vols., Būlāq, Egypt, *1285*/1868-69; reprint ed., Beirut, Dār al-Fikr lil-Jamī', *1390*/1970, vol. 20 p.122.
8. Ibid., vol. 20 pp.122-30.
9. al-Bakrī, op.cit., vol. 1 p.184.
10. Musil, *Arabia Deserta*, p.552.
11. Abū Isḥāq Ibrāhīm bin Muḥammad al-Iṣṭakhrī al-Fārisī, *Kitāb Masālik al-Mamālik*, ed. M.J. de Goeje, Leiden, E.J. Brill, 1870, p.23, quoted in Musil, *Arabia Deserta*, p.512.
12. Musil, *Arabia Deserta*, pp.511-12.
13. *Encyclopaedia of Islam*, New ed., s.v. "Kalb b. Wabra: I.-Pre-Islamic Period", by J.W. Fück.
14. See, e.g., Yāqūt al-Ḥamawī, vol. 3 p.245.
15. Ḥamd al-Jāsir, *Fī Shimāl Gharb al-Jazīra*, pp.504-05.
16. For a history of the events relating to the Battle of Marj Rāhiṭ and to the blood feuds, see al-Ṭabarī, vol. 2 pp.472-86; Hitti, pp.192, 280-81; Julius Wellhausen, *Arab Kingdom and its Fall*, trans. Margaret Graham Weir, ed. A.H. Harley, London, Curzon Press, 1973, pp.170-84, 201-07; *Encyclopaedia of Islam*, s.v. "Kalb b. Wabra: II. – Islamic Period", by A.A. Dixon.
17. *Encyclopaedia of Islam*, s.v. "Kalb b. Wabra: II. – Islamic Period", by. A.A. Dixon.
18. Ibid.

19. Most probably, the progeny of al-Asbagh bin 'Amr, the leader of the Kalb, or a faction of the Kalb, at the time of the second Muslim expedition to Dūmat al-Jandal.
20. *Encyclopaedia of Islam*, s.v. "Kalb b. Wabra: II. – Islamic Period", by. A.A. Dixon; *Encyclopaedia of Islam*, s.v. "Ḳarmaṭī", by W. Madelung.
21. Ḥamd al-Jāsir, *Fī Shimāl Gharb al-Jazīra*, pp.43, 154-55.
22. Ibid., pp.44, 122.
23. Ibid., pp.122, 155.
24. Ibid., p.122.
25. Aḥmad bin Yaḥya bin Faḍl Allāh al-'Umarī, "Masālik al-Abṣār fī Mamālik al-Amṣār", unpublished MS, no. 3417, Ayā Ṣūfiyā (St. Sophia) Museum, Istanbūl, vol. 4, leaf 29, quoted in Ḥamd al-Jāsir, *Fī Shimāl Gharb al-Jazīra*, p.122.
26. Ḥamd al-Jāsir, *Fī Shimāl Gharb al-Jazīra*, pp.44, 123.
27. Ibid., p.44.
28. Muṣṭafā al-Dabbāgh, *al-Jazīrat al-'Arabiyya: Mawṭan al-'Arab wa Mahd al-Islām*, 2 vols., Beirut, Dār al-Ṭalī'a, *1382*/1963, vol. 1 p.174, quoted in Ḥamd al-Jāsir, *Fī Shimāl Gharb al-Jazīra*, p.43; Ḥamd al-Jāsir, *Fī Shimāl Gharb al-Jazīra*, pp.43, 122, 156.
29. al-Hamdānī, p.272. Ḥamd al-Jāsir reads Bayāḍ Qarqara as Bayāḍ Qarqar and says that al-Hamdānī names the Wādī as Bayāḍ Qarqar. Ḥamd al-Jāsir, *Fī Shimāl Gharb al-Jazīra*, p.43. Alois Musil says that Qarqar, or Qarāqir, are watering places in the Wādi'l-Sirḥān 180 km. south-east of 'Ammān, at the intersection of two important transport roads. Musil, *Arabia Deserta*, pp.494-95.
30. Ḥamd al-Jāsir, *Fī Shimāl Gharb al-Jazīra*, pp.44, 122, 155-56.
31. Wallin, p.32.
32. Ḥājī Khalīfa, op. cit., p.530, cited by Musil, *Arabia Deserta*, p.553.
33. Palgrave, vol. 1 p.61.

18
Architectural Monuments of the Period

The Mosque of ʻUmar bin al-Khaṭṭāb, Dūmat al-Jandal

One of the most important monuments of Dūmat al-Jandal is the mosque attributed to ʻUmar bin al-Khaṭṭāb, the second Caliph. The most valuable study of the mosque is that of Dr Geoffrey King, then of King Saʻūd University,[1] who visited the site in *1395*/1975. G.A. Wallin, who visited the area in *1260-61*/1845, had previously given a brief description of the building.[2]

Dr King describes the mosque as an ancient stone building, part of which has been reconstructed. The Āl Saʻūd initiated the rebuilding of the mosque during the first Saʻūdī state, according to Wallin, who also states that in *1261*/1845 the minaret was the only one in Dūmat al-Jandal. This is not entirely surprising, however, as many mosques in Arabia lacked minarets. Wallin suggests that the mosque might have been a church before Islam; though Christians lived in the area before Islam, there is no reason to accept this.

In his description of the mosque, Dr King states that the *qibla* wall lies south-south-west and borders an unpaved street which passes through the minaret base by means of a passage. The minaret is set at the south-west corner of the mosque, independent of the rest of the building. The entire building is of stone – the principal building material in pre- and early Islamic times – and the masonry of both the prayer-hall and the minaret may include material taken from the Qaṣr Mārid, which overshadows the mosque.[3] One enters the mosque through a wooden door on the south side. An unroofed passage gives access to the prayer-hall and to the stone staircase leading to the roof and to the minaret. The interior of the prayer-hall is divided by three rows of piers running parallel to the *qibla* wall. The roof supported by these piers is flat, constructed of the traditional wood and thatch. There are a number of niches in the *qibla* wall for keeping the Holy Qur'ān. Some interior areas are plastered and there is also some whitewash. On the north side of the prayer-hall is an open rectangular courtyard.[4]

The *qibla* wall is interesting, for to the west of the *miḥrāb* recess is a second recess, with a fixed *minbar* within it (a feature of mosques in several parts of Arabia). It is possible to discern the position of the *miḥrāb* on the exterior surface of the *qibla* wall by shadow projection from the line of the rest of the wall.[5]

The height of the minaret is about 15 m. The minaret is square in ground-plan. Its walls have a raked tapering form, with a slightly convex curve, and culminate in a pyramid-like shape at the summit. Its design is unique among the minarets of the Kingdom. Internally, the minaret has four levels, built above the platform formed by the roof of the passage-way to the street. The entrance of the minaret is at the height of the prayer-hall roof, and gives on to the lowest floor. The upper floors were originally connected by stone staircases, but parts of these have collapsed. Light enters the minaret through small windows in the walls.[6]

Interior of the 'Umar Mosque at Dūmat al-Jandal.

Qaṣr Za'bal

This small castle, standing on the summit of a sandstone hill on the northwestern edge of Sakākā, is, in the words of Winnett and Reed, the most impressive structure in the town.

The Qaṣr Za'bal is a fortress of irregular shape, built of mud-brick and stone. It has four towers, one at each corner, only one currently in good condition. From the Qaṣr there is a fine view of Sakākā, with its green farms and gardens and the desert beyond. The castle is reached by ascending the mountain along a very narrow and winding track. There are small water reservoirs inside the Qaṣr to compensate for the absence of a well, the castle's main disadvantage.

The present structure dates back about 140 years, for the local people report that the castle was rebuilt after the conflict between the Āl Rashīd and Āl Sha'lān during the early 1850s.[7] Wallin, who visited al-Jawf in 1845, records that Sakākā "contains an old half-decayed castle named Za'bal. . .".[8] Ḥamd al-Jasīr suggests that this castle was built in the pre-Islamic period.[9]

The people of al-Jawf relate that of the Prophet's (P.B.U.H.) companions, the first to come to the area was buried near the foot of this mountain. Not far from the Qaṣr Za'bal is a rock cave called Ghār Ḥaḍra.[10]

Al-Qudair Castle

Situated to the south of Sakākā and west of Qārā on the edge of a sandstone hill, this small but important castle of irregular shape, measuring about 7 m. by

6.5 m., is dated to the year *518*/1124. It is built of random rubble, with mud filling here and there. It has two towers, one large and the other small. There is an open space divided by a wall in the centre.[11]

Muwaisin Castle

This castle, built on a low hill, lies 12 km. north-east of Dūmat al-Jandal and 30 km. south-west of Sakākā. Rectangular in shape and measuring 27 m. by 10 m., the castle comprises two sections. The west section consists of two rooms, still intact, whereas the east section has a courtyard with three rooms that are utterly ruined.[12]

Khaleel al-Muaikel, from his study of the pottery sherds excavated from inside the castle, suggests that "the castle was built probably between the third and sixth century A.D."[13]

To the west of Muwaisin castle there is a mountain called Qārat al-Nayāṣa (the Mountain of Porcupines), on the face of which there is a large number of panels of early Arabic inscriptions from the *2nd-3rd centuries*/8th-9th centuries. This area lies on the disused pilgrim route from lower Mesopotamia,[14] and the inscriptions may have been the work of the passing pilgrims.

Al-Madāra

Before concluding this section it would be pertinent to mention here another find of this period. At al-Madāra, a place near al-Rajājīl, a small earthenware jar was found, filled with coins, apparently Fāṭimid. On comparison, two coins from this collection were found to be similar to two Fāṭimid coins listed (at No. 369 and 387) by G.C. Miles in his book *Fāṭimid Coins*.[15] The two coins found at al-Madāra were struck in Egypt in the time of al-Mustanṣir (*427-87*/1036-94). The larger coin weighs 4.27 gm. and has a circumference of 22 mm. The second weighs 1.58 gm. and has a circumference of 20 mm. They both have concentric discs with inscriptions that include the *shahāda* as is normal in coins of this type.

---

1. Geoffrey King, "A Mosque Attributed to 'Umar b. al-Khaṭṭāb in Dūmat al-Jandal in al-Jawf, Saudi Arabia", *Journal of the Royal Asiatic Society*, 1978, pp.109-23.
2. Wallin, pp.27-28.
3. King, "Mosque Attributed to 'Umar b. al-Khaṭṭāb", p.110.
4. Ibid., pp.110, 120.
5. Ibid., pp.120-21.
6. Ibid., pp.121-22.
7. al-Muaikel, vol. 1 pp.141-42.
8. Wallin, p.37.
9. Ḥamd al-Jāsir, *Fī Shimāl Gharb al-Jazīra*, p.147.
10. Ibid., with some difference in details.
11. al-Muaikel, vol. 1 pp.146-48.
12. Ibid., vol. 1 pp.143-45.
13. Ibid., p.102.
14. Ibid., p.143.
15. G.C. Miles, *Fatimid Coins*, Numismatics Notes and Monographs, no. 121, New York, 1951, pp.36, 38 and plate IV.

PART FIVE

THE MODERN HISTORY OF AL-JAWF REGION

19

Al-Jawf and the First Sa'ūdī State

The power of the Sa'ūdī state during its first period reached al-Jawf in the time of 'Abd al-'Azīz bin Muḥammad bin Sa'ūd I, who had succeeded his father, the founder of the state, as imām. Al-Jawf was incorporated into the realms of the Āl Sa'ūd in *1208*/1793. According to Ibn Bishr, the circumstances were as follows:

> 'Abd al-'Azīz bin Muḥammad bin Sa'ūd I ordered the people of Washm, al-Qaṣīm and Jabal Shammar to come along with their chiefs for going to a military expedition. The people of Washm came with Muḥammad bin Mu'aiqal, those of al-Qaṣīm came with Muḥammad bin 'Abd Allāh Āl Ḥasan, and those of the Jabal arrived with their chief Muḥammad bin 'Alī. 'Abd al-'Azīz ordered them to go to Dūmat al-Jandal, known as Jawf Āl 'Amr, in the north. They went [to al-Jawf] under the command of Muḥammad bin Mu'aiqal, clashed with the people there, seized three settlements and besieged the rest. They killed a number of men, whereas among the members of the raiding party killed was 'Amhūj bin al-Mu'arqab.[1]

G.A. Wallin, the first European on record as having visited al-Jawf, briefly mentions this episode in the account of his travels to the area in *1261*/1845, although without naming the individuals. He reports as follows:

> In the early times of the Wahhâbies, one of the generals of Ibnu Sa'ood entered the town with an army, and destroyed an old tomb in the quarter of Alder', which was adorned by a cupola, and respected by the inhabitants as the sepulchre of Dhoo Alkarnein. Having levied upon the inhabitants the Zakà tax, ordained in the Korân as one of the five fundamental dogmas of Islâm, he issued forth to other conquests, leaving a substitute to govern the town in the name of Ibnu Sa'ood. Learned Imâms, or Khatîbs, as they are called here and in all Negd, educated and instructed at the expense of Ibnu Sa'ood in Almedînâ and Der'iyé, were sent hither to teach the people the Islâm religion, purged and regenerated as it had been by the doctrine of 'Abdu-l-Wahhâb. The feuds and wars were extinguished, justice administered, public safety restored throughout the extensive dominions of Ibnu Sa'ood, and every one still remembers those times with enthusiasm.[2]

It has been speculated that the purpose behind the occupation of al-Jawf by the Sa'ūdī state was to test how far the Ottoman governors of Syria would go to resist the Sa'ūdī incursions (into Syria) in the years to follow.[3] The first Sa'ūdī advance into Syria came about only four years later, in *1212*/1797. Gradually the sphere of influence of the Sa'ūdī state extended far beyond al-Jawf into the Syrian desert.[4]

The biggest expedition to Syria via al-Jawf occurred in *1225*/1810. According to 'Abd al-Raḥīm 'Abd al-Raḥmān, the aim was to fight the strong Syrian tribes in the Jawf region. The tribes, however, on learning of the Sa'ūdī expedition, shifted their strongholds to new positions in the Jordan valley.[5] 'Uthmān bin Bishr gives more details about the expedition. He says that an army comprising eight thousand men set out from Dir'iyya under the command of Imām Sa'ūd for Nuqrat al-Shām, a plain in the Syrian valley, on an expedition against the 'Anaza, Banū Ṣakhr, and other tribes. Men from al-Jawf also participated in the expedition. The enemy became aware of their advance and took refuge in 'Ain al-Qahwa in the Ḥawrān mountains and afterwards in al-Ghawr depression. The Sa'ūdī forces campaigned around al-Muzairīb and Bostra, but the enemy succeeded in eluding them and took refuge in the strong al-Muzairīb fort. Seeing no advantage in an assault on the fort, the Sa'ūdī forces returned, with a large amount of spoils.[6]

After the incorporation of al-Jawf into the first Sa'ūdī state, the area remained linked administratively with Ḥā'il, whose amīr, Muḥammad bin 'Alī, had been one of the commanders of the Sa'ūdī expedition to the area.

The Sa'ūdī presence in al-Jawf continued until the fall of the first Sa'ūdī state at the hand of Ibrāhīm Pāshā in *1233*/1818, following which al-Jawf lay open to encroachment by the Ruwala tribe under its Āl Sha'lān amīrs, who were currently strengthening their position in the northern part of the Peninsula. Nevertheless, no governor or representative of the Āl Sha'lān is recorded to have been appointed in al-Jawf at this period.

---

1. 'Uthmān bin 'Abd Allāh ibn Bishr, *'Unwān al-Majd fī Tārīkh Najd*, 2 vols. Riyadh, Maṭābi' al-Qaṣīm, *1385*/1965-66, vol. 1 p.123.
2. Wallin, p.32.
3. 'Abd al-Raḥīm 'Abd al-Raḥmān 'Abd al-Raḥīm, *al-Dawlat al-Sa'ūdiyyat al-Ūlā, 1745-1818 C.E./1158-1233 A.H.*, Cairo, Ma'had al-Buḥūth wa'l-Dirāsāt al-'Arabiyya, 1975, p.216.
4. Ibid., pp.216-18.
5. Ibid., p.220.
6. Ibn Bishr, op.cit., pp.183-84. Commenting on this incursion, J.G. Lorimer says that the Sa'ūdī forces ". . . struck terror into the heart of Syria by a sudden foray into the Haurān district, where, in the space of three days, they sacked no less than 35 villages; and the provincial capital of Damascus would probably have fallen, had they cared to attack." See J.G. Lorimer, vol. 1 pt.1B, p.1080.

20
Al-Jawf and the Second Sa'ūdī State

The second Sa'ūdī state was established under Imām Turkī bin 'Abd Allāh Āl Sa'ūd in *1238*/1823, and consolidated by his son and successor, Imām Faiṣal.[1] Local accounts vary as to when the area was brought under the authority of the Āl Sa'ūd after the rise of the second Sa'ūdī state. It is said that Faiṣal bin Turkī sent Muḥammad bin 'Alī Āl 'Arfaj, former amīr of Buraida, as amīr of al-Jawf. Muḥammad Āl 'Arfaj was a native of al-Qaṣīm. He was born in Buraida and belonged to the Tamīm tribe. On several occasions he was appointed governor of Buraida by Imām Turkī bin 'Abd Allāh, but was eventually dismissed and imprisoned on the order of Imām Faiṣal, who appointed one of Muḥammad's cousins, 'Abd al-'Azīz bin Muḥammad Āl 'Arfaj, in his place. Released from prison, Muḥammad Āl 'Arfaj was sent to al-Jawf as amīr, and there composed a poem expressing his passionate attachment to his home town. It includes the following lines:

> Oh, have mercy on me. Sweet slumber was stolen from my eyes;
> I was kept awake by the freezing cold.
>
> Pressing thoughts burdened my mind, and I was not able to sit still;
> I suffered like a man with a broken shin.
>
> The freezing winter brought to mind sweet memories of my homeland;
> A worldly paradise and a life of ease.
>
> . . . . .
>
> Ride your mount for two days, and on the third
> You will alight at Jubba by sunset.
>
> At midday on the morrow you will approach Faid;
> Press on and don't dismount from your camel.
>
> At sunset on the fifth day you will reach the town of my kin:
> Men of strong will and grand designs who foil the schemes of their adversaries.
>
> . . . . .
>
> O messenger, give my greetings to all and tell them:
> Here in al-Jawf I am plagued by vexation and hardships.
>
> I wonder if there is among you, dear ones,
> A discerning man with good judgement,
>
> Who would counsel me concerning a night visitor;
> I was asleep and I woke up disturbed.[2]

It appears that Muḥammad Āl 'Arfaj came to al-Jawf in *1243*/1828 and remained as governor till his return to al-Qaṣīm, where he was killed in *1258*/1841. Imām

Faiṣal bin Turkī Āl Sa'ūd appointed 'Abd Allāh Ibn Rashīd as amīr of Ḥā'il in *1250*/1834, and Ḥā'il and Jabal Shammar were to remain under the Āl Rashīd until the late King 'Abd al-'Azīz took the region in *1340*/1921. Once 'Abd Allāh Ibn Rashīd had made himself secure in Ḥā'il, he sent his brother 'Ubaid on an expedition to al-Jawf in *1254*/1838. 'Ubaid, accompanied by 3,000 camel riders, compelled the inhabitants of al-Jawf to pay *zakāt* but left neither a representative nor any forces to garrison the oasis when he withdrew.[3]

In *1269*/1853, Ṭalāl bin 'Abd Allāh Āl Rashīd repeated his father's action, and sent his uncle 'Ubaid and his brothers Mit'ab and Muḥammad on a campaign against al-Jawf. On arrival, they laid siege to the town. The amīr of the oasis at that time, according to Carlo Guarmani, the Italian traveller who visited Arabia in 1864, was Ḥaṭṭāb bin al-Sarrāḥ, who paid tribute to the Ruwala chieftains. Guarmani writes that after a siege of twenty days, the town fell to the Āl Rashīd, in spite of a heroic defence. "Emir . . . [Ḥaṭṭāb] was taken prisoner and is still alive, a prisoner in irons, in the castle of . . . [Ḥā'il] while his sons retired to the . . . [Wādi'l-Sirḥān] . . ."[4] Charles Doughty says that Muḥammad bin 'Abd Allāh Āl Rashīd "was wounded . . . [on this occasion] by a ball in the foot which lodged in the bone . . ."[5] Within two years, the Jawf region had garrisons from Jabal Shammar in a number of important places. Throughout this period, Ṭalāl bin 'Abd Allāh recognized the suzerainty of his own overlord, Imām Faiṣal bin Turkī, in Riyadh.[6]

During the period of their pre-eminence in the region, the Āl Rashīd amīrs found a power vacuum in the northern part of the Peninsula into which to extend their authority. 'Abd Allāh al-'Uthaimīn gives the following account of the establishment of 'Abd Allāh Ibn Rashīd's power in the Jawf area, which explains how the Āl Rashīd were able to gain control of the oasis.

> There was fighting between the quarter of al-Dalhamiyya and al-Sarrāḥ on the one side and Khadhmā' and al-Jar'āwī on the other. In this fighting, al-Jar'āwī quarter was destroyed. Its inhabitants were related to al-Ramāl group of the tribe of Shammar. Some of these people had moved from Jubba to al-Jawf. In about the year *1254*/1838, the amīr of the Jabal [Shammar] sent his brother 'Ubaid to put an end to the fighting. As a result of this, al-Jawf came under the authority of 'Abd Allāh [Ibn Rashīd]. Al-Jawf started paying the *zakāt* but without Ibn Rashīd having any representative there.[7]

Elsewhere, al-'Uthaimīn explains the underlying motives for Ibn Rashīd's initial interest in al-Jawf:

> It is not surprising or unexpected that Ibn Rashīd wished to spread his power into the Jawf area once his affairs in Jabal Shammar were in good order. Among the factors which encouraged Ibn Rashīd to campaign in this area was the consideration that it had been related to Ḥā'il in administrative matters in a period not long before his tenure of office.[8]

In the course of the march of his forces to the north through the Nafūd desert, Ibn Rashīd was helped by the people of Jubba. Their support for him stemmed from the friendly relations established between him and the people of Jubba when he, with his brother 'Ubaid, had fled from Ḥā'il during a reverse of fortune and took refuge with them. (He could not go to Riyadh because the power of Imām Faiṣal bin Turkī had also been briefly eclipsed.) On that occasion, Ibn Rashīd had composed the following lines:

Harken, whoever is my true friend,
 Have pity on me, my dear ones.
Can't you see that my tears are flowing freely?
 For so long I have been crying, tears have burned my cheeks.
I can't bear the sight of the young lady with firm breasts,
 Toiling with her long sleeves tied behind and walking bare-footed,
Sharp thorns piercing her tender soles,
 With no leatherware for protection.

. . . . .

May thunderous clouds pour over Jubba their copious rains of the early season,
 Drenching all the lands bordered by the mountains of Umm Sinmān.
For only in Jubba does the fugitive find refuge.
 Whoever seeks refuge there will find it, as he would within the sacred shrine of Makka.
Ibn Rakhīṣ, who was camped near al-Ajrād,
 Gave us a hearty welcome and asked us to alight by his camp.

. . . . .

'Īsā claims that war is costly;
 I say: victory and good luck will bring us wealth.
'Īsā claims that war is baneful;
 I say: ask the smith why he gave the sword a curve.
If we cannot use the sword with the sharp edge against our enemies,
 Give it to al 'Arfajiyya and she will show you how to use it!
Even if I [have to come] from beyond the bridge of Baghdād,
 I vow to meet my enemy as surely as a man would face his fate on the day of judgement.

THE PEOPLE OF AL-JAWF AND THEIR OPPONENTS

The people of al-Jawf frequently showed boldness and resoluteness in resisting the attempts made in the *13th*/19th century to dominate their area. Where the stories of this resistance are not recorded in history books, its memory is preserved in popular poetry, in which are recounted some of the incidents of the campaigns of the Āl Rashīd amīrs in al-Jawf. This record is all the more useful since the amīr of Ḥā'il, 'Abd Allāh Ibn Rashīd, and his brother 'Ubaid were both poets. There were poets in al-Jawf, too, including the chief of the oasis, Ḥaṭṭāb al-Sarrāḥ, his son Ghālib, and Mufaḍḍī al-'Aṭiyya.

Among the poems describing the intense struggle for the control of al-Jawf is the following by 'Ubaid al-'Alī al-Rashīd, recited by him in answer to a letter from Dūmat al-Jandal asking him earnestly to wage war against Khalīf and Ḥaṭṭāb:

O Munificent Lord who gives with generosity,
You bestow your bounty graciously.
O Great Lord, forgiver of sins,
You rendered Moses victorious over the Pharaoh.
Open for us a door of victory with your grace;
Send us the helping angels you sent [with the Prophet
Muḥammad] to the battle of Badr.
Please Lord, answer my prayers and fulfil my wish,
O Almighty who creates with the power of His word.
Hail, rider on a spirited mount.
You see its body bouncing like a crazed beast.
After marching for four nights you alight near my comrades:
Gallant defenders of the homeland since ancient times.
Tell him that even if he did not send a call for help,
Surely we were intent on heading his direction in due time.
You complain about the doings of Khalīf and Ḥaṭṭāb;
God will punish those who break their promises.
Should you ask for my help against Bedouin raiders,
Know that I am ready to face the adversary with my sharp sword.
We will pursue those brigands incessantly;
We are only waiting for our deputies to return from India.
When they come back, by the Grace of the Lord, with the cannons,
We will deal the adversaries blows as hard as you can remember.
I will answer your call with multitudes, who are rough-mannered and harsh;
They will rout whoever dares to meet them.
We are lions; we sacrifice our lives and our possessions.
We give all that we have in the defence of our friends.

Ghālib bin Ḥaṭṭāb answered with the following poem:

O ʻUbaid, if you come to us, we will open the gates for you;
We will stand by to see if your hordes dare enter the town.
You will face Khalīf and Ḥaṭṭāb in al-Jawf;
They are not nomads who scamper from your way.
You do not scare us with your armies and cannons.
This is the land of al-Sarrāḥ; we will defend it to the last man.
Your cohort whom you ply with gifts:
His advice will bring you ruin.
You claim your intention is [to collect] *zakāt* and [appoint] religious teachers here;
This is a façade to hide your real intention.
Remember, O ʻUbaid, when you were a friend of Ḥaṭṭāb,
He stocked your larder with delicious dates.

After one of the battles between ʻUbaid Ibn Rashīd and the people of al-Jawf, ʻUbaid recited the following verses:

Generous hands will be recompensed
With the gracious bounty of the Good Lord.

We rise above other tribes;
  We do not live by empty words.
O Great Lord, Creator of light,
  Grant us a quick, eminent victory.
It was so imprudent to fight the people of al-Jawf:
  Gallant warriors who beat rugged enemies on the battlefield.
We wore shiny broadcloth to the battlefield and they wore coarse wool.
  They attacked us like a thirsty herd of camels headed for water.
Our wounded were carried tied to their saddles.
  Ninety of our best riflemen lay dead in the sand dunes.

In another poem, addressed to Ḥaṭṭāb bin Sarrāḥ, 'Ubaid Ibn Rashīd recited the following lines:

Who will deliver to Khalīf and Ḥaṭṭāb the cheerful news of my raid against them?
  News as cheerful as the routing of the Pharaoh by Moses.
He who shoots at us with bullets, we shoot at him with cannon-balls.
  We shall turn your haughtiness, by the grace of the Lord, into submission.
I shall bring against you cannons from India,
  Brought by our deputies who spent ninety days on the road.
I am not like those merchants who peddle henna;
  I am the scion of noble ancestors, who trades in the art of warfare.

Amīr 'Ubaid Ibn Rashīd was able to capture Ḥaṭṭāb and his son Ghālib, in Dūmat al-Jandal.[10] The circumstances of their capture are stated in a poem by Ghālib saying that this step was expected of 'Ubaid. Though 'Ubaid's words superficially did not imply that he would try to apprehend them, had they been a little more cautious, they could have eluded him. In the following verses Ghālib blames his father for their misery. The poem was composed while they were in the prison of Ibn Rashīd in Ḥā'il.[11]

I moan like an exhausted and emaciated camel;
  I grieve over a homeland we left behind.
We were her protectors and shields before;
  But now the dirty feet of the enemy defile her pure soil.
O Ḥaṭṭāb, this is not the time to feel sorry;
  We are reaping the reward of your innocent trust of the enemy.
You should have listened to my advice when we were up on the roof;
  When you chose one approach and I another.
Kasb dates have become a delicacy to me;
  Before, I would eat only the Ḥilwa dates.[12]
Would weeping be of any use I would weep over Muraifa,
  The lush palm garden that has been possessed by the enemy.
Verily, 'Ubaid came upon us like a pestilence;
  Verily, he came upon us like a plague from the heaven above.

In another poem, Mufaḍḍī al-'Aṭiyya of al-Jawf described a battle between Mit'ab Ibn Rashīd[13] and the people of al-Jawf:

At the end of the twin months[14] Mit'ab fell upon us.

Exchange of gun-fire at Mārid sounded as loud as the beating of blacksmiths
at work.
He wanted to push us against the wall but could not.
We charged at him, not paying heed to his threats.
Glory to those among us who fell on the battlefield;
And glory to the youths who distinguished themselves on that day.
I wish to God that Mit'ab had waited a while longer.
We discharged all our ammunition at his men.
Mit'ab charged upon us, intending to put down our palm gardens,
But in the end he saw his troops lie dead at al-Qaniyya.

---

1. Apart from the well-known Najdī chroniclers, there are two studies on the second Sa'ūdī state: R. Bayly Winder, *Saudi Arabia in the Nineteenth Century*, London, Macmillan, 1965, and, more recently: 'Abd al- Fattāḥ Ḥasan Abū 'Aliyya, *al-Dawlat al-Sa'ūdiyyat al-Thāniyya, 1256-1309 A.H./1840-1891 C.E.*, Riyadh, Dār al-Marrīkh, *1405*/1985.
2. *Muntakhabāt min al-Shi'r al-Nabaṭī li ashhar al-Shu'arā' Najd [Selections from the Nabaṭī Poetry of the Most Famous Poets of Najd]* (n.p., n.d.), pp.18-20. Muḥammad Āl 'Arfaj is regarded as one of the greatest poets of Najd. Among his verses are love poems. Selections from his poetry appear at pp.18-46 of this anthology.
3. Musil, *Northern Neğd*, pp.238-39; Wallin, p.32.
4. Guarmani, p.102.
5. Charles M. Doughty, *Travels in Arabia Deserta*, 2 vols., Cambridge, Cambridge University Press, 1881, vol. 2 p.18.
6. Musil, *Northern Neğd*, pp.239-40.
7. 'Abd Allāh Ṣāliḥ al-'Uthaimīn, *Nash'at Imārat Āl Rashīd*, Riyadh, Riyadh University Libraries, *1401*/1981, pp.118-19; see also Wallin, pp.30-32.
8. al-'Uthaimīn, p.119.
9. Musil, *Northern Neğd*, p.238.
10. Cf. the version of Carlo Guarmani on this point. Guarmani, p.102.
11. This poem is given by 'Abd al-Raḥmān bin 'Aqīl in a version which differs somewhat from the one that follows. *al-'Arab* 17, Ramaḍān-Shawwāl *1402*, p.274. 'Abd al-Raḥmān bin 'Aqīl has ascribed it to Ḥaṭṭāb bin Sarrāḥ, whereas actually it is by his son Ghālib.
12. The excellence of the dates of al-Jawf is well known. Ḥilwa is one of the distinguished varieties. The Kasb dates are the ordinary varieties which have not been given any name.
13. Mit'ab bin 'Abd Allāh bin 'Alī bin Rashīd ruled Ḥā'il for a short span of time after the death of his brother Ṭalāl in 1868. He was killed by his nephews Bandar bin Ṭalāl and Badr bin Ṭalāl.
14. In the Hijri calendar there are two pairs of "twin" months: Rabī' I and Rabī' II, and Jumādā I and Jumādā II—months 3 to 6. Here the poet means that Mit'ab came in Jumādā II.

21
Al-Jawf and the Ottoman Rule

In the latter part of the *13th century*/1870s, the Ottoman government decided to extend their rule to al-Jawf, and in so doing, challenged the Āl Rashīd position in the north. The circumstances surrounding the extension of direct Turkish authority to al-Jawf, their motives for coming to the oasis, and their departure after only a short period reflect the tenuousness of their connection with al-Jawf. The background of the attempt to exercise direct rule in al-Jawf by the Ottoman Turkish government must be seen in the context of their dominion at the time over most of the Arab lands.

There are various, at times contradictory, reports of the arrival of the Turks in al-Jawf. Nevertheless, the reports of two European travellers and a number of official Ottoman documents are helpful in explaining the Turkish adventure. Among the latter, some of which are reproduced towards the end of this chapter, is one showing that an amīr of the Āl Sha'lān, of the Ruwala tribe, assisted the Turks in wresting al-Jawf from the hands of the Āl Rashīd and attaching it to Syria.

It reads as follows:

> To the Governor of Syria
> In view of the services rendered and exertions made by Hazzā' al-Sha'lān towards wresting the area of al-Jawf, which falls within the great province [Syria], from the hands of Ibn Rashīd, and based on the feeling of your government of the necessity of rewarding the above-mentioned [Hazzā' al-Sha'lān] by a royal order of the third degree and with a sword worth one thousand or two thousand *ghirsh* – to be bought and presented to him – approval [to take these actions] has been given after having received permission from the higher department of the Royal Dīwān. The matter has been entrusted to the Finance Ministry for taking the appropriate steps towards this end. This has been issued to fulfil the demand. (Book of Samples, no. 905) *11 Rabī' al-Awwal 1289*/19.5.1872.

This letter, dated 19 May 1872, helps to determine the date of the arrival of the Turks in al-Jawf. Read with the report of Charles M. Doughty (see pp. 98–99, below), who gives the year of the event as 1872, and studied in the light of the more reliable of the chronologies of the Jabal Shammar confederacy[1], this document enables us to narrow down the date of the arrival of the Turks in al-Jawf to between 1 February and 15 May 1872.

After the opening of the Suez Canal in 1869 the Turks were persistently trying to extend the areas under their influence. Thus they tried in the early 1870s to expand their rule to the Yemen, 'Asīr, and al-Aḥsā'. It is against this broader Arabian context that their attempts to control al-Jawf should be seen, although they were not able to maintain their hold for long.

There are various accounts of the Turkish expedition to al-Jawf. A local report from al-Jawf gives the following information: In the time of ʻUbaid Ibn al-Rashīd there was a struggle between two families in al-Jawf (Dūmat al-Jandal) over a piece of land. The case was brought before ʻUbaid Ibn al-Rashīd, who gave judgement in favour of one of the parties. The man who had received the adverse judgement returned to al-Jawf and communicated with the Ottoman government, which sent ʻAbbās Pāshā, supported by a small force, to take over as governor of al-Jawf. ʻAbbās stayed there for a whole year, but then wanted to return to Turkey. ʻUbaid Ibn al-Rashīd told ʻAbbās that he (ʻUbaid) could deputise for him and could send the Ottoman government the prescribed amount of dates and grain as a tax from the area and act in ʻAbbās's absence. This idea appealed to ʻAbbās and he departed. Thus ʻUbaid Ibn al-Rashīd returned to power, and put to death the man who had communicated with the Turks.

On this occasion ʻUbaid Ibn Rashīd is said to have composed a poem, part of which reads as follows:

> O land lying behind the sand dunes,
> Do not think that long absence will cause me to forget you.
> O dear land, I left you for the sake of ʻAbbās;
> But I shall not leave you to Ibn Shaʻlān.
> I shall pay you a visit soon, accompanied by cannons, swords and helmets;
> I shall raze to the ground all your high buildings.

This local report fails on account of the fact that ʻUbaid died in 1869,[2] that is, sometime before the Turkish incursion. There is no doubt that ʻUbaid was the driving force behind the Jabal Shammar confederacy. As mentioned by Lorimer, according to one authority, he was the virtual ruler after the death of his brother ʻAbd Allāh,[3] during the reigns of his nephews Ṭalāl and Mitʻab. He might have given the above-mentioned verdict during Mitʻab's reign – as the regent in Mitʻab's absence – but, so far as the rest of the story is concerned, it is certain that he did not live to see the fall and recovery of al-Jawf, which most probably occurred in 1872 and 1873, respectively.

The second account of the Turkish adventure to al-Jawf is by the celebrated British traveller Charles Montagu Doughty, who visited Arabia in 1876-1878. Though Doughty did not visit al-Jawf, he assiduously collected most of the available information regarding this episode in the history of the area and the Rashīdī-Turkish relations.

Doughty records that "in or about the year 1872" an expedition was sent by the Turkish government of Syria to bring al-Jawf under its authority. The small force, commanded by a Kurdish Pāshā named Muḥammad Saʻīd, consisted, according to one of Doughty's sources, of 70 irregular soldiers and a motley crew of serving men-at-arms, and according to another of his informers, two hundred troopers, one hundred police soldiery and fifty *ageyl*[4] of the Ḥajj service. The force assembled at Maʻān and after a march of nine days stopped near Dūmat al-Jandal for the night, lighting campfires in a very wide area in the plain.

This gave the townspeople the impression that the whole wilderness was burning. Some bedouin tribesmen on good terms with the Turkish government passed by the Turks and, arriving at the town, gave highly exaggerated reports of the strength of the forces gathered outside. Doughty records that "the sheukh went out and delivered the keys the same night, and surrendered themselves to the Pasha, who in the morning peaceably occupied the place."[5]

According to Doughty, when Muḥammad Ibn al-Rashīd, the prince of Ḥā'il, learned that al-Jawf had been taken by the Turks, he sent a letter to the Turkish commander saying, "As thou hast entered Jauf without fight, now in like manner depart from it again; and if not, I come to put you out."[6] Doughty relates that Ibn Rashīd then crossed the Nafūd with (according to Doughty's source) a force of ten thousand men, though Doughty himself estimates it at "perhaps one thousand at most". On Ibn Rashīd's arrival in al-Jawf, fighting started in which the Turks compensated for the disparity in numbers by the use of artillery. After a short while, Ibn Rashīd, perceiving that his enemies were holding secure positions and that sustaining the attack would be of no avail, invited the Pāshā for talks. "In the end it was accorded between them that Jauf should be still the Prince's town but tributary to the Dowla; Ibn Rashîd covenanted to pay every year for the place, at Damascus, 1500 mejîdy crowns: and a kaimakàm with his Syrian garrision was to be resident in the place."[7]

Doughty further relates that when the Pāshā departed and the *qā'im-maqām*, or resident deputy administrator, took charge, he committed one of the towers of the Mārid castle of Dūma to certain Maghribī soldiers in his employ, while entrusting the other tower to a few Syrian soliders. But after a time the men from the West mutinied on account of not having received their stipends, while the Syrians held out for the Turkish government against them. Doughty reports that

> . . . the Moors had the upper hand, and when this tiding was brought in haste to Hâyil, the Emir returned with his armed men, and reoccupied the place which he had lately lost with so much displeasure. The Moors – fifteen persons – were transported to Hâyil; where they became [members] of the Prince's armed service . . . Jauf was thus recovered, by the defection of the Moors, four years before my coming to Hâyil.[8]

Another important source for the history of al-Jawf for this period is the account of the German traveller Julius Euting,[9] who gives a detailed description of the Turkish rule. According to him, at the end of 1869 or the beginning of 1870/*1286*, the *Shaikh* of the Ruwala tribe, Saṭṭām bin Sha'lān, went to Damascus to meet Ṣubḥī Pāshā and Muḥammad Sa'īd Pāshā, who were leaders of the *Ḥajj* caravan. Saṭṭām said to them that he knew of a fertile area rich in water and which, if villages were established there, could yield a considerable sum in taxes. He also said that the Ruwala tribes were prepared to abandon their nomadic life to settle in the villages and to pay the taxes to the Ottoman government. When the Turkish officials asked where this potentially valuable land was, he explained that he was speaking of the Wādi'l-Sirḥān and that the Turks, however, would

A yard scene in Dūmat al-Jandal (*1330*/1911-12). Photograph by Alois Musil (from *Arabia Deserta: A Topographical Itinerary*).

A draw-well in Dūmat al-Jandal (*1330*/1911-12). Photograph by Alois Musil (from *Arabia Deserta: A Topographical Itinerary*).

Nawwāf bin Nūrī al-Sha'lān in his Qaṣr in Dūmat al-Jandal (1909). This photograph, and the one below, were taken by Alois Musil during the period of exchange of hostilities between the Āl Rashīd Emirate and the Āl Sha'lān amīrs (from *Arabia Deserta: A Topographical Itinerary*).

A scene outside Nawwāf's Qaṣr (from *Arabia Deserta: A Topographical Itinerary*).

An orchard in al-Jawf (*1330*/1911-12). Photograph by Alois Musil (from *Arabia Deserta: A Topographical Itinerary*).

Breakfast in the Qaṣr Mārid with 'Āmir al-Mushawrib, the deputy of the Āl Sha'lān, 1914. Photograph by Captain William Shakespear (*Royal Geographical Society*).

Inside view of the Qaṣr Mārid, 1914. Photograph by Captain William Shakespear (*Royal Geographical Society*).

Dūmat al-Jandal as it appeared from the Qaṣr Mārid, 1914. Photograph by Captain William Shakespear (*Royal Geographical Society*).

An old quarter of Dūmat al-Jandal.

The ancient wall of Dūmat al-Jandal.

An old street in Sakākā.

The ancient castle of al-Ṭuwair.

Inscriptions on the base hillock of the castle of al-Ṭuwair.

Qaṣr Za'bal in Sakākā.

Bi'r Saisara (Saisara well) in Sakākā.

Qaṣr Mārid in Dūmat al-Jandal.

Minaret of the 'Umar bin al-Khaṯṯāb Mosque in Dūmat al-Jandal.

Al-Raḥmāniyya Mosque at the ʻAbd al-Raḥmān al-Sudairī Foundation complex: elevation.

Dār al-Jawf lil-'Ulūm: the 'Abd al-Raḥmān al-Sudairī Foundation's public library in Sakākā.

Al-Nusl Hotel in Sakākā: elevation.

A view of modern Dūmat al-Jandal.

A general view of Sakākā.

have to occupy al-Jawf in the first instance, in order to protect the Ruwala's proposed villages from attack by other tribes. These local Turkish officials responded favourably to the proposal and set about making plans, but without telling their superiors; thus, if the project failed the government would escape blame, while if it succeeded, they would be praised and honoured. Discreetly, the expedition was assembled far from Damascus, and at the end of February 1870, the Ottoman force set out from Ma'ān with 200 cavalry, 60 infantry and 80 bedouin, with Muḥammad Sa'īd Pāshā at their head, and Ḥusain Bek al-Sharaksī as *qā'im-maqām* of the area to be conquered. Since Ḥusain knew no Arabic, Maḥmūd Āghā (subsequently Euting's servant) was appointed as interpreter to the expedition.

Eight days after leaving Ma'ān they reached al-Jawf; half a day away, the Turks met with local elements with whom they had already been in contact. They camped in the quarters of al-Mārid and "Khzâm" (i.e. al-Khadhmā') in Dūmat al-Jandal and planted their small cannon on a knoll, to observe the situation for a day or two. However, on the very next day followers of Muḥammad Ibn al-Rashīd arrived, under Ṣāliḥ bin Rakhīṣ, and camped in al-Dir' quarter. The Turks naively asked him why he had come, and Ibn Rakhīṣ casually replied that he had no other purpose for visiting than to see what was happening. On the third day after the arrival of the Turkish expedition, Ibn al-Rashīd himself appeared in Dūma with 8,000 men and many horses. He sent a letter to the Turks in the morning demanding that they depart from al-Jawf forthwith. As the Turks showed no reaction, Ibn al-Rashīd began to attack less than half an hour later, but without success as the Turks were well entrenched. Ibn al-Rashīd therefore decided to negotiate, and after a brief exchange he left al-Jawf for Ḥā'il. As for the Turks, Muḥammad Sa'īd Pāshā departed with 120 soldiers and the bedouin force to al-Salṭ in Transjordan, leaving behind only Ḥusain Bek with about eighty troops as a garrison. They were able to stay unharmed in Dūma, and the new *qā'im-maqām* was able to go as far as Sakākā, Qārā and al-Ṭuwair to inspect his domains. However, he started to levy new and heavy taxes on barley and salt, and within two months the opposition to the Turkish rule turned dangerously bitter. The people of al-Jawf began plotting to get rid of the Turks. A banquet was arranged and a plan was made to kill all the Turks who attended. The Turks, however, saw through the plot and were unhurt, though they no longer dared to venture out of their restricted quarters.

Muḥammad Sa'īd Pāshā wrote to Ḥusain Bek encouraging him to remain in al-Jawf until reinforcements arrived, while, simultaneously, Ibn Rashīd offered Ḥusain Bek 1,000 liras to leave voluntarily, ensuring him safe passage to Boṣrā in the Ḥawrān. Ḥusain Bek turned down the offer, but four months later he was to bitterly regret his decision, for, surrounded by enemies and finally running out of food he had to withdraw from al-Jawf, eight months after his arrival.

Euting is mistaken about the date of the arrival of the Turkish expedition. As we have seen, the most likely date is the first half of 1872 and not 1870.[10] Likewise, he is mistaken about the date of the final lifting of the Turkish occupation, which will be discussed later.

There follow below translations of documents relating to various phases of the Turkish occupation of al-Jawf. The first is in Arabic and was obtained from Dūmat al-Jandal. The rest are in Turkish and come from the official archives library of the Prime Minister's Secretariat in Istanbūl. A brief critical analysis of the events of the Turkish occupation, based on the contents of some of the documents, follows the translation. Copies of the original documents are given in Appendix II, in the order in which their translation has been recorded. The last document relates to Hazzā' al-Sha'lān, discussed at the beginning of this chapter.

DOCUMENT NO. 1

The first document, in Arabic, bears on the upper right-hand corner the seal of Muḥammad Sa'īd Pāshā, Governor of Syria, and is dated *Muḥarram 22, 1290*/22 March 1873. Since it is smudged, a general meaning is given, rather than a direct translation.

The document provides for the establishment of an administrative council in the *qaḍā'*[11] of al-Jawf and for the nomination of *al-Shaikh* 'Abd Allāh Ṣāliḥ of Dūmat al-Jandal as a member of that council "in view of his proper obedience to the commands of the Porte".

He is to get a monthly salary of 150 *ghirsh* (piaster), which he will draw from the treasury of the *qaḍā'*, duly documenting its receipt.

The decree advises *Shaikh* 'Abd Allāh Ṣāliḥ to co-operate with the *qā'im-maqām* of Ma'ān and the other members of the council and to decide all administrative matters in accordance with the principles of justice. It also draws his attention to the requirement that his conduct conform with what pleases the Porte and that he avoid doing anything unbecoming for which he could be answerable.

DOCUMENT NO. 2[12]

To the Exalted Province of Syria

In view of the abolition of the *mutaṣarrifiyya*[13] of Ma'ān, it has been decided that the administration of the *qaḍā'* of al-Jawf be at the level of a *qā'im-maqāmiyya*. The province of al-Madīnat al-Munawwara has demanded that the said *qaḍā'* be annexed to it, with a view to giving it under the Ibn Rashīd administration, which includes both the Jabal [Shammar] and al-Qaṣīm, and the areas under their control. But, in view of the strong relationship, as mentioned in your telegram, between the salt-producing area [of Qurayyāt al-Milḥ] situated in the said *qaḍā'* and your province, the question of annexing the said salt-producing area has been postponed. For the same reason it has also been decided to let the administration of the *qaḍā'* continue as at present, and not to permit Ibn Rashīd to interfere in its affairs. The province referred to above has been informed about

this accordingly. This letter has been written to inform you of the matter.
[Issued on *23 Rabīʿ al-Awwal 1290*/21.5.1873]

DOCUMENT NO. 3[14]

To the Province of al-Madīnat al-Munawwara

In view of the abolition of the *mutaṣarrifiyya* of Maʿān, it has been decided to have the administration of the *qaḍā'* of al-Jawf at the level of a *qā'im-maqāmiyya*. His Excellency[15] has requested for the annexation of the said *qaḍā'* [al-Jawf] to the Province of al-Madīna, with a view to giving it under the Ibn Rashīd administration, which includes both the Jabal [Shammar] and al-Qaṣīm, and the areas under their control. However, a telegram has arrived from the governor of Syria, stating the need of that province [Syria] for the salt-producing area which is there in the said *qaḍā'*. The telegram also states that the matter of annexing the salt-producing area to either of the two provinces should be decided later and that it should be communicated to His Excellency not to permit Ibn Rashīd to interfere in the affairs of that *qaḍā'*.

Therefore till the time a notification is issued determining the side to which the said *qaḍā'* will be subordinate, Ibn Rashīd must not be allowed to interfere in the affairs of the *qaḍā'*. It is obvious that the demand for annexing the *qaḍā'* to the Ibn Rashīd administration is based upon a particular view [of the whole problem]. Hence, this document is issued so that His Excellency re-examines his opinion and remarks concerning this matter.
[Issued on *23 Rabīʿ al-Awwal 1290*/21.5.1873]

DOCUMENT NO. 4[16]

To the Exalted Province of Syria

At the time when the Council of State was holding a meeting to discuss the proposals of His Excellency the former Pāshā [governor] of Syria regarding the creation of a *mutaṣarrifiyya* in Maʿān so as to unify the *aqḍiya*[17] of al-Jawf, al-Karak and Maʿān, the Special Committee of the Deputies completed a study of the letters received from your administration and found that your schemes and proposals accord with the interest of the state.

In this respect it was found that the situation requires the immediate abolition of the said *mutaṣarrifiyya* [Maʿān] and the restoration of the previous arrangement, notwithstanding our initial intimation through our telegram dated *11 Ṣafar 1290* [10.4.1873] for establishing the *mutaṣarrifiyya*. The situation requires that Saʿīd Pāshā [the ex-governor] stay in Syria and that all the orders issued in this regard be carried out. It also requires stopping all related expenditure that has not yet been incurred. Instructions regarding this have been given to the said Ministry [the Ministry of Finance] just as this letter has been issued for carrying out the orders. All this is in accordance with the decision and the notification.

[Issued on *2 Rabī' al-Ākhir 1290*/30.5.1873]

DOCUMENT NO. 5[18]

To the Exalted Province of Syria

The (brilliant) letters coming from your province and the recommendations contained therein have been studied. These letters insist on the need for annexing the *qaḍā'* of al-Jawf to the province of Syria. It has been gathered from their contents that the people of the *qaḍā'* of al-Jawf are suffering from the excesses of Ibn Rashīd, that if the administration of the *qaḍā'* is with the province of Syria, then the [Turkish] Government will gain the existing revenues of the *qaḍā'* as well as the revenues of the salt-producing area, which lies within the *qaḍā'* at a distance of two days from Ḥawrān, that the [annual] customs dues expected from the salt-producing area amount to 150,000 *ghirsh*, that after paying off the expenses the Government would get a net income of around 50,000-60,000 *ghirsh* and that besides this the Government will get the money which Ibn Rashīd collects from the Sharārāt tribe, who winter in the region, as well as the money which he collects from the other bedouin as *zakāt*.

[On the other hand] the letters received from the province of al-Madīnat al-Munawwara say that the said *qaḍā'* has been under the administration of the *Shaikh* of Jabal Shammar [Ibn Rashīd] for twenty years, and that the castle inside that was also built by him. Thus the letters point out the advantages of keeping the administration of Ibn Rashīd in it and say that it would facilitate the implementation there of the reforms which have been planned. Those letters were placed before the Special Committee of the Deputies, and after a discussion on what was written by both sides it has been decided to annex the said *qaḍā'* to [the province of] al-Madīnat al-Munawwara and to place it under the administration of Ibn Rashīd in view of the facts that it is situated in the desert and is far from Syria.

But seen in the context of Your Excellency's submissions regarding Ibn Rashīd's injustice and excesses, particularly, the intensification of the enmity existing between him and the two clans of al-Ḥaṣn [al-Ḥasan] and Ruḥaibī – following the assistance given by the said clans to Sa'īd Pāshā – leaving the *qaḍā'* under the administration of Ibn Rashīd would put their lives in danger. Forsaking them in such a condition does not befit the eminent position of the Exalted Government. The matter, therefore, demands putting an end to the fears of the tribes and relieving them of his injustice decisively. Similarly, it is one of the duties of the Exalted Government to ensure the security and safety of the people and amīrs of the two clans and the general public of the area. Therefore, the province of al-Madīnat al-Munawwara has been directed to get firm guarantees from Ibn Rashīd so as to link this matter with explicit undertakings.

From the information contained in the letters received from Your Excellency and al-Madīnat al-Munawwara, it has been observed that the said salt-producing area is not under the above-mentioned *qaḍā'*. In view of its being close to Ḥawrān, it has been decided to have the administration of the salt-producing area with the exalted province [Syria]. The province of al-Madīnat al-Munawwara has been informed of this decision.

This letter is being issued to Your Excellency to implement what the situation demands *per se*.

[Issued on *14 Rajab 1290*/7.9.1873]

DOCUMENT NO. 6[19]

To the Province of al-Madīnat al-Munawwara

Letters have come from the province of Syria saying that the people of the *qaḍā'* of al-Jawf are suffering from the excesses of Ibn Rashīd, that if the said *qaḍā'* is annexed to the province of Syria, then the [Turkish] Government will have control over the existing revenues of the *qaḍā'* as well as the revenues of the salt-producing area, which lies within the *qaḍā'* at a distance of two days from Ḥawrān, that the annual customs dues expected from the salt-producing area amount to 150,000 *ghirsh*, that after paying off the expenses the Government will get a net income of 50,000-60,000 *ghirsh*, and that besides this the Government will get the money which Ibn Rashīd collects from the Sharārāt tribe, who winter in the region, as well as all the money which he collects from the other bedouin as *zakāt*.

On the other hand, letters have arrived from Your Excellency[20] regarding this matter saying that if the said *qaḍā'* is annexed to the province of al-Madīnat al-Munawwara, it would lead to the improvement of the administration of the *qaḍā'* and would consequently facilitate the implementation there of the planned reforms and improvements which Your Excellency has promised to carry into effect. After discussion of this matter in the Special Committee of the Deputies and appraisal of the contents of the letters received from both sides [i.e. al-Madīna and Syria], it has been decided to annex the said *qaḍā'* to the province of al-Madīnat al-Munawwara and give it under the administration of Ibn Rashīd in view of the fact that it is situated in the desert and is far from Syria.

But as understood from the information coming from the said province [Syria], Ibn Rashīd's injustice and excesses continue unabated. Particularly, the enmity and hatred between him and the two clans of al-Ḥaṣn [al-Ḥasan] and Ruḥaibī have become more intense as a result of the assistance given by those two clans to Sa'īd Pāshā.[21] Because of this, putting the said *qaḍā'* under the rule of Ibn Rashīd would endanger the security and lives of the people. Forsaking the clans does not befit the power and high position of the Exalted Government, and it is incumbent upon her to relieve them of those acts of injustice and those dangers. In fact, it is the sacred duty of the Exalted Government to protect the security and stability of the people and amīrs of the two clans, and the general public of the area. Hence I inform Your Excellency that firm guarantees and promises should be obtained from Ibn Rashīd regarding protection of the public and the above-mentioned clans so that the Government could then put the said *qaḍā'* under his administration.

Lastly, it is considered suitable to attach the salt-producing area, as mentioned in Your Excellency's letter of 25 Jumāda'l-Ūlā 1290 [21.7.1873], to the province of Syria, because it is so close to Ḥawrān. The said province [Syria] has been informed of this, and this document has been issued to carry the needful into effect.

[Issued on *14 Rajab 1290*/7.9.1873]

DOCUMENT NO. 7[22]

To the Exalted Province of Syria

Letters emanating from the headquarters of your exalted province, indicating the need for placing the *qaḍā'* of al-Jawf along with its tribes and its attached surrounding areas under the administration of the *qā'im-maqām* and annexing it to the *sanjaq (liwā')*[23] of Ḥawrān, have been received. In these letters details [of various aspects of the matter] and the necessary budgetary provisions for it [the *qaḍā'*] have been given. These papers were passed on to the Special Committee of the Deputies, which has completed their study. Notwithstanding the fact that these letters comprise the explicit opinions and thoughts of His Excellency the ex-governor, in view of his transfer it is appropriate to refer to Your Excellency's views and also to ascertain and present the views of the local people on this matter so that a second debate on it could be completed. This task is deputed to Your Excellency, and this document is issued to state the position.

[Issued on *12 Ramaḍān 1293*/1.10.1876]

DOCUMENT NO. 8[24]

To the Province of al-Madīnat al-Munawwara

It has been decided to separate the *qaḍā'* of al-Jawf from the province of Syria and place it under the administration of Ibn Rashīd, which is subordinate to the province of al-Madīnat al-Munawwara. This decision has been made at the suggestion of His Excellency[25] and also in view of the fact that in it lie the possibilities of straightening the affairs of the *qaḍā'* and the ease in carrying into effect the reforms planned for it. But in view of what had been learned from the letters coming from the said province [Syria] about the harshness of Ibn Rashīd and his revenge-seeking by causing fright among the tribes, His Excellency was asked through a special letter on *14 Rajab 1290* to get undertakings and assurances from Ibn Rashīd that he would abstain from tyrannizing the general public and the clans so that the placement of the said *qaḍā'* under his administration could be completed following that.

Further evidence of the cruelty and treachery of the above-mentioned [Ibn Rashīd] has been provided by a plaint from the elders and notables of the said *qaḍā'* addressed to Ṣubḥī Pāshā, one of the members of the Government's advisory council, in which they have expressed their desire to keep the *qaḍā'* under the previous administration and also mentioned that in case the previous administration is allowed to continue, the revenues of the Government would be according to its wishes.

This document has been issued to inform His Excellency about the situation there [in the *qaḍā'* of al-Jawf] and to [request him to] express his opinion and observations on this matter.

[Issued on *1 Dhu'l-Ḥijja, 1290*/31.1.1874]

On studying the Turkish documents 2 and 3 we find that up to 30 May 1873, the Turkish Government had not responded favourably to the requests for incorporation of al-Jawf in the Madīna province so as to enable the Governor of that province to pass it to the control of Ibn Rashīd. This means that until then al-Jawf had not been re-occupied by Ibn Rashīd. The documents numbered 5 and 6, dated 7 September 1873, show that there was a dramatic change in the Turkish approach to the question of al-Jawf. We find the Ottoman government not only complaining of Ibn Rashīd's harshness towards some of the people of al-Jawf on account of their collaboration with the Turks, but also arguing in favour of placing al-Jawf under Ibn Rashīd's administration. This proves that Ibn Rashīd had gained control of the area in the meantime. Further evidence of this is provided by Doughty's generalized statements that al-Jawf was recovered by Ibn Rashīd four years before his own coming to Ḥā'il, on 22 October 1877, and that after regaining the control of al-Jawf, Ibn Rashīd "commanded to cut off the right hands of many who were gone to the faith of the Dowla", that is, the Ottoman government. Thus we can conclude that al-Jawf passed under the control of the Rashīdīs some time between the last week of May 1873 and 31 August 1873.

The question arises, what did the Turkish government intend to achieve, after the control of the area had passed to Ibn Rashīd, when it said that "firm guarantees and promises should be obtained from Ibn Rashīd regarding protection of the public and the above-mentioned clans so that the Government could then put the said *qaḍā'* under his administration"?[26] The answer lies in the fact that Ottoman Turkey, as the dominant imperial power in the Middle East, was recognized as exercising some nominal suzerainty over most of the areas not directly ruled by her. So far as the Jabal Shammar area is concerned, D.G. Hogarth pointed out in the beginning of the 20th century that "Turkey has always had a certain hold over the Rashid family at Hail, and the Ottoman sultan's name has always been included in the public prayers".[27] It is clear that after the defection of their own soldiers and the consequent loss of al-Jawf to Ibn Rashīd, the Turks realized that their adventure to al-Jawf was not well judged and was not worthy of being repeated. They were, therefore, looking for a face-saving solution which could show that they still enjoyed that nominal suzerainty over the areas. Obviously, it was with this objective that the Turkish government was communicating to the concerned provinces its decision to place al-Jawf under Ibn Rashīd's control. Beyond doubt, it is the *de jure* control of al-Jawf which the documents are referring to and not the *de facto* control, which had already passed to Ibn Rashīd.

---

1. All authorities agree on the fact that Muḥammad Ibn Rashīd himself came hurriedly to al-Jawf to face the Turkish challenge. Most authorities, among them Lorimer, Huber and Ibn 'Īsā, say that Muḥammad came to power in *1289* (11 March 1872 to 28 Feb. 1873). See J.G. Lorimer, vol. 1 pt.1B, pp.1165-67; Philip Ward, *Ha'il: Oasis City of Saudi Arabia*, Cambridge, England, Oleander Press, 1983, p.410, which gives a translation of parts of Charles Huber's *Journal d'un voyage en Arabie (1883-84)*; Ibrāhīm bin Ṣāliḥ bin 'Īsā, *Tārīkh Ba'ḍ al-Ḥawādith al-Wāqi'a fī Najd . . .*, Riyadh, Dār al-Yamāma, *1386*/1966, p.184. Lorimer even says that the event occurred immediately after Muḥammad's accession in 1872.
2. Lorimer, vol. 1 pt. 1B, p.1164; Musil, *Northern Neğd*, p.241; cf. Doughty, vol. 2 p.28.
3. Lorimer, vol.1 pt. 1B, p.1164.
4. Arabic, 'aqīl: troopers and armed dromedary riders who used to escort Ḥajj caravans.
5. Doughty, vol. 2 p.34.
6. Ibid.
7. Ibid., p.35.
8. Ibid., p.33. Doughty entered Ḥā'il on 22 October 1877.
9. Julius Euting, *Tagbuch einer Reise in Inner-Arabien*, 2 vols., Leiden, Brill, 1896-1914. The account of the Turkish incursion is given at pp.131-34 of vol. 1.
10. Another gentleman who has made some more glaring mistakes in respect of the chronology of the events in his account of the Turkish expedition to al-Jawf is the Arab writer Fahd al-Mārik. He puts the episode in the year *1309*/1891-2 and insists on the accuracy of his chronology! He states that the inhabitants of al-Jawf were tired of the rule of Muḥammad bin 'Abd Allāh [Ibn Rashīd], Amīr of Ḥā'il, and it seemed to them that they could use the Turks to get rid of him, preferring in any case the rule of the Turks to that of Ibn Rashīd. A delegation therefore met Sulṭān 'Abd al-Ḥamīd II, who was at Damascus at the time, to seek from him the protection of the Turkish Government. The Sulṭān agreed and sent a contingent under the command of Muḥammad Sa'īd Pāshā. As soon as Ibn Rashīd heard of this, he brought together a large army and set out for al-Jawf. Fahd al-Mārik then goes on to narrate at length the events that followed, concentrating mostly on the bravery of an Arab horseman named Rāḍī bin Jady. However, in his dating of the event and his story regarding the meeting of a delegation of the people of al-Jawf with Sulṭān 'Abd al-Ḥamīd II – who became the Ottoman Sulṭān in September 1876, around three years after the departure of the Turks – he is wide of the mark. (See Fahd al-Mārik, *Min Shiyam al-'Arab*, 4 vols., Beirut, al-Maktabat al-Ahliyya, 1963-65, vol. 3 pp.132-43.)
11. *Qaḍā'*: an administrative district in a province, usually headed by a *qā'im-maqām*.
12. Extracts Notebook No.902.
13. *Mutaṣarrifiyya (Mutaṣarrifliq* in Turkish): an administrative division of a province governed by a *mutaṣarrif.* It was of a higher level than a *qaḍā'*.
14. Extracts Notebook No. 873.
15. His Excellency: the Governor of al-Madīnat al-Munawwara.
16. Extracts Notebook No. 903.
17. *Aqḍiya*: plural of *qaḍā'*.
18. Extracts Notebook No. 905.
19. Extracts Notebook No. 871.
20. Your Excellency: the Governor of the Province of al-Madīnat al-Munawwara.
21. Sa'īd Pāshā: the Kurdish Pāshā who led the Turkish expedition to al-Jawf.
22. Extracts Notebook No. 905.
23. *Sanjaq*, or *Liwā'*: The highest-level division in a province administrated by a *qā'im-maqām*.
24. Extracts Notebook No. 873.
25. His Excellency: the Governor of the Province of al-Madīnat al-Munawwara.
26. See document nos. 5 and 6.
27. D.G. Hogarth's comments in Butler, p.534.

22

Al-Jawf in the First Half of the *14th*/20th Century

In the early *14th*/20th century, the Āl Rashīd rulers of Ḥā'il gradually lost effective control of al-Jawf, with their authority being challenged in the oasis by the Āl Sha'lān clan of the Ruwala tribe. The Āl Sha'lān are a clan of Mar'aḍ of Jam'ān of the Ruwala, and as amīrs they held power in parts of Syria, flourishing in the *13-14th*/19-20th centuries. The tribe is mentioned in the following lines by the Arabic poet Muḥibb al-Dīn al-Khaṭīb:

> Ruwala are Arabs whose tents are their palaces;
> Ḥamāt and Damascus are their home.

The region of Dūmā in Syria is considered to be their most important area of habitation. Their power spread southwards to Qurayyāt al-Milḥ, and in the past they competed with the Āl Rashīd for the control of the Wādi'l-Sirḥān and al-Jawf. Āl Rashīd power was challenged in the area by Saṭṭām bin Sha'lān. Muḥammad bin 'Abd Allāh Ibn Rashīd became amīr in Ḥā'il in *1289*/1872 and subsequently, after the failure of the Turkish incursion, re-established his amīrate's authority in al-Jawf. The oasis of al-Jawf remained nominally under the Āl Rashīd until *1337*/1918, although, as Āl Rashīd power declined, their authority in al-Jawf was increasingly contested. Alois Musil writes that after *Muḥarram* *1327*/January 1909, Nūrī Ibn Sha'lān began to gain control of parts of the oasis of al-Jawf and appointed his son Nawwāf to rule the occupied parts.[1] When Sa'ūd bin 'Abd al-'Azīz Ibn Rashīd became amīr of Ḥā'il after the murders of Sa'ūd bin Ḥamūd Ibn Rashīd and Ḥamūd bin Sabhān, he sent letters to Nūrī Ibn Sha'lān, seeking peace between himself and the Āl Sha'lān. However, nothing substantial arose from this. Once the situation in al-Jawf had resolved itself to his advantage, Nawwāf Ibn Sha'lān placed 'Āmir al-Mushawrib as amīr of al-Jawf, while he himself continued on northwards to al-Qurayyāt before moving up into Syria. In al-Qurayyāt, Nawwāf appointed Ḥamd bin Muwaishīr as amīr. (Nawwāf himself died in *1339*/1921.)

The outcome of al-Mushawrib's rule in al-Jawf is recorded by Sa'd al-Junaidal, who relates:

> 'Āmir al-Mushawrib indulged in moral corruption and debauchery. The people of al-Jawf complained about him to Nawwāf Ibn Sha'lān, who, realizing that 'Āmir's rule would bring adverse effects, promised to remove him. However, some local leaders who had relations with Nawwāf advised him to let al-Mushawrib stay. Ibn Sha'lān, therefore, hesitated about removing him. Al-Mushawrib meanwhile strengthened his position in the region, and his wrong-

> doing increased, with offences against women being committed. The more zealous members of the population deliberated over doing away with him and ridding themselves at the same time of the rule of Ibn Sha'lān. This movement was led by Rajā' bin Muwaishīr, one of the inhabitants of Sakākā. When he had reached an agreement on this plan with those among the people who were of the same mind, he wrote to his brother Ḥamd bin Muwaishīr, the governor of al-Qurayyāt on behalf of Ibn Sha'lān, informing him of what he intended to do. Rajā' then carried out his plan and killed 'Āmir al-Mushawrib and 'Āmir's brother as well as a certain al-Qubaisī, who was one of their companions. When the news reached Ḥamd bin Muwaishīr of what his brother and his followers intended to do, he transferred all the weapons under his control in al-Qurayyāt to al-Jawf and himself proceeded to it in all haste. War then broke out between Ibn Muwaishīr and Ibn Sha'lān.[2]

Al-Mushawrib was killed in *Rabī' I 1337*/December 1918. With the hostilities between the parties not abating, Ibn Muwaishīr sought aid from the amīr of Ḥā'il, Sa'ūd Ibn Rashīd, and the latter, taking advantage of the discomfiture of Ibn Sha'lān, raided al-Jawf to extend his own control over it. Ibn Rashīd appointed al-Shuwai'ir as governor of al-Jawf, but on the death of Sa'ūd Ibn Rashhīd, al-Shuwai'ir departed from al-Jawf, a year and a half after the Rashīdī expedition to al-Jawf, leaving Ibn Saif as his deputy.[3]

During this period, the people of al-Jawf were in touch with the Sulṭān of Najd, 'Abd al-'Azīz Ibn Sa'ūd, and expressed to him their desire to merge al-Jawf with the Sa'ūdī state. 'Abd al-'Azīz eventually sent an expedition led by 'Assāf al-Ḥusain in the year *1341*/1922. When 'Assāf reached al-Jawf, he found that Sulṭān bin Nawwāf Āl Sha'lān had established himself as the ruler after the fall of the Āl Rashīd amīrate in Ḥā'il in *1340*/1921. 'Assāf entered al-Jawf and took over the amīrate from Sulṭān bin Nawwāf, who then departed from al-Jawf.

Since that day al-Jawf has been a part of the Sa'ūdī state.[4]

1. Musil, *Northern Neğd*, pp.247–48.
2. Sa'd bin 'Abd Allāh bin Junaidal, p.137.
3. Ibid., p.138.
4. The Sa'ūdī state at that time was known as the Sultanate of Najd and its Dependencies. With the annexation of al-Ḥijāz, the name was changed in 1926 to the Kingdom of the Ḥijāz and of Najd, which in turn became in 1932 the Kingdom of Sa'ūdī Arabia.

23
Al-Jawf and the Third Sa'ūdī State

With the extension of the authority of the third Sa'ūdī state to the region of al-Jawf in *1341*/1922 in the reign of King 'Abd al-'Azīz bin 'Abd al-Raḥmān Āl Sa'ūd, the feuds and lawlessness of the nomadic past came to an end, and a new era of peace and stability dawned.[1] Like all other parts of the third Sa'ūdī state, al-Jawf became a constituent part of the Kingdom of Sa'ūdī Arabia in 1932, enjoying in the course of time greater opportunities for a higher standard of living.

The administrative area of al-Jawf – now the province, or amirate, of al-Jawf – was established soon after the passing of al-Jawf under the control of the third Sa'ūdī state. Much of the history of the third Sa'ūdī state relating to al-Jawf is still not fully documented. The 'Abd al-Raḥmān al-Sudairī Foundation has plans to document what material it can gather and, if there is sufficient information, to publish the work. For the present we can only give a brief outline of the tenures of the amīrs of al-Jawf during the third Sa'ūdī state. Appendix I, *Recent Development in al-Jawf Province*, gives details of al-Jawf's advancement since its coming under the control of the third Sa'ūdī state.[2]

The first amīr of the region was Amīr 'Assāf al-Ḥusain, who assumed office at the start of *D͟hu'l-Qi'da 1341*/June 1923, having led the Sa'ūdī expedition to the area a year before. He was relieved of his office at the end of *S͟ha'bān 1343*/March 1925 to be replaced by Amīr 'Abd Allāh bin 'Uqayyil, who arrived in al-Jawf at the end of *Ramaḍān 1343*/May 1925 and served for around two years. The next amīr to come to the region was Amīr Turkī bin Aḥmad al-Sudairī, who assumed office in *D͟hu'l-Ḥijja 1345*/June 1927, immediately after the 'Īd al-Aḍḥā festivities. He continued as amīr for one year, until the 'Īd al-Aḍḥā of *1346*/June 1928, and he was replaced by Amīr 'Abd al Raḥmān bin Sa'īd in the beginning of the next Hijri year, *1347*/June 1928. After a little less than two years, Amīr Ibn Sa'īd was recalled by Amīr 'Abd al-'Azīz bin Musā'id, amīr of the Ḥā'il region. Amīr Ibrahīm al-Nas͟hmī was deputed – after his return from the Ḥuwaiṭāt campaign – to work as the acting amīr of al-Jawf in place of Ibn Sa'īd, and he continued as such until *Ramaḍān 1349*/January-February 1931.

To succeed Amīr Ibn Sa'īd, Amīr Turkī bin Aḥmad al-Sudairī was once again sent to al-Jawf, in *Ramaḍān 1349*. It was during his tenure that the amirate headquarters were transferred from Dūmat al-Jandal to Sakākā. Amīr Turkī remained here until the end of *1351*/April 1933. In the month of *D͟hu'l-Ḥijja 1352*/March-April 1934, Amīr Turkī's brother Amīr 'Abd al-'Azīz al-Sudairī arrived to take charge of the office of amīr, unfilled for some months. Amīr 'Abd al-'Azīz remained in al-Jawf until *15 Muḥarram 1357*/17 March 1938 and was replaced by Amīr Muḥammad bin Aḥmad al-Sudairī, who remained in al-Jawf until *5 Ramaḍān 1362*/5 September 1943. The office of amīr was then taken over (on 5

Amīr ʻAssaf al-Ḥusain.

Amīr ʻAbd Allāh bin ʻUqayyil.

Amīr Ibrāhīm al-Nashmī.

Amīr Turkī bin Aḥmad al-Sudairī.

Amīr ʻAbd al-ʻAzīz bin Aḥmad al-Sudairī.

Amīr Muḥammad bin Aḥmad al-Sudairī.

Amīr ʻAbd al-Raḥmān bin Aḥmad al-Sudairī.

Amīr Sulṭān bin ʻAbd al-Raḥmān al-Sudairī.

September 1943) by Amīr 'Abd al-Raḥmān bin Aḥmad al-Sudairī. Amīr 'Abd al-Raḥmān retired, after a long tenure of office, on *1 Rajab 1410*/27 January 1990. On the same date Amīr Sulṭān bin 'Abd al-Raḥmān al-Sudairī became amīr and remains so to the present date.

With its headquarters at Sakākā, the amīrate of al-Jawf has the following districts or sub-districts:[3]

1. Dūmat al-Jandal
2. Zallūm
3. Ṣuwair
4. al-Shuwaiḥiṭiyya
5. Ṭal'at 'Ammār
6. al-Ṭīrī
7. 'Adhfā'
8. al-Laqā'iṭ
9. Khaw'ā
10. al-Ṭuwair
11. Qārā
12. al-Murair
13. al-Shaqīq
14. Maiqū'
15. al-Nabk Abū Qaṣr
16. Ṭabarjal
17. Abū 'Ajram
18. al-Thaniyya
19. al-'Assāfiyya
20. al-Fayyāḍ
21. al-Sulaimāniyya

To meet the growing economic and social needs of the people, the Kingdom of Sa'ūdī Arabia has introduced, over the decades, numerous development projects, which have helped in raising the standard of living. To oversee the phased implementation of these projects, various government departments, societies and organizations have been established in al-Jawf Province down the years. These are listed in Appendix III in the order of their establishment.

---

1. The consolidation of al-Jawf region into the Sa'ūdī state occurred at a time when the Syrian revolt against the French colonial rule was gaining momentum. During the 1925-26 uprising several of the leaders of the Syrian war of independence flocked to the domain of King 'Abd al-'Azīz and took refuge in the Wādi'l-Sirḥān area of al-Jawf Province. Among them were Sulṭān Bāshā al-Aṭrash, al-Amīr 'Ādil Arsalān and a few other chiefs from the Arsalān family, Khair al-Dīn al-Ziriklī, al-Ḥāj Amīn al-Ḥusainī, and Adīb Khair.
2. The historical and other related aspects of al-Jawf since its joining the third Sa'ūdī state are discussed further in the following chapters: *Western Travellers to al-Jawf*; *The Settlements of the People of al-Jawf Province*; and *The Traditions of the People of al-Jawf*.
3. By virtue of a royal decree promulgated in *1414*/1993, al-Qurayyāt Province was merged in the province of al-Jawf. This has laid the foundation for the reorganization of the districts and sub-districts in the Province.

PART SIX

WESTERN TRAVELLERS TO AL-JAWF REGION

24
Early Travellers

During the *13th-14th*/19th-20th centuries, the area of al-Jawf attracted the attention of a number of Western travellers whose accounts provide us with important information about life in those times.

These travels to al-Jawf took place in the context of European exploration of the Arabian Peninsula as a whole, in an age when this part of the world started gaining more attention for a number of reasons.

The places these travellers visited were in those days very difficult to reach, but what posed a greater difficulty was the cultural barrier, the difference of language, religious practice and customs.

Most travellers were received with courtesy and hospitality, if some initial suspicion. Their reasons for visiting the Arabian Peninsula varied. Some came with political aims, some with zeal for scientific exploration, others were merely adventurers, and yet others came with the urge to make a name for themselves. What all had in common were courage and fortitude, and some knowledge of Arabic and of the customs of the people they were to visit.

These travellers have preserved much information and provided useful insights and comments. On occasions, however, the opinions, comments, or observations given by these men were made from the point of view of a foreigner who does not necessarily understand or grasp the whole context of the subject. It goes without saying that the writings reflect the thinking and opinion of their authors, a matter that we do not necessarily agree with all the time.

With a view to providing a background for the accounts of the visitors to al-Jawf itself, it is appropriate to give first a brief survey of the earliest reports and books written by the most prominent of the travellers who visited Arabia (but not al-Jawf).

The tradition of modern scientific exploration of Arabia begins in the south-west of the Peninsula with Carsten Niebuhr, who was born in Germany but was of Danish nationality. He was a member of an expedition that set out from Denmark in *1176*/1762 to explore the Yemen. His book *Travels through Arabia* was the first attempt by a European to describe an area of the Peninsula and the customs of its people in a serious scientific manner. Niebuhr discussed bedouin life, although he did not really encounter this in Yemen itself but rather in the course of his journeys in Sinai, 'Irāq and Syria. Among the succession of travellers to south-western Arabia a century later was Joseph Halévy, who, in *1287*/1870, became the first European to explore Ma'rib and to record its inscriptions. The German archaeologist Edward Glaser was to visit Ma'rib and its area 18 years later. Further east, J.R. Wellsted had been able to explore Oman in *1251*/1835, while Adolf von Wrede managed to reach Wādī Ḥaḍramawt in *1259*/1843 to investigate some of the ancient remains still visible there. Other noteworthy explorers of the south of Arabia were Leo Hirsch (*1311*/1893), and Theodor Bent, who travelled there with his wife in the same year.

Turning to western Arabia, two accounts that long pre-date Niebuhr's expedition are those of Lodovico Varthema (*909-914*/1503-1508) and Jospeh Pitts (c. *1098*/1687). A remarkable visit was also made to the Ḥijāz by Domingo Badia y Leblich, a Spaniard who travelled under the name of 'Alī Bey al-'Abbāsī and visited the Holy Cities and their surrounding areas in *1221-2*/1807.

After 'Alī Bey's visit, the number of European travellers to the Ḥijāz and to other parts of Arabia gradually increased, the most notable of these being Johann Ludwig Burckhardt. Burckhardt, born in Lausanne, Switzerland, in *1189*/1784, was the first to explore Petra in southern Jordan and, because he spoke Arabic and travelled as a Muslim, was able to travel in the Ḥijāz with ease. In *1229*/1814 he visited Jeddah (Arabic, Jidda), al-Ṭā'if and Makka; then, taking the western coastal route, he reached al-Madīna in *1230*/1815. His *Travels in Arabia* was published in London in *1244-5*/1829. Another of his books, *Notes on the Bedouins and Wahabys*, can be regarded as a historical source for the first Sa'ūdī state.

Another European traveller to Makka and al-Madīna in the *13th*/19th century was the Englishman Sir Richard Burton, who visited Makka during the *Ḥajj* of *1269*/1853. His book, *Personal Narrative of a Pilgrimage to al-Madinah & Meccah*, appeared in *1271*/1855. In order to study the Ḥijāz, Burton arrived in al-Wajh and Yanbu' disguised as an Afg͟hān pilgrim. From Yanbu' he went first to al-Madīna and then to Makka. Some years later, he was able to provide further geographical information on Arabia, for he was sent by Khedive Ismā'īl to prospect for gold ores said to be in the Midian region in the northern Ḥijāz.

Information about central Arabia remained very much more sparse. In *1234-5*/1819, an English officer, Captain G.F. Sadleir, became the first European to cross Arabia from the Gulf coast to the Red Sea, in the course of a diplomatic mission to make contact with Ibrāhīm Pās͟hā, the commander of the Turco-Egyptian forces which had invaded Najd. Sadleir went first to al-Qaṭīf and then to al-Aḥsā', al-Manfūḥa, al-Dir'iyya and al-Rass, from where he travelled to al-Madīna, Yanbu' and Jeddah, following Ibrāhīm Pās͟hā's army as it withdrew westwards. It was thus by accident rather than design that Sadleir became an Arabian explorer, keeping an informative diary which provides a unique record of central Arabia, long before any other European traveller penetrated the country.[1] It was not until some twenty-five years later that an extensive exploration of central Arabia was attempted by Georg Augustus Wallin. He and his successors added greatly to the knowledge of the central areas of the Peninsula and are particularly important for our purposes, since a number of them visited al-Jawf itself.

The following pages draw on those travellers whose accounts give a detailed picture of al-Jawf region.

ULRICH SEETZEN

Ulrich Seetzen was the earliest European explorer to turn his attention to al-Jawf. Although Seetzen did not actually visit the oasis himself, he went to considerable trouble to gather reports about it and central Arabia generally.[2] Seetzen was in the Russian Imperial diplomatic service in the Near East and was an Arabist as well as a botanist. He made the pilgrimage as a Muslim in *1225*/1810, and then went south. However, he died near Ta'izz, and no full account of his studies was ever published.

Before Seetzen went to Arabia, he sent one Yūsuf al-Mālikī from Palestine to al-Jawf and the Nafūd to investigate the area on his behalf. The following account was written in *Ṣafar 1221*/May 1806 after Yūsuf returned and described to Seetzen his trip.

> One day's journey more and you come to a rocky region called Kleiah, and at the end of the following day you reach Dschof [al-Jawf]. The district of Dschof is without doubt the same that Bussching mentions under the name of Dschof al Sirhan, and which belongs to Nedsched [Najd]. One must not confuse this district with Bellad al Dschof which is part of Arabia Felix. In Dschof are several small villages; Yūsuf remembered seeing about seven, but knew the names of only three of them – Sūq al-Dir', Sūq al-Sa'idiyyīn and Sūq 'Ain Umm Sālim. All of these villages lay at a very short distance from each other. The houses of each village are built more or less in a circle, connected with only one main door for each house. The houses are built of mud and have flat roofs. Each house has behind it a small plantation of date palms. The inhabitants have only well water, which they draw up through a camel-powered pulley . . . For nearly twenty years they have been under the rule of the followers of 'Abd al-Wahhāb [*al-Shaikh* Muḥammad bin 'Abd al-Wahhāb], and just a few years previously these towns constituted the western limits of their territory. By these villages stands an old building which should be examined by scholarly visitors. There is a square tower which is built of large quadrants and pointed on top, a sort of obelisk. Artfully, a winding staircase leads upstairs, whose small rooms are attached to the side. The height of this tower must be considerable; Yūsuf affirmed it was more than two to three times the height of the tallest local minaret.[3]

Thereafter, Yūsuf claimed to have continued to the south side of the Nafūd. However, his account of the country beyond al-Jawf lacks the precise detail that marks his account of Dūmat al-Jandal. (His description of the square tower is undoubtedly a precise account of the minaret of the mosque of 'Umar bin al-Khaṭṭāb.)

GEORG AUGUSTUS WALLIN

Although Seetzen was the first European to report on al-Jawf, the first European recorded as actually reaching the area was the scholar-explorer Georg Augustus Wallin, Swedish by blood and tongue, but a native of Finland. He had a sound knowledge of Arabic and was awarded a grant by the University of Helsinki – where he had studied – to travel in Egypt and Arabia "chiefly for the purpose of the comparative study of Arabian dialects". Before setting out for the east, he studied medicine for a period of six months so as to be able to treat the people he met during his journey. He undertook his travels as a Muslim, taking the name of *al-Shaikh* ʻAbd al-Walī.

This wandering European scholar made two journeys to northern Arabia, the first in *1261*/1845 and the second in *1264*/1847-48, and greatly impressed the learned circles of Europe with his wide-ranging knowledge of Arabia. In his travel account he dwelt upon such diverse topics as tribal migrations, inter-tribal relations, ancient history, local government, agriculture, irrigation, and archaeology and places of archaeological interest.

Wallin greatly admired the people of al-Jawf (which he visited in *1261*/1845), praising their hospitality and good manners.[4]

He begins his description of the area with the Wādi'l-Sirḥān, parts of which he had crossed to reach Dūmat al-Jandal. He mentions that among desert lands, Wādi'l-Sirḥān was one of the most fertile, and that whenever the rainfall was adequate, the surface was covered with pasture and foliage.[5] Describing al-Jawf, he says:

> The valley of Algawf has pretty nearly the form of a regular circle, surrounded on all sides by the chain of Gâl-Algawf, which rises, with almost equal height, about 500 feet above the level of the bottom. These mountains consist of sandstone, and descend with steep and rugged walls, partly covered with sand, towards the valley . . . In the last slope of this calcareous mountain lies the town of Algawf, in a semicircle, whose chord from W.N.W. to E.S.E. measures about 3,500 paces. Nearly in the centre of this semicircle, facing almost full N., there stands the old castle of Almârid, on a precipice of the limestone mountain, overlooking the town and the whole valley.[6]

Continuing his account of Dūmat al-Jandal, Wallin records:

> Most of the houses are provided with a room, generally separated from the other buildings, which is called the coffee-room, where strangers are lodged and guests receive their daily meals and coffee. The orchards and palm plantations are all laid out separately from the houses, at the foot of the limestone mountain, and extend more or less along the bottom of the valley. Each orchard is enclosed by a wall, dividing it from the others; and between these walls narrow lanes lead, serving as streets for the owners, and as channels for the water which night and day is led over the plantations from the springs. According to the extent of every orchard, part of this irrigation is allotted to it for a certain number of hours, which during the day are determined by the hours of prayer, and at night by the stars. As this irrigation, however, does not suffice for all plantations, every orchard contains

> generally one or more wells, which supply the defect of the springs. Water is easily found in this valley; nor is it so deep in the earth as in many other places in the neighbourhood, the average depth of the wells here not exceeding 10 fathoms. Besides the date-palm, which appears to be first here indigenous, almost every fruit, common to these climates, is cultivated in Algawf, though in small quantities, as figs, apricots, peaches, oranges, grapes, &c. The pomegranate, which in the villages along the Syrian pilgrim-road, and also in Negd, is cultivated with great success, does not thrive here. Vegetables are grown, but in very small quantities, and much less than in Negd. Between the trees in the orchards the inhabitants sow corn, the produce of which generally suffices for their wants, which is very seldom the case in other villages of the desert.[7]

Contradicting Neibuhr and Seetzen, who according to him mention al-Jawf as Jawf al-Sirḥān, Wallin says that he never heard any Arabs of this area adding "al-Sirḥān". Wallin states that the inhabitants of Dūmat al-Jandal, of various tribes, had closer links with Syria than with 'Irāq as far as trade was concerned, and that the itinerant traders visiting the town were exclusively from Syria.[8]

Giving a general description of the various divisions of Dūmat al-Jandal, Wallin writes as follows:

> Every quarter [which he also calls "sook" (Arabic *sūq* = market)] is surrounded by a wall . . .which divides it from the contiguous quarters on both sides; but within this wall the houses are disposed in no regular order, being often separated from each other by intervening small orchards and deep pits, formed in course of time by digging up clay or sand. The streets are narrow and irregular, without any pavement whatever; and in every quarter there is an open space, where strangers . . . first let their camels kneel down. In this place also, the people of the quarter generally assemble in the afternoon to pass the hour immediately preceding sunset in conversation about their mutual affairs.[9]

Wallin goes on to describe the 12 quarters into which the town was divided at the time.[10] In view of their importance in the history of Dūmat al-Jandal, we have included a summary of Wallin's description in an appendix (Appendix IV).

After naming the quarters of the city, Wallin deals with its history before Islam, during the reign of Ukaidir, the Islamic conquest, and the various military campaigns of the Muslims, subjects already discussed. He then moves on to describe aspects of life in al-Jawf, mentioning that the young studied the fundamentals of religious law and that reading and writing were generally more widespread than in the Turkish-ruled areas of Arabia. Describing the characteristics of the people, he says that they were very hospitable and civil hosts. He records that he had never met even an Arab tribe of the desert which outdid them in this respect. He also mentions their love of poetry, and that their gatherings were often accompanied by music.

Wallin observes that the dates in al-Jawf were of the best quality, better than those of Baṣra and Baghdād. In the course of his four month stay, dates were his "principal and almost only food", yet he never grew weary of them. He records that "there is a proverbial saying, that no dates are to be compared with those of Algawf and Teimâ; but while there is, strictly speaking, only one species in the latter town of an exquisite quality, every one of the numerous and different species which occur in Algawf is, almost without exception, the very best of its kind."[11] He notes 15 varieties regarded as being especially distinguished.

Wallin relates that the people of al-Jawf considered their town to be the centre of the world, calling it *Jawf al-Dunyā* (the belly of the world, as he translates it). He records that one could reach Damascus from al-Jawf in seven days, and he gives the watering places on the way as follows: "Nabk (one day from Algawf, in Wâdi Sirhân), Mureira, Ghurâb, Kurâkir, Alhâzim, Azrak, Bisrá (a village in Nukrát Alshâm), Hureirá, Ruzdaly on the pilgrims' way, Al'awig, Damascus."[12]

According to Wallin, the route from al-Jawf to Riyadh which was normally used crossed Jabal S̲hammar and al-Qaṣīm and took some twelve or thirteen days. However, if one crossed the Nafūd, the route took about seven days. The route to al-Madīna via Taimā' and al-Ḥijr (now called Madā'in Ṣāliḥ) took nine days, while the route to 'Irāq crossed what Wallin called "Nufood land" to the north-east of al-Jawf.[13]

WILLIAM GIFFORD PALGRAVE

The next traveller to al-Jawf, William Gifford Palgrave, was an Englishman. Palgrave left Ma'ān for Najd on *17 D̲hu'l-Ḥijja 1278*/16 June 1862 and arrived in Dūmat al-Jandal on *2 Muḥarram 1279*/30 June 1862. In the account of his journey to central Arabia, he provides a long description of al-Jawf,[14] which is quite accurate, although some of his other reports were sufficiently curious to suggest to H. St.J. B. Philby that he had failed to reach all the places that he claimed to have visited.[15] Nevertheless, it is clear that Palgrave did indeed visit al-Jawf. He was so weary by the time he reached it that it seemed to him a paradise. He praises the people for their friendliness, hospitality and courage, which may well have encouraged subsequent travellers to visit al-Jawf.

Palgrave was Jewish but became a Jesuit. After his Arabian journey, however, he converted to Protestantism. He travelled under the name "Saleem Abou Maḥmood-el-'Eys" and was accompanied by a Greek teacher from a school in Zaḥla in Lebanon, named Geraigiri, who travelled as "Barakāt-esh-S̲hāmee"; Palgrave presented himself everywhere in the guise of a Syrian doctor accompanied by a companion.

It is generally accepted that Napoleon III sponsored Palgrave's journey and that he was a spy sent by the French Emperor to determine the political situation in Arabia. The security of the countries close to the Suez Canal, the construction of which had started shortly before Palgrave's journey, was a matter of paramount interest to the French.[16]

Whatever his motives, Palgrave is no less important than Wallin for the detailed account that he gives of his visit to al-Jawf. He recounts the rigours of the journey and the sharp contrast offered by the beauty of Dūmat al-Jandal itself with its greenery and gardens. To illustrate this contrast he quotes an Arab poet who, while describing some similar locality in Algeria, says, "Like the Paradise of eternity, none can enter it till after having previously passed over hell-bridge."[17]

On the outskirts of Dūmat al-Jandal they were welcomed by two horsemen, both well-dressed in the fashion of the area, who came towards them from the direction of the town and saluted them. They laid out dates and a waterskin and invited Palgrave and his companion to partake of them. Hungry and thirsty, the travellers found the dates to be of the finest quality and the water fresh and cold.

The elder of the two men was about forty, tall and well-built, his appearance suggesting importance and intelligence. His name was Ghāfil al-Ḥabūb, leader of the Āl Ḥabūb of al-Jawf. The other, whose name was Ḍāfī, appeared younger and was less richly clothed, although he wore a sword with a silver hilt.

These two then disputed amiably between themselves as to which should have the honour of taking Palgrave and his companion to his house until, finally, Ghāfil al-Ḥabūb brought them home, overriding the younger man.[18]

Palgrave describes Ghāfil's house as follows:

> . . . Ghāfil halted before a portal high enough to admit a camel and rider, and, while we modestly dismounted to await further orders, entered alone the dwelling to see if all had been duly got ready for our reception, and then quickly returned, and invited us to follow him indoors.
>
> We traversed a second entrance, and now found ourselves in a small courtyard, three sides of which were formed by different apartments; the fourth consisted of a stable for horses and camels.[19]

Palgrave then entered the *qahwa* or coffee room, which, according to him, was similar to others found throughout the Peninsula:

> The K̇'hāwah was a large oblong hall, about twenty feet in height, fifty in length, and sixteen, or thereabouts, in breadth . . . The roof of timber, and flat; the floor was strewd with fine clean sand, and garnished all round alongside of the walls with long strips of carpet, upon which cushions, covered with faded silk, were disposed at suitable intervals.[20]

Palgrave describes in detail the method of making coffee and serving it. After the better part of a day spent in reception and rest, in the late afternoon his host took Palgrave and his companion to visit the orchards of the oasis.

Palgrave gives an account of the geographical limits of al-Jawf as follows:

> This province is a sort of oasis, a large oval depression of sixty or seventy miles long, by ten or twelve broad, lying between the northern desert that separates it from Syria and the Euphrates, and the southern Nefood, or sandy waste . . .[21]

Palgrave's journey to al-Jawf took place in summer when the fruits ripen, and he makes the following observations:

> The gardens of the Djowf are much celebrated in this part of the East, and justly so. They are of a productiveness and a variety superior to those of Djebel Shomer

> or of Upper Nejed, and far beyond whatever the Hedjaz and its neighbourhood can offer. Here, for the first time in our southward course, we found the date-palm a main object of cultivation; and if its produce be inferior to that of the same tree in Nejed and Ḥasa, it is far, very far, above whatever Egypt, Africa, or the valley of the Tigris from Baghdad to Basra can show. However, the palm is by no means alone here. The apricot and the peach, the fig-tree and the vine, abound throughout these orchards, and their fruit surpasses in copiousness and flavour that supplied by the gardens of Damascus or the hills of Syria and Palestine. In the intervals between the trees or in the fields beyond, corn, leguminous plants, gourds, melons, &c. &c., are widely cultivated. Here, too, for the last time, the traveller bound for the interior sees the irrigation indispensable to all growth and tillage in this droughty climate kept up by running streams of clear water, whereas in the Nejed and its neighbourhood it has to be laboriously procured from wells and cisterns.[22]

Continuing his description, Palgrave writes:

> The gardens just described are everywhere enclosed by high walls of unbaked brick, and are intersected by a labyrinth of little watercourses passing from tree to tree and from furrow to furrow. Among all their different kinds of produce one only is considered as a regular article of sale and export – the date; and from this the inhabitants derive a tolerable revenue, not, indeed, by traffic within the limits of the Djowf itself, where every one is supplied from his own trees, but from the price received in exchange at Tabook or Ḥā'yel, Damascus and Baghdad, for even so far is this fruit carried.[23]

Palgrave then describes Sakākā, and the villages in the area. He mentions that Sakākā was less fertile than Dūmat al-Jandal, but it was nearly its equal in population. According to him, the "united population" of the two localities, Dūmat al-Jandal and Sakākā, was "about thirty-three or thirty-four thousand souls", while the entire population of the region, in his opinion, was not more than "forty or forty-two thousand".[24]

He discusses at length the political situation of the area, how Ṭalāl Ibn Rashīd was able to conquer the area in the 1850s, and how he held sway over it at the time of Palgrave's visit.[25]

Palgrave mentions that the people of al-Jawf were originally of the Ṭayyi' tribe and that they were "tall, well-proportioned, [and] of a tolerably fair complexion, set-off by long curling locks of jet-black hair . . ." According to him, the people were "eminently good specimens of what may be called the pure northern or Ismaelitish Arab type . . ." He says that they were "a very healthy people . . . [who kept up] their strength and activity even to an advanced age". In his view, the "good and dry" climate and their "habits of out-door life" contributed to the maintenance of their health and vigour.[26]

The most distinctive characteristic of the inhabitants of al-Jawf, according to Palgrave, was their hospitality and he declares that there was no other area, even in Arabia, where the guest was "better treated, or more cordially invited to become in every way one of themselves. Courage, too, no one denies them . . ."[27]

On the second day in al-Jawf, Palgrave and his companion moved to a house near Ghāfil's where they were able to trade the articles which they had brought with them, such as coffee beans, cloth, knives and so on. Palgrave's desire to sell was as great as the desire of the people to buy, and some bought for cash, others on credit. Palgrave remarks that all credit was later paid off in full, something which had not always been the fortune of the merchants in the High Street in Oxford, in his experience.[28]

Palgrave and his companion clearly spent a pleasant time in al-Jawf; "invitations rained in on all sides", and they were never "left to dine twice under the same roof". The time came for them to resume their journey to Jabal Shammar, and although the people tried to persuade them to stay longer until the dates were harvested, they insisted on moving on. Eventually they departed and, for their southwards journey, were lucky enough to accompany a group of the Sharārāt who were also on their way across the Nafūd to Ḥā'il.

CARLO GUARMANI

Carlo Guarmani, an Italian expert on the Arabian horse, was Palgrave's immediate successor, making a journey to central Arabia and al-Jawf in *1280*/1864.[29] There was much interest in Europe at the time in Arabian horses, and Guarmani's expertise on the subject was demonstrated by his book *El Kamsa* (Rome, 1864). The title means "the five", a reference to the five strains of the Arab horse. Guarmani was commissioned to purchase Arab horses in Najd by Emperor Louis Napoleon III of France, and the Italian king, Victor Emmanuel II, although there may have been ulterior political motives, just as there appear to have been in Palgrave's case.

Guarmani's route took him through Taimā', east to Khaibar, 'Anaiza and Ḥā'il and then in a circuitous route to al-Jawf via Taimā' once more. He also claims to have been in al-Jawf during an earlier expedition. His journey began in Jerusalem, and he headed towards Ma'ān with a group of four Palestinian bedouin, who took him from tribe to tribe. This gave him the opportunity to compare the customs of the various bedouin groups – from al-Ta'marī, Banū Ḥamīda, Banū Sakhr and Sharārāt – with whom he came into contact. No European had previously had the opportunity for such close contact. Travelling in Arab dress and speaking Arabic fluently, he made precise observations on the subgroups and branches of the various tribes and noted the names of their *shaikhs*. He also gives in his book an account of the prevailing political situation in the area, particularly with regard to the Āl Rashīd and the tribes of north Arabia.[30]

In the course of his journey, Guarmani purchased three stallions from Ibn Rubai'ān, a *shaikh* of the 'Utaiba tribe, in exchange for 100 camels. He received a fourth horse as a gift – a mark of the good relations that he had established with the bedouin and their *shaikhs*. He passed through 'Anaiza as well as Ḥā'il, where he met Ṭalāl Ibn Rashīd, amīr of Jabal Shammar, staying three days as his guest before setting out for Taimā' to claim back the money he had left with his travel companions during his first visit to that town. He then returned to Ḥā'il a second time, and took his leave of the amīr once more to cross the Nafūd for Jubba and al-Jawf. He records that during this journey it had been raining for "thirty-six hours consecutively". When he reached his destination, he found the amīr of Ḥā'il encamped at Sakākā. Guarmani went to pay his respects and to offer his thanks for the amīr's help, for Guarmani expected, rightly, that this would be his final departure from the country. He was embraced by the amīr, who was clearly pleased to see him again. Guarmani then travelled back to Dūmat al-Jandal and from there, with a caravan of 182 men, women and children, travelled along the Wādi'l-Sirḥān. On their way they came under attack from a group of Ruwala bedouin, and one of his horses was shot dead. Guarmani finally reached Kāf at the north end of the Wādi'l-Sirḥān and, eventually, Damascus.[31]

Guarmani gives quite a long account of Dūmat al-Jandal:

> Giof-Amer is a small town of 6,000 inhabitants. It is built, as are most of the Nejd towns, of sun-baked bricks and layers of sandy earth made into a paste and also baked in the sun, and even some small rough chalk stones taken from the Hememie.
>
> The city wall, originally enclosing its fourteen quarters, having been destroyed, each quarter now possesses its own wall, like Aneizeh in Cassim, so that it might be said that Giof consists of thirteen villages (since El-Delhamie has been ruined), each one being united to the next by continuous groves of palm trees. But it is less confusing to call it a town, for there are plenty of villages in the vicinity.
>
> The palm groves, from El-Husseni to Diret-Cattab, are planted from west-north-west to east-south-east, and the rest from north-west to south-east. El-Husseni is the first district on the west-north-west, after it come Aal el-Garb, El-Zarai, El-Gait, El-Dera, and Diret-Cattab; in the broader portion of the strip turning towards south-east are El-Selman, El-Habbub, El-Seidan, El-Rakebin, El-Aladge, Ain-Zogba, Kadema and the ruin of El-Delhamie. These districts are almost in a straight line; the whole area occupies a space 50 m. march in length, but in no place more than 10 m. in breadth; the widest point is Diret-Cattab, 20 m. from El-Husseni and 30 m. from the ruins of Delhamie.
>
> The fort of Mared stands on a sandstone hill, to the south-west of Diret-Cattab, abutting on to its houses, and to the south-south-west of El-Dera, to which it is joined by a high wall. It is very ancient and very roughly built. Mared must have been rebuilt several times; the upper part is of baked earth, while the lower two-thirds are of stone. The original shape was rectangular, flanked by four round towers, with a higher tower in the centre from which the surrounding plains could easily be searched. The big tower has fallen into ruins, and the frequent additions, in order to hold it up, have spoilt its former shape.
>
> At Kadema there is a spring of the purest water. There are more springs, though slightly salt, to be found in the other quarters, and several wells have been dug in the palm groves and the fields, which produce the same crops as do the Gebel and Teime, as well as the *semek*.
>
> Giof-Amer takes its name from the deep valley (*Giof* in Arabic) in which it is situated, and to the Beni-Amer who constructed it on the site of the ruined Duma el-Gendalie, sometimes called Duma el-Gendal; this ancient town was conquered by Kaled-eben-Walid and became celebrated for the arbitration which decided the fall of Ali-eben-Abu-Taleb, the greatest Arab warrior of his day.[32]

In the course of his narrative, Guarmani makes a curious remark: "During the day I visited the town [Dūmat al-Jandal], with which I was already acquainted, for I had been there in 1851 [*1267-68*]."[33] It is unfortunate that Guarmani makes no other reference to this visit, and there is no explanation either of the purpose of this earlier trip or of the circumstances under which it was made.

CHARLES DOUGHTY

Charles Doughty is considered one of the greatest of European explorers in Arabia, travelling mainly in areas in the north of the Peninsula from *1293 to 1295*/1876-78. During this time he witnessed closely the life of the Arabs in the desert and subsequently described it in his book *Travels in Arabia Deserta*, with particularly precise and vivid accounts of his journeys. The book is a great work of literature in its own right. In the course of these travels, Doughty visited Ḥā'il, Taimā', Khaibar, Buraida, 'Anaiza, al-Ṭā'if and Jeddah, though not al-Jawf. (We have included his brief report since his book gives very useful information about some events in the history of al-Jawf.) In addition to the detailed description of his journey, he includes an account of the geology of the country, which he mapped as far as he could. He notes the presence of ancient flint implements that indicated very early settlement, and he provides an extensive description of the Nabaṭaean monuments at Madā'in Ṣāliḥ. He mentions ancient bronze coins that he found and refers to the *awsām* used by the tribes to brand their camels and livestock.

Few other travellers to central Arabia recorded the life of the bedouin in as much detail as Doughty did. He lived among them for two years, travelling with them and sharing their hardships. Doughty differs from other travellers in another respect: he travelled solely for the sake of travelling, putting his life at risk in the process.

Charles Doughty was born in England in *1259*/1843, and began his wanderings when he was 28, first in Europe and then in the Arab world. He initially went to Palestine and Syria, where he spent a year improving his Arabic. He joined a pilgrim caravan headed for the Holy Cities and remained with it as far as Madā'in Ṣāliḥ, from where he began his journey into central Arabia.[34] Whilst in Ḥā'il, Doughty heard about the Turkish campaign to al-Jawf which had ended in failure some years before his arrival in Arabia. This aroused his interest in the oasis and the surrounding areas. His account of the Turkish expedition has been given in the chapter *Al-Jawf and the Ottoman Rule*.

LADY ANNE BLUNT AND WILFRID SCAWEN BLUNT

Lady Anne Blunt was born in England of an aristocratic family, a daughter of William Noel, first Earl of Lovelace, and grand-daughter of Lord Byron the poet. She married Wilfrid Blunt in *1286*/1869, and after an initial visit to the Near

East, they undertook an expedition into the Syrian desert to purchase Arab horses.[35] On *16 Dhu'l Ḥijja 1295*/13 December 1878, they set out on a second expedition into the desert to buy yet more pure-bred Arab horses and arrived in al-Jawf about a month later. Lady Anne subsequently recounted their journey in her book *A Pilgrimage to Nejd*, of which a lengthy section is devoted to al-Jawf.[36]

The party, which set out from Damascus, consisted of six others besides Lady Anne and her husband. It included Muḥammad bin Aruk ('Arūq), the son of the ruler of Tadmur (Palmyra) in Syria, who had come to contract a marriage with a relative in Najd. Lady Anne made the journey in a mixture of European and Arab garb, wearing her ordinary travelling ulster (a long overcoat) covered by an *'abā'a*, and a *kūfiyya* in place of a hat. In Kāf in the Wādi'l-Sirḥān, they met some relatives of Muḥammad bin Aruk, who was acting as their guide, and learned that other relatives were living in al-Jawf. After travelling for five days through the Wādi'l-Sirḥān, they were raided by a group of Ruwala, who attacked Blunt and broke the butt of his gun over his head. When Lady Anne saw there was no escape, she cried to the nearest horseman "*Anā dakhīlak*," that is, "I am under your protection." On asking who they were, the Ruwala were informed by Muḥammad that they were "Franjīs" (i.e. Europeans), friends of the Ruwala *shaikh*, Ibn Sha'lān, and thus under his protection. At this, the raid abruptly and amicably ended, and the Blunts' company and the Ruwala sat and shared dates before parting.[37]

Lady Anne Blunt describes the Wādi'l-Sirḥān at great length, largely in an appendix to her travel book. She writes that the "Wady Sirhán is a curious chaotic depression, probably the bed of some ancient sea like the Dead Sea . . ."[38] Later, she comments:

> . . . the Wady was and is the great receptacle of the plain, and corresponds pretty closely with its neighbour, the still existing Dead Sea, while the Wady-er-Rajel entering it from the north, holds towards it the position of the Jordan. . . . The abundance of water obtainable from its wells along a line extending 300 miles from the frontier of Syria, to within 200 of the frontier of Nejd, points out Wady Sirhan as the natural high road of Northern Arabia, and such it must from the earliest times have been.[39]

After a journey of eight days from Kāf through the Wādi'l-Sirḥān, the group arrived at Dūmat al-Jandal, where they met emissaries from the town and were invited to the castle of the Amīr, who was absent at the time. His deputy, Dawwās, received them, and they were given a meal including meat of which, Lady Anne relates, she had never tasted the like before. The Blunts believed that it was antelope. They were probably right; it could have been oryx.[40]

Dawwās informed them of the necessity of obtaining permission from the Amīr, Jawhar, who was at Sakākā, if they wished to continue their journey to Ḥā'il. They stayed in Sakākā for three days with Muḥammad's relatives (and this period concluded with the marriage of Muḥammad to one of his relatives). There the Blunts visited Amīr Jawhar and presented him with gifts of fine clothes; for his part, Jawhar arranged for a guide to lead them across the Nafūd to Ḥā'il.

The Blunts found the Nafūd "interesting beyond . . . [their] hopes". Lady Anne described her first encounter with the Nafūd as follows:

> At half past three o'clock we saw a red streak on the horizon before us, which rose and gathered as we approached it, stretching out east and west in an unbroken line. It might at first have been taken for an effect of mirage, but on coming nearer we found it broken into billows, and but for its red colour not unlike a stormy sea seen from the shore, for it rose up, as the sea seems to rise, when the waves are high, above the level of the land. Somebody called out "the Nefûd", and though for a while we were incredulous, we were soon convinced. What surprised us was its colour, that of rhubarb and magnesia, nothing at all like the sand we had hitherto seen, and nothing at all like what we had expected. Yet the Nefûd it was, the great red desert of central Arabia.[41]

Elsewhere she expresses her feelings as follows:

> The transition from the smooth hard plain to the broken dunes of the Nefûd is very startling. The sand rises abruptly from the plain without any transition whatever; and it is easy to see that the plain is not really changed but only hidden from the eye by a super-incumbent mass. Its edge is so well defined that it is hardly an exaggeration to say that with one foot a man may stand upon the Hamád, and with the other on the Nefûd; nor is there much irregularity in its outline . . . No traveller can see this desert of red sand for the first time without acknowledging its individuality. It is as little like the ordinary sand dunes of the desert, as a glacier is like an ordinary snow field in the Alps. It seems, like the glacier, to have a law of being peculiar to itself, a law of increase, of motion, almost of life. One is struck with these in traversing it, and one seems to recognise an organism.[42]

After a journey of two days from al-Jawf, they reached the wells of al-Shaqīq in the Nafūd, where they filled their water skins. From this point began the hard part of the journey, five days or more across the Nafūd without any wells whatsoever. In the meantime, their guide recounted frightening tales of those who had perished in the desert, and how a whole Turkish military detachment of some 500 men had died of thirst in the Nafūd on their way from Ḥā'il back to Syria.[43]

JULIUS EUTING

Julius Euting was a German scholar who made a journey in the northern part of the Peninsula in *1300-01*/1883-84 and subsequently wrote a book about his travels, a chapter of which is devoted to al-Jawf,[44] with a section on the Turkish expedition, which has already been described above.[45] Euting's account of al-Jawf is extremely detailed and is in the form of a daily diary, extracts of which have been translated from the original German and are given below. Euting travelled with an Alsatian, Charles Huber, parts of whose account are also given further on. Huber's account, however, is less detailed than Euting's work.

Euting describes the Jawf region as follows:

> The oasis of el-Gyôf [al-Jawf], taken in a broad sense, includes a number of villages which are located to the north-east in isolated valleys, up to one day's journey away. . . . These are the villages of Skâkah (8,000 inhabitants), Ḳârah (1,000 inhabitants) and Ṭuwêr (about 300 inhabitants). The settlements of Sehârah, Gun (?) Hâsiah, Gâwah, and Mu'eizen, mentioned by other travellers, seem to be deserted. The principal place, however, is el-Gyôf [Dūmat al-Jandal], with a concentration of about 12,000 inhabitants. . . . Until the coming of Shammarī control, the twelve sections (Sûḳ; plural, Aswâḳ) of the town resembled individual fortifications, in a constant state of siege.[46]

Euting says that the population of Dūmat al-Jandal was a mixture of different tribes. Although the harsh measures of 'Ubaid and Ṭalāl of Jabal Shammar had brought security and order to the area, there were neither any trades or crafts, nor any stores or bazaars.

His description of the town continues:

> Narrow alleys between high garden walls and groups of houses provide no glimpse of the interiors. Almost all the better houses have a tower, 30-40 feet high, with scallops, loopholes and gun embrasures. Formerly, they would be furnished as the position of defence and refuge in case of war. Nowadays, they are only decorations, and signs of affluence.[47]

Euting goes on to describe Qaṣr Mārid and other defences of the town.

Euting and Huber arrived in Dūmat al-Jandal on Tuesday, *6 Dhu'l-Ḥijja 1300*/9 October 1883 and went directly to visit the governor's palace, where Jawhar, the governor – whom the Blunts had met five years previously – welcomed them. For their part, they presented Jawhar with fine sabres and other gifts. Euting relates that they seated themselves among the assembled guests and were questioned exhaustively about their journey. Meanwhile, incense was passed to them, and they were given sweetened coffee followed by real coffee, and large sweet dates with liquified butter and flat bread. After this reception, Euting left the gathering in order to refresh himself:

> In the courtyard I let Maḥmûd [Euting's servant] pour several pails of water over my head, and also shave my head. Then I dressed in clean clothes. I felt like a newborn, and then I went outside the Ḳaṣr in order to do some sketching. First, however, I laid down on the ground and stretched out – O God, how great – and fell into a deep sleep.[48]

That evening, dinner consisted of extremely peppery rice and mutton. The next day, 10 October, at 8 a.m. Huber and his former guide, Muḥārib, made an expedition to Sakākā, Qārā and Ṭuwair, while Euting stayed behind in al-Jawf, to be told once more the story of the abortive Turkish occupation of al-Jawf, which he had heard in Kāf. During the evening, in Jawhar's Qahwa, the discussion centred on the troubles being faced at the time by Ottoman Turkey.

On Thursday, 11 October, Euting received news of the collapse of his friend

Muḥaiṯhal, outside his house. The man had a high fever, and Euting decided to visit him that afternoon. As his house, in Sūq al-Hawīdī, was rather isolated, Jawhar insisted that Euting go by donkey. Euting's party included a man who bore his sabre, his servant Maḥmūd, who carried the medicines, and two soldiers following. Euting describes his trip as follows:

> From the Ḳaṣr the road went down steeply to the broad valley. Between endless garden walls and past ancient sandalwood trees, we now and then passed groups of people, who greeted us politely. On the way, Maḥmûd showed me a square which had a small hillock in the centre. This is the place where the Turks had planted their cannon [in *1289*/1872], and where the discussions between Ibn Raschîd and Muhammed Sa'îd Pascha had taken place. After a half hour's ride we arrived at Muḥêtil's house, which was hidden in a shadowy and well-watered garden. Upon entering I found my travel companion in a very serious condition; without shirt or head-dress, just wrapped in a cloak, he was lying semiconscious on a clay bank, unable to rise and too tired to speak. He answered my greeting with a nod of acknowledgement. I talked to him encouragingly and began to examine him. He had a very high temperature as well as cough, his pancreas was very sensitive and his belly felt hard; obviously he was suffering from typhoid fever. Therefore, I administered a Calomel powder, and for emergencies I left an additional dose with him. I instructed his son in how to administer six quinine powders during the next three days, after which he could come to me for more. . . . While coffee was being prepared, I wanted to visit the well-kept garden. Besides palm trees there were fig trees, vines, pomegranates, apricots, peaches, cucumbers, melons, and assorted greens.[49]

That evening, for the first time in his life, Euting ate camel meat. He remarks that, boiled in water, it was not particularly different from the meat of goat or sheep, except that it was rather tougher, and darker in colour. Coffee after the dinner was taken at the house of a camel dealer, Ḥusain, outside the *qaṣr*.

Starting the description of the events of the next day, he says:

> Friday, 12 October 1883. A strong wind that started during the night blew our possessions all over the roof. The watercolour sketch I had made of Gyohar [Jawhar] very quietly was so well received by the model that from then on he was very eager to sit for me. He liked the light treatment I had given his dark skin and was very happy that I had painted him with his pipe.[50]

It surprised Euting how fast news in the desert spread, for later he found that knowledge of the portrait had reached widely scattered places. The amīr of Ḥā'il was to ask to see the portrait and criticized it for making Jawhar appear too light-skinned.

This was the day of the Ḥajj. The following day being the 'Īd al-Aḍḥā, a camel was killed in preparation for the occasion, and everyone "suddenly displayed a great urge for cleanliness . . . [Men had] their heads washed [and] their beards trimmed, and had changed into clean clothes."

On the morning of the 'Īd itself – Saturday, 13 October – Jawhar held a reception at his Qahwa and received the greetings of the people. Large copper plates were brought in, piled high with camel meat on mounds of rice, the diameter of each plate approaching one metre.

Euting and Huber had intended to depart on Sunday, 14 October. However, they encountered difficulties in hiring camels, and their own camels were a day away, grazing in the Nafūd. They feared a five-day waterless ride, for they were not certain of being able to use the wells at al-Shaqīq; so they were particularly concerned to carry sufficient water for this length of time. Ultimately, they were able to give a final shape to their travel arrangements, though not to the full satisfaction of their host, Governor Jawhar.

In the afternoon of that day, Euting and Huber made a trip up to the cliffs at the edge of the valley. On their way back, they saw a remarkable sight. Here is how Euting describes it:

> On the level part of a square between the walls of a garden, an unusual dance was being performed. With a distance of 20 paces between them, a row of about a dozen girls was facing a row of the same number of boys. Between the two rows, two girls were dancing without any head-dress, their loose hair combed towards the back and their eyes turned modestly towards the ground.[51]

They were dancing to the tune of an accompanying song, although Euting could not understand the words. He was told that the dance was called La'b al-Daḥḥa. Euting writes that J.L. Burckhardt had recorded a similar dance among the bedouin. He also mentions other reports of such dancing, adding that he was later informed that in Syria the dance was known as "Dabka".[52]

Early next morning – Sunday, 14 October – with the camels well-watered, Euting and Huber set out to cross the Nafūd for Ḥā'il and left al-Jawf behind them.

CHARLES HUBER

Charles Huber, a French traveller of Alsatian origin, made two journeys to Arabia, the first in the summer of *1295*/1878 when he reached Ḥā'il, and the second in *1300-01*/1883-84, when he returned with Julius Euting, as described above. Huber and Euting visited al-Jawf together on that occasion, but later parted company. Huber's book *Journal d'un Voyage en Arabie (1883-1884)* was published posthumously in *1308*/1891. The book is really a compilation by his editors from his daily journal of his second Arabian journey. His book pays special attention to the measurement of distances and orientations as well as keeping an accurate record of his own movements by the hour and even by the minute. In addition, he included observations on the people and rulers of the country. As the book is so detailed a journal of factual observations, for the non-specialist reader it can be somewhat tedious and exasperating. We give here a number of translated extracts to give a general impression of his account:

> Wednesday, 3 October (1883) *En route* for al-Jauf. At 8:20 a.m. left Kāf to proceed towards S.30°E.; at 8:45 a.m. towards S.45°E.; at 8:55 a.m. to S.70°E.; at 9:05 a.m. to S.80°E.; at 9:08 a.m. to S.85°E.; at 9.25 a.m. to N.80°E.; at 9:30 a.m. to S. 80°E.; at 10:22 a.m. to N.E.E.; at 11:19 a.m. arrived at Etsery [Ithra].[53]

His diary for 6 October reads:

> At 0:08 a.m. set out to S.70°E.; at 0:20 a.m. to S.50°E.
> In one hour 4,350 paces.
> For seven hours arid gravel desert.
> At one hour began to meet the first hills of the Nafud; here there is a place where in 1877 a battle occurred between the Shararat and the Suqūr; the latter came to make a raid (razzia) on the former, and 90 men were cut down.
> Stayed there for five minutes.[54]

As described in Euting's account above, Huber left Dūmat al-Jandal for Sakākā on the morning of 10 October. His account reads as follows:

> At 11.35 a.m. a white *tell* (15 metres in height) which is to be found half way between al-Jawf [Dūmat al-Jandal] and Sakaka . . . at 3:50 p.m. reach Sakaka. I enter by a street with Suq M'adel on the left and Suq Qrous in front of me. . . . Sakaka has an air of freshness, cleanness and prosperity; the palm trees are beautiful and their produce is of the same quality as that of the dates of al-Jawf [Dūma].[55]

At Sakākā, Huber made a number of topographical notations:

> Thursday, 11 October
> Climbed up to the Qasr [Za'bal?] this morning but it was impossible to determine the angle of the sun as it rose behind clouds. . . .
> Sakaka has about 10,000 souls; 6 suqs I was told. . . .
> The densest concentration of the population is found in the north, to the east of the qasr.[56]

He continues his diary for the day, noting down his observations *en route* to Dūmat al-Jandal:

> At 7:15 in the morning left Sakaka . . . at 7:59 a.m. at the far edge of the town. From 7:59 a.m. to 9:00 a.m., 4,900 paces.
> At 9:00 a.m. arrived at Ātoueir [al-Ṭuwair] at the qoulban [wells] of Shaykh Hamed, the back of whose house adjoins the rock which supports the qasr [Qal'at al-Ṭuwair]; the base of the rock is covered by inscriptions. . . .
> From the summit of the qasr at Ātoueir, the following observations were made:

Qasr of Sakaka	168°
Summit of Umm el Çeqour	153°
Summit of Yabes	144°
Summit of Lagāiṯ	140°
Qārā area	31°[57]

Huber describes Dūmat al-Jandal in the same manner, with a complete lack of attention to the town and its people and their way of life, merely logging his movements precisely:

Saturday, 13 October
Youm el-'Aïd, the great public feast in front of the qasr. . .
At 3:25 p.m. I leave to visit the North of el-Gouf; at 3:45 p.m. at the Qasr Marid; at 3:55 p.m. Shârâ is on my left at 400 metres . . . at 4:10 p.m. I am at the edge of Gouf.
At 4:20 p.m. arrive at the enclosure wall that the people call these days the amara ['imāra] of Okeïdir [building of Ukaidir], and made the following observation: Shârâ at 1 kilometre or 1 km. 200 m., towards 256°. . . .[58]

Unfortunately, his account of al-Jawf is sparse throughout, in contrast to that of his companion, Euting, which is far more detailed and useful. However, it is possible that, had Huber not met his death[59] before he had time to write up his travels, he might have provided a fuller account of his travel to al-Jawf.

Charles Huber and Euting left Dūmat al-Jandal for Ḥā'il on Sunday, 14 October – the time of starting from the *qaṣr* precisely recorded by Huber as 8:30 a.m.

BARON EDUARD NOLDE

The last European to travel to al-Jawf and to Ḥā'il and beyond in the 19th century was an Austrian aristocrat of the Hapsburg Empire (which broke up in 1918), Baron Eduard Nolde. The purpose of this visit, according to him, was to experience the difficulties and hardships of such a journey but, like those who went before him, he had an ulterior motive. It is said that he worked for the Secret Service of the Russian Czar. He himself mentions in his posthumously-published travel account in German[60] that he was carrying a letter of introduction for Muḥammad Ibn Rashīd, the amīr of Ḥā'il, from the Ottoman Sulṭān. It can be inferred from the ceremonious reception accorded him in Ḥā'il that he was on some important political mission.

The adventurous Baron was already a widely-travelled man before coming to Arabia in 1893 at the age of 44, having been to South America, Africa and the Middle East, amongst other places. His account makes interesting reading, owing to the exceptional circumstances in which he undertook the journey and to the lively and thrilling narrative. He displays a good knowledge of the history of the Middle East and the political circumstances of the time.

Having made preparations for his journey with consummate skill, Nolde, accompanied by a party of 36 servants, 40 camels, six horses, and several mules and donkeys, set out from Damascus on 1 January 1893. On the special orders of the Ottoman Sulṭān, a mounted escort consisting of 26 Kurdish soldiers, with their additional 25 camels, accompanied him to Dūmat al-Jandal.[61]

When this awe-inspiring caravan, following the Wādi'l-Sirḥān route, reached the outskirts of Dūmat al-Jandal, Nolde sent his trusted 'Irāqī guide, Nasroullah, to Jawhar, the Āl Rashīd governor of al-Jawf, to announce his visit. Jawhar, in the meantime, learning of the arrival of so many riders and soldiers, and doubting their intentions, decided to check before allowing them to enter the castle. When Nolde and his party arrived at the gate of Qaṣr Mārid, he found it locked. On enquiring about the whereabouts of Nasroullah he was told that he was inside the castle.[62]

Nolde writes that after a short while "Nasroullah appeared on the platform of the tower overlooking the gate and explained to me that both he and his two soldiers had been disarmed and were apparently being held hostage in the castle; he begged me to be careful . . ."[63] Continuing his narrative of the events when Jawhar personally appeared on the tower, Nolde writes as follows:

> I suggested to him . . . an agreement on the following basis: he had not the least to fear from me as I was undertaking a peaceful journey to the Nedjd with the main objective of visiting Djohar's own master, Emir Ibn-Raschid. The presence of a few Turkish soldiers was easily explained because so far my journey had taken me through dangerous, lawless country and such an escort had been necessary. Of course, now that I had reached the lands of the Emir, this was no longer essential and the soldiers would be sent back to Damascus. . . . This would occur before my own departure from Djouf. . . . If Djohar wished to show me his own goodwill and good intentions, he should free Nasroullah, and I would prove my trust by immediately coming to the castle alone. . . .
>
> I have never found the Arabs to be untruthful or treacherous. . . . Without further delay Djohar declared that if I were to publicly give my word in front of his and also my own people to carry out my suggestion, he would agree. This was done. . . . Nasroullah and the two soldiers were set free and sent to me. A few minutes later I stepped into the castle [alone]. . . . Standing directly behind the gate, which was quickly closed behind me, Djohar, surrounded by his most important people, was expecting me. . . . [After the routine embrace] I was escorted to a large reception room and coffee hall. On the way we passed the gallows and torture chambers. . . . My lips had hardly touched the cup [of coffee] when Djohar gave the order to throw open the gate immediately. This happened almost with theatrical speed, for barely another minute had passed when more than 50 of my armed men filled the hall to be served with coffee. At that moment the most cordial relations between me and my camp, on the one side, and Djohar, the fort, and the town of Djof, on the other side, were struck.[64]

Nolde briefly describes Dūmat al-Jandal and his stay of four days there as follows:

> For Arabia, Djof is quite a considerable town with at least 10,000 to 12,000 inhabitants. Water is good and plentiful, gardens beautiful and extensive, and the dates of Djof rightfully have the reputation of being the finest in the world because of their flavour.
>
> I had no difficulty in Djof in purchasing as many sheep, calves and chickens as I liked besides also various other provisions for my journey. Djohar and I alternately held great feasts and everyone, my people, the soldiers and the fort staff lived most opulently. . . .[65]

For his journey from al-Jawf to Ḥā'il, Nolde opted for the route passing through Ḥayyāniyya, instead of the one through the oasis town of Jubba, which was followed by the other Europeans travelling from al-Jawf to Ḥā'il. His party, accompanied by the two guides provided by Jawhar, started their journey through the Nafūd on 28 January 1893, the Kurdish soldiers already having left in the night for Damascus. Their first night in the Nafūd was spent at Khaw'ā. Nolde describes Khaw'ā and the wildlife of the Nafūd:

> . . . here at Hoa it seemed, especially by the shine of the setting sun, that blood had been poured over the ground on which one trod, the desert and the surrounding cliffs. A little later the cries of the animals, drawn here because of the water, seemed pretty uncanny in this wild terrain: the wailing of the jackals, the shrill laughter of the numerous hyenas and, finally, the roaring of the leopards which echoed far in the night.[66]

Nolde keenly observed the sudden temperature changes in the desert. He records the following:

> I have never experienced either in Mexico, in the Himalayas, in the Caucasus, or in upper Armenia, such drastic and sudden temperature drop as that which we were registering here in the Nefud. As evidence I quote from my travel diary the following, by no means the only, example: 1st February, at 12 o'clock noon the thermometer reads + 5.5, rises only very slowly because of the cold winds; at 2 o'clock in the afternoon + 6, at 4 o'clock + 7.5. Now the mercury suddenly rises to 25.5 until 7 o'clock in the evening (shortly before sunset);[67] after which, even more suddenly, that is within the first 15 minutes after the sun has disappeared, it falls by 33 C., i.e. to -8 which became -11 towards morning. It was like this every day, generally with strong cold winds which, as so often in the desert, could start up just as suddenly as they ceased.[68]

Nolde witnessed a phenomenon rarely seen in the Nafūd. He records that on the 2nd day of February "there was a heavy snowfall covering the Nefud far and wide with several inches of snow, so that it resembled a Russian winter landscape rather than what one expects to find in the middle of Arabia." The bedouins told him they had heard that in that part of the Nafūd snowfall did occur, though very rarely, and that the last time had been about 50 years previously.[69]

ARCHIBALD FORDER

Archibald Forder was an English Protestant lay preacher, who had lived for some time at Karak in Jordan and who, in *1318*/1900, was residing at Jerusalem when he determined to make a winter trip to north Arabia. Forder's book on his life and travels in the Near East[70] includes a long section on al-Jawf and Dūmat al-Jandal,[71] which was the last point of his itinerary. He introduces his account of his Arabian journey with the following words:

> Previous failures had not discouraged me sufficiently to make me give up the idea of reaching the district and town of the Jowf, the most important and largest town in Northern Arabia.[72]

Although Forder's visit to al-Jawf is discussed here at length, this is not for any inherent historical value – it adds little to our knowledge of the area beyond what other travellers had observed – but because his expedition differs from the journeys of the others in its remarkable aim: propagating the Christian faith in, as Forder puts it, the land and birthplace of Islam, that is, Arabia. To achieve this, he carried with him four cases filled with copies of the Bible translated into Arabic as well as other publications calling people to Christianity. As for his personal necessities, these were restricted to the basics.

Forder knew Arabic, and he dressed in Arab clothes during his journey. He first came to Kāf in the Wādi'l-Sirḥān, which was then under the authority of Ibn Rashīd, and then proceeded to Ithra, where some of his belongings were stolen. However, on his return nearly three months later, he found that the *shaikh* of Kāf had regained his possessions from the thieves and had kept them for him. Eventually, the caravan that he was travelling with reached Dūma, about which Forder gives the following first impression:

> Before us in the distance could be seen the palms of the Jowf, and rearing itself above the palms was the fine old circular castle, no one knows how old. . . . About four in the afternoon we entered this secluded desert-bound town, and were soon lodged in the spacious guest-room of the three sons of the chief, whose name was Johar – or Aboo Amber, i.e. the father of Amber.[73]

Turning back to the scene of his arrival at the town, Forder writes:

> Soon after sighting the old castle I saw men, women and children coming out to meet their relatives and friends that were arriving from the desert journey with its dangers and fatigue. For a time all attention was taken off me by the greetings, salutations, and welcomings of the long-separated relatives. But soon it was discovered that a stranger was with the party, and for him there was no word of welcome.[74]

Then he continues with a description of the town and its people:

> I was much interested in the old mud towers that I saw on all hands as I entered the Jowf from the north. I found out afterward that they were for the purpose of defence. It was impossible to get any pictures of them because of the constant eyes on me. We rode along the side of this beautiful oasis in the desert. The beauty and prosperous condition of the thousands of palms impressed me. The Jowf as a town is about two miles long, and on an average, a quarter of a mile wide. . . . I learned from the chief, later on, that there were about forty thousand inhabitants in the Jowf, all told. The buildings, except the castle, are all of mud and sand brick, dried in the sun; some of the houses have three stories, built, of course, in a very primitive style. The roofs are all flat, protected by a wall about waist high. The women, there secluded, frequent these roofs, as they are free from all observation. . . . Most of the houses are doorless, owing to the scarcity of wood. The people live mostly out of doors, in the hottest months seeking the shade of the palm groves and gardens, and in the cooler months basking in the sun on the sand. Rain is scarce in the Jowf; they told me three falls a year were about all they had. The water supply is good, drawn up by camels from springs

> deep down in the earth. There are some warm, sulphurous springs there, used by the people for ablution purposes. I saw no shops in the town, and on asking how the people got the necessities of life, such as clothing, cooking utensils, coffee, etc., they told me they relied on caravans that came from Mecca, Baghdad, or Damascus.[75]

Forder goes on to mention how the men of al-Jawf made their *'abā'as* or cloaks, their head-ropes, saddle-bags and carpets. He bought an al-Jawf *'abā'a* for three-and-a-half dollars. He says that the *'abā'as* from al-Jawf were greatly prized in Palestine and Syria. He then goes on to give a description of the gardens of Dūmat al-Jandal and what grew in them from fruit trees and vegetables, in addition to date palms:

He then continues:

> Many of the men smoke, not all. I was agreeably surprised to find so many of the men and boys able to read intelligently, and also to see that many of them possessed watches. The ignorance of outside affairs surprised me. Absence of posts, telegrams, newspapers, and railways keeps them isolated. . . . The government of the Jowf, as also Ithera and Kaf, is in the hands of Abdul-Azeez-Ibn Rasheed, who resides at Hayel, a city six days' journey from the Jowf. He is represented in the Jowf by a very influential old man named Johar, whose fame I had heard some years before. Just, liberal, open-hearted, and firm, he is feared and respected by all that know him or have anything to do with him.[76]

Forder then describes his first visit to Jawhar, his reception and how Jawhar asked the purpose of his journey. Forder replied: "To see the Jowf and its people, also to sell God's Word to any that will buy."[77] This visit took place during the month of *Ramaḍān 1318*/January 1901, but in spite of this, Jawhar ordered dates to be brought for Forder, saying: "We are fasting and dare not eat. You must be hungry; don't be ashamed; 'kool wahud ala deenoo' – every one to his religion. Eat."[78]

ALOIS MUSIL

Alois Musil made a number of journeys to the northern and north-western parts of the Arabian Peninsula as well as to the desert areas of Syria and 'Irāq. These journeys are of particular importance for the detailed observations that he made of the country, its people, its antiquities and its history. Musil was to become Professor of Oriental Studies at the University of Prague in Czechoslovakia, where he wrote several of his major studies on Arabia and its northern neighbours. His series of journeys, which provided him with the material on which his books were based, were made between *1313 and 1333*/1896 and 1915. His books on Arabia were published in English under the auspices of the American Geographical Society, although his earlier works had appeared in German.

Musil began his journeys in Arabia in the period *1313-20*/1896-1902 with an exploration of the district known in ancient times as Arabia Petraea and corresponding roughly to eastern and southern Jordan. After this, Musil turned his attention to the Syrian desert, undertaking journeys there in *1326*/1908, *1330*/1912 and *1333*/1915. The information thus collected formed the basis of his book on Palmyra (Tadmur). Another journey made in *1328*/1910 was to produce a study of the northern part of al-Ḥijāz. Over the period *1330-33*/1912-15, Musil also explored a fourth region, beginning at Palmyra and going to the middle reaches of Euphrates and the central part of ʿIrāq. He continued his explorations into northern Najd, the desert of Samāwa, and southern ʿIrāq. His 1908-09, 1912 and 1914-15 expeditions to the northern parts of Arabia, including al-Jawf region, during which he spent much of his time with the Ruwala and other tribes, were to provide him with the material for his book *Arabia Deserta*.

Musil's work was of a dual nature. He tried to record the current conditions of the northern parts of the Arabian Peninsula as he saw them and also to assemble material for maps to be prepared later. His accounts are accompanied by a journal relating to his travels. He paid a great deal of attention to correlating ancient and modern place names. His historical accounts and commentaries on the places that he visited provide a comprehensive overview of the main civilizations which have flourished in the region over successive historical periods, and they are still of considerable value to scholars studying Arabia.

Although he travelled extensively in north Arabia, Musil was unable to give in his book *Arabia Deserta* very detailed descriptions of al-Jawf, where he first arrived in *1327*/1909. At that time there were serious disturbances following the decline of the power of the Āl Ras͟hīd and the attempts by different forces, including the Āl S͟haʿlān, to gain control of the oasis. As a result of this, Musil's freedom of movement was restricted in Dūmat al-Jandal. Although he took a number of photographs of historical significance, he was not able to produce – unlike his works on other areas to which he made exploratory travels – a scholarly study of the antiquities of al-Jawf. Nevertheless, he gives a detailed account of the history of al-Jawf, using the Assyrian sources, Greek and Latin texts, and the works of the Arab geographers and historians of the Islamic period. As a result, his study constitutes a major research tool for the student of the history of the area.

In *Rabīʿ I 1333*/January 1915, Musil made a further visit to al-Jawf and described the area in some detail:

> At 1.28 p.m. we sighted al-Gowf, or Dûmat al-Ǧandalijje, as this settlement is rightly called. Far off beyond the arid, grey plain, almost on the southern border of the basin, appeared the dark green of plentiful date palms, in welcome contrast with the bare rosy slopes over which we were toiling. Among the palms the high yellow walls and towers of the settlement gleamed in the sunshine. Looming above the walls and palms was the main tower of the Mâred surmounted by four smaller but substantial towers; to the right of the Mâred on the top of a slope rose the quadrangular tower of al-Farḥa and north of it the smaller al-Frejḥa.[79]

During his stay in Dūmat al-Jandal, Musil visited the governor, ʿĀmir, who had been appointed by Nawwāf Ibn Sha'lān, and made enquiries about ancient inscriptions found in the town:

> I hastened to look for 'Âmer, Nawwâf's regent, and finally found him in a large room that had no windows, sipping his coffee by the western wall, near a corner in which he could not be shot from the door. After greeting me, he seated himself in the foremost place and awaited my interrogations. I handed him the message from Nawwâf and then directed him to show me all the inscriptions there were in al-Ǧowf in languages that the people did not understand. He answered that while deepening the well in the Mâred tower they had found a number of marble slabs bearing strange inscriptions, but that nobody seemed to know what had become of them. He also told me that in a street near the Mâred there was set in the wall a stone with strange writing. I told him that I was going to look at the stone and that meanwhile he must see to it that those marble slabs were found. On squeeze paper, with a brush and water, I made an impression of the Nabataean inscriptions on the stone in the wall and then, as there was no wind in the narrow street, I let the paper dry on the stone . . .[80]

Musil was brought two fragments of Nabaṭaean inscriptions, but the people were unable to locate any others, and he assumed that the other inscriptions had been taken up north to Syria, or that they had been built into the walls of Qaṣr Mārid during repairs.[81]

On the Jawf region as a whole, Musil makes the following observations:

> The settlements of al-Ǧowf (the basin, the cavity) are situated, as the name itself implies, in a basin extending from the west northeastward. This basin is about one hundred kilometres long, about ten kilometres wide, and forty to fifty meters deep. The run-off flows down the surrounding heights into it and remains throughout the year on the underlying rocks under a layer of coarse sand and gravel, emerging at many places in the form of springs and elsewhere filling wells from four to twenty meters deep. In the deepest wells the water is quite tepid and somewhat salty. It is, of course, the abundance of water that accounts for the presence of men and settlements at al-Ǧowf. The largest settlement is called by the inhabitants Dûmat al-Ǧandalijje, while the appellations al-Ǧowf and al-Ǧûba refer to the entire basin with the remainder of the settlements.
>
> Dûmat al-Ǧadalijje comprises about four hundred dwellings and is subdivided into ten precincts: on the west, Sûḳ al-Ṛarb, Sûḳ as-Sḥara, Sûḳ al-Wâdi, Sûḳ aš-Šâjbe, Sûḳ Mâred; north of these, Sûḳ Sarrâḥ, Sûḳ ar-Rḥejbijjîn, and Sûḳ 'Alâǧ; south of the Mâred, Sûḳ al-Ḫadne, and finally, Sûḳ an-Nžejb. In the neighbourhood of the town are small gardens: an-Nwêḳîṭ, al-Wusî'a, Ǧâwa, al-Ḳnejje, 'Ujûn Kibre, 'Ajn aš-Šejḫ, ar-Ršejde, etc.[82]

Musil was quite sure that there had been a large Nabaṭaean settlement at Dūmat al-Jandal but was unable to locate the graveyard which he believed to have existed. He was told that old caves in the area of Mārid were unearthed, but that nothing was found in them, and they were covered up immediately after their discovery.[83]

Departing from al-Jawf for the Nafūd, Musil saw the valley one more time and records the sight:

> Beyond al-Ğerâwi, where stand a few etel trees, we ascended the slope enclosing the basin al-Ğowf and for the last time enjoyed the view presented by the residence of Emir Nawwâf eben Ša'lân. Violet is the dominant colour of the environs of the Mâred. To the north, near the settlement of al-Wâdi, there are two dome-like elevations composed of three horizontal strata, the lowest being red, the middle blue, and the highest white. The tops of the palms looked quite dark, the drifts of sand around us shone yellow, and the heated air over all the landscape trembled, so that every remoter object seemed to loom through a mysterious veil. However, the most beautiful impression was that conveyed by the rounded peaks of the rugged and disconnected range of al-Ḥamâmijât to the northeast of al-Ğowf. At 3.40 they were a golden brown at the base, violet about the center, and a clear pink at the top.[84]

CAPTAIN S.S. BUTLER AND CAPTAIN L. AYLMER

On *9.12.1325*/9 January 1908, Captain S.S. Butler accompanied by Captain L. Aylmer, set out for al-Jawf from Baghdād in a caravan of merchants and with a bedouin guide. The two English officers were taking leave from their posts in East Africa and had decided to use the opportunity presented to return to England via the Arabian Gulf, Baghdād, al-Jawf and Damascus: the Baghdād-al-Jawf-Damascus route was not at that time familiar to Europeans. The account of their travel was written by Butler.[85]

Butler and Aylmer's guide, a bedouin from the Bishr section of the 'Anaza tribe, insisted that the travellers wear Arab dress for the desert journey, a precaution which Butler considered wise in retrospect. In the course of their journey towards al-Jawf, they spent some time with the 'Anaza, moving on two occasions with them as the bedouin searched for pasture for their animals and for water. In their company, as the tribe made these migrations, Butler counted some 250 tents. Subsequently, they came on a group of Ṣulaib tribesmen, one of whom guided them to al-Jawf. In the course of their journey towards al-Jawf, they several times saw gazelle in herds, and numerous lesser bustard and sand-grouse, as well as the odd partridge and hare. Huntsmen in the area would use not only guns but hawks, of which the bedouin had many.

Like other travellers before them, Butler describes al-Jawf as he saw it:

> The district of El Jauf is a large hollow, which gives one the impression of having once been a big lake, or inland sea. The ground in this big depression is very rocky, and is covered with great flat layers of purple and reddish sandstone. The town of El Jauf, that takes its name from the district, lies on the west edge of this basin, in a hollow about 2 miles broad; but coming from the east the first town to be reached in this hollow is not El Jauf, but Skaka, which is about 30 miles east of El Jauf. Skaka is an oasis, consisting of many thousand date palm trees, which yield the most delicious fruit, and about three or four hundred houses, all built of mud, but solidly constructed, and many of them having two storeys, and all, of course, with the flat roofs of the East.[86]

Compared with earlier travellers, Butler estimated the population of Sakākā lower, at 1,700. He says that at the time of their visit, Sakākā appeared to be the more thriving town, with merchants from 'Irāq living there. He writes:

> Water there is in abundance from wells both sweet and brackish, the crops of barley, such as they are, and the date palms being watered from the latter by means of the "jarrad", or skin bucket, drawn up by oxen or camels, and emptied automatically. This method of watering the crops is common all over Eastern Turkey-in-Asia and Northern Arabia. The water is carried off by means of little channels to the date gardens and patches of barley. The sweet-water wells were about 50 to 60 feet to the water. At the north end of the town there is an old castle perched on a rock, called Gasr el Zabl, of, I think, ancient Arabic origin, which, the inhabitants told us, is now sometimes used as a prison. Arriving at Skaka total strangers, and not pretending to be Mohammedans, we were, nevertheless, at once put up and treated with the utmost hospitality by a meshedani . . . and all we met in Skaka treated us in an equally hospitable way.[87]

Al-Jawf at the time was under the Āl Rashīd of Ḥā'il, and the governor was Faiṣal Ibn Rashīd, who had only recently arrived in Dūmat al-Jandal, where he resided in a castle. Given permission to depart from Sakākā to Dūma, Butler and Aylmer travelled to Dūmat al-Jandal and were received there by the Amīr.

> Arrived at El Jauf, we were taken at once to the emir's castle, a large building made of mud and stones, and about 90 yards long by 50 broad, with walls about 40 feet high and a tower at each corner about 60 feet high. It is built entirely for defence, there being no windows, and the door is in an angle of the wall, and strongly barricaded. We were shown into a waiting-hall and given coffee, and after a minute or so were led out into a courtyard (where we saw the two old cannons of English make mentioned by Lady Anne Blunt) and up a staircase to inverview Feysul Ibn Rashid.[88]
>
> . . . We found Feysul Ibn Rashid sitting in a low room, the roof of which was supported by wooden pillars. All round the sides of the room were spread carpets, on which sat his viziers and members of his court. He himself sat behind the open fireplace, the opposite side of the room to the door, and on our entrance, rose and came forward to greet us.[89]

Butler and Aylmer spent five days in Dūmat al-Jandal altogether, and Butler gives the following comments on the town as he saw it:

> The town runs north-west and south-east, and lies in a belt of date palms about 2½ miles long by half a mile broad. At the north end is the old castle Maarid and the "suk" or bazaar, and at the south end is the emir's castle, a building made in the middle of the last century. The "suk" is not worthy of the name, being merely a cluster of houses round the castle, and there are no shops there, all buying and selling being done in the private houses of the merchants, both here and at Skaka. In neither place was there anything to be bought when we were there, except a little coffee and flour, there being no sugar, rice, tea, onions, or anything at all in the shape of luxuries to be had anywhere from the merchants.[90]

Butler estimated the population of Dūma at only 2,500-2,750, far lower than Palgrave or Forder had suggested in earlier years. The houses that Butler and Aylmer saw in Dūma were well-constructed in mud, some two storeys high. He also comments, like other travellers before him, on the fine quality of the water from wells in al-Jawf and of dates produced in the area. In Dūma he found that the principal industry was the manufacture of *'abā'as*, saddlebags, headstalls for camels, and swords. The *'abā'as* of Sakākā were also excellent, and like Forder before him, Butler states that these were famed from Baghdād to Damascus. After their visit to al-Jawf, Butler and Aylmer departed north-westwards along the Wādi'l-Sirḥān to Azraq and the Ḥawrān. Their account was subsequently presented as a lecture to the Royal Geographical Society in London, and the published article was accompanied by a map of their route prepared by Aylmer. During the discussion at the lecture, the possibility was raised of the practicality of a railway line from Suez to Baṣra via al-Jawf,[91] and, although not the principal objective of Butler and Aylmer's expedition, it would seem, the question was to arise again over a decade later in British quarters.

---

1. George Forster Sadleir, *Diary of a Journey across Arabia (1819)*, Cambridge, England, Falcon-Oleander, 1977.
2. See U.J. Seetzen, "Beyträge zur Geographie Arabiens", *Monatliche Correspondenz zur Beförderung der Erd-und Himmels-kunde* vol. 46, November 1808, pp.386-88.
3. Ibid.
4. See Wallin, pp.24-45.
5. Ibid., p.25.
6. Ibid.
7. Ibid., p.26.
8. Ibid., pp.26-27.
9. Ibid., pp.25-26.
10. Ibid., pp.27-30.
11. Ibid., p.35.
12. Ibid., pp.36-37.
13. Ibid., p.37.
14. See Palgrave, vol. 1 pp.46-86.
15. Zahra Freeth and H.V.F. Winstone, *Explorers of Arabia from the Renaissance to the End of the Victorian Era*, London, Allen & Unwin, 1978, pp.158, 174-75.
16. Ibid., p.157.
17. Palgrave, vol. 1 pp.46-47.
18. Ibid., pp.47-49.
19. Ibid., p.49.
20. Ibid., pp.49-50.
21. Ibid., p.56.
22. Ibid., pp.58-59.
23. Ibid., pp.59-60.
24. Ibid., pp.60-61.
25. Ibid., pp.61-65.
26. Ibid., pp.65-66.
27. Ibid., p.67.
28. Ibid., pp.70-71.
29. For an account of his travel, see Guarmani.
30. Freeth and Winstone, pp.195-223.
31. Ibid.
32. Guarmani, pp.101-02.
33. Ibid., p.59.
34. Freeth and Winstone, pp.228-36.
35. Ibid., pp.270-71.
36. See Blunt, vol. 1 pp.111-51.
37. Ibid., pp.102-07.

38. Ibid., p.88.
39. Ibid., vol. 2 p.511.
40. Freeth and Winstone, p.274.
41. Blunt, vol. 1 pp.155-56.
42. Ibid., vol. 2 pp.514-16.
43. Ibid., vol. 1 pp.174-75.
44. See Euting, vol. 1 pp.123-40.
45. See pp.99, 115–16, above.
46. Euting, vol. 1 p.124.
47. Ibid., p.125.
48. Ibid., p.130.
49. Ibid., pp.135-36.
50. Ibid., p.137.
51. Ibid., pp.139-40.
52. Ibid., p.140.
53. Charles Huber, *Journal d'un Voyage en Arabie (1883-1884)*, Paris, Société asiatique, 1891, p.35.
54. Ibid., pp.39-40.
55. Ibid., p.43.
56. Ibid., p.44.
57. Ibid., pp.44-45.
58. Ibid., p.48.
59. Huber was killed by his own guides at Rābigh on 29 July 1884 while he was on his way to Jeddah.
60. See Baron Eduard Nolde, *Reise nach Innerarabien, Kurdistan und Armenien, 1892*, Brunswick, Friedrich Vieweg, 1895.
61. Ibid., pp.5-6.
62. Ibid., p.11.
63. Ibid., pp.11-12.
64. Ibid., pp.12-14.
65. Ibid., pp.14-15.
66. Ibid., p.17.
67. On 1 February the (natural) day in the centre of the Nafūd is ten hours and fifty-two minutes long. On this date, the sunrise time at Sakākā and Ḥā'il, according to the present Sa'ūdī Arabian standard time, is 7.11 and 7.00, respectively, whereas the sunset time is 5.59 and 5.55, respectively!
68. Nolde, pp.18-19.
69. Ibid., pp.19-20.
70. See Archibald Forder, *Ventures among the Arabs in Desert, Tent, and Town*, Boston, W.N. Heartshorne, 1905. His account of travel to northern Arabia is given at pp.151-233.
71. Ibid. pp.206-33.
72. Ibid., p.151.
73. Ibid., p.205.
74. Ibid., p.206.
75. Ibid., pp.206-08.
76. Ibid., p.209.
77. Ibid., p.211.
78. Ibid., p.212.
79. Musil, *Arabia Deserta*, p.467.
80. Ibid., p.470.
81. Ibid., p.471.
82. Ibid., p.472.
83. Ibid., p.474.
84. Musil, *Northern Neğd*, p.2.
85. Butler, pp.517-35.
86. Ibid., pp.524-25.
87. Ibid., pp.525-26.
88. Ibid., p.526.
89. Ibid., p.527.
90. Ibid., pp.529-30.
91. Ibid., pp.534-35.

25
Later Travellers

DOUGLAS CARRUTHERS AND G.E. LEACHMAN

In the years preceding World War I, there were a number of European visitors to north Arabia. Among them were Douglas Carruthers,[1] who travelled extensively in northern Arabia in 1909 to do some mapping work, and Captain G.E. Leachman,[2] who travelled from Baghdād to the camp of the amīr of Ḥā'il in the spring of 1910. However, neither provides any new information on al-Jawf, although their explorations added to the knowledge of the scholarly world regarding the area as a whole. On the eve of World War I, two more English travellers visited north Arabia. One of these, Gertrude Bell, crossed north Arabia to Ḥā'il in *1332*/early 1914, but although she passed across the east Jordan desert via the wells at Bāyir and down into the Wādi'l-Sirḥān, she decided not to pass through al-Jawf.

CAPTAIN WILLIAM SHAKESPEAR

The second traveller of the same year, Captain William Shakespear,[3] made his way to al-Jawf in the course of a journey to Cairo from his former appointment in Kuwait as British political agent. Like Butler and Aylmer before him, Shakespear was using the opportunity of his leave to visit Arabia, in response to an earlier invitation from His Late Majesty King 'Abd al-'Azīz, then amīr of Najd.

Shakespear set out from Kuwait with a small caravan and travelled first to Riyadh by way of Zilfī and al-Ghāṭ. After visiting the late King in Riyadh and holding disucssions with him, Shakespear headed north towards the Rashidī capital of Ḥā'il, before continuing on to al-Jawf. He arrived at Dūmat al-Jandal on *1 Jumādā II 1332*/28 April 1914 and found the Jawf region under the control of 'Āmir al-Mushawrib, the deputy of Nawwāf bin Nūrī al-Sha'lān of the Ruwala tribe. Shakespear held discussions with him and presented him with a message from the amīr of Kuwait. Shakespear also gave him a medicine chest as a personal gift. 'Āmir al-Mushawrib and his English visitor then had a shooting competition using guns that Shakespear had with him.[4] On 1 May 1914, Shakespear set out again on the next stage of his journey. While on its way, the party came under attack but Shakespear managed to reach the camp of *al-Shaikh* 'Awda bin Ḥarb Abū Tāyih, the "chief of the Abu Thiya (Tawāyiha) section of the Ḥuwaiṭāt" tribe, and from there, after another march of several days, 'Aqaba and the Egyptian frontier.[5]

In the winter of the same year, after the outbreak of World War I, Shakespear returned to Arabia, this time to the court of His Late Majesty King ʻAbd al-ʻAzīz as official British representative. However, a short time later – on 24 January 1915 – Captain Shakespear was killed while accompanying the King and his army at Jurāb during a campaign against Ibn Rash̲īd.[6]

Although Shakespear never wrote of his Arabian travels, he kept a diary, which has been accessible to scholars. While travelling he also took numerous photographs, a number of which are now held by the Royal Geographical Society in London. Some are of al-Jawf.

ʻABD ALLĀH (H.ST.J.B.) PHILBY

ʻAbd Allāh Philby's journeys to Arabia began with his mission to Riyadh to meet the late King ʻAbd al-ʻAzīz in *1336*/1917-18. Landing on the eastern coast to march to Riyadh, he went west to reach the Red Sea and became the second European to cross Arabia from coast to coast. Subsequently, he became well-acquainted with the Āl Saʻūd and resided for many years in Saʻūdī Arabia. By publishing the accounts of his numerous journeys and explorations, he added much to the geographical knowledge of the Arabian Peninsula.

His expedition to al-Jawf[7] took place in *1340*/1922 and was made in the company of Major A.L. Holt. Philby at the time was a British political official based in ʻAmmān and was interested in the Wādi'l-Sirḥān and al-Jawf from the standpoint of his political duties. The British in the area had no clear idea at this time of the circumstances prevailing in al-Jawf in the aftermath of the fall of Ḥā'il to the Āl Saʻūd the previous summer. Major Holt accompanied Philby specifically to study the terrain and the possibility of extending a railway from ʻAmmān across the desert to ʻIrāq.

Philby's party set out with cars and camels, making a false start and getting no further than Kāf and Qurayyāt al-Milḥ at the north end of the Wādi'l-Sirḥān. They set out again on *4 Ramaḍān 1340*/2 May 1922 for Kāf and took the route along the Wādi'l-Sirḥān to al-Jawf. They passed through various oases in the Wādī, but the insecurity of the area forced them to leave the valley for the final part of their journey, so that Philby had no chance to describe the southern part of the Wādī. Nevertheless, he gives more information for the northern part than do some earlier travellers.

At the time Philby and his party reached Dūmat al-Jandal (on 20 May), a rebellion by Ibn Muwaish̲īr against the Āl S̲h̲aʻlān rulers in favour of King ʻAbd al-ʻAzīz had just started at Sakākā, and Philby's movements were consequently restricted. However, in Dūmat al-Jandal they had no difficulty. As Dūma was well-known from the reports of the earlier travellers, Philby contented himself with giving only a brief description of the town, where they stayed for three days, but he took a number of photographs.[8] About Dūmat al-Jandal he writes:

> . . . I need only mention the great mediaeval (Arab) fortress of Qasr Marid built on a conmanding [sic] eminence with recently constructed mud towers replacing

> their stone predecessors; the copious well-springs, which provide slender running streams for the irrigation of the oasis; the ruins of the central hamlets of Suq and Suq al-Hattab, which would seem to be of the same period as Marid itself, the houses being built of uncemented stone slabs; and the species of red marble abundant in the neighbourhood, out of which they make coffee-mortars. There is no town properly so called, but a population of about 5000 souls is distributed over some dozen hamlets.[9]

Philby and his companion Holt were invited by Sulṭān bin Nawwāf al-Sha‘lān to Sakākā, where they remained his guest for ten days. Philby describes Sakākā as follows:

> Sakaka, like Jauf, has no town but consists of a considerable area of palm groves dotted here and there with pretty hamlets, each peopled by one of the many units which compose the population of some eight thousand souls. It has practically supplanted Jauf as the political and commercial capital of the Juba district, and it appears to be in frequent trade communication with Mesopotamia, whence it draws the bulk of its supplies of foreign commodities – piece-goods, rice, coffee, tea, and sugar being the chief articles of import. The oasis is picturesquely situated within a semicircle of fantastic sandstone hills, on one of which, close to the oasis and detached from the main range, stands the old castle of Za‘bal, reminding one of the mediaeval fortresses perched on eminences along the Rhine.[10]

However, Philby could not examine the castle because it was occupied by Ibn Muwaishīr's supporters.

The party was allowed to continue towards ‘Irāq. On 2 June, they left Sakākā for ‘Ar‘ar, eventually reaching Karbalā' on 11 June. Within a month of leaving the oasis of al-Jawf, Philby heard that the late King ‘Abd al-‘Azīz Āl Sa‘ūd had taken control of it.

MAJOR A.L. HOLT

Major Holt, as we have seen, accompanied Philby to al-Jawf in the spring of *1340*/1922 with the specific objective of examining the terrain and the area generally to assess the possibility of linking the coast of Palestine with ‘Irāq by railway. Holt published a report on his conclusions as well as a map of the journey made by him and Philby from ‘Ammān to ‘Irāq.[11] The circumstances of the period made the question of improving the speed of communication between the eastern parts of the British Empire and the Mediterranean a matter of considerable importance to Britain. With the technology of the time, it took a steamship between 27 and 31 days to carry the Baghdād mail to London, while an aircraft flying across the desert route from Baghdād to London took a little less than six days. It was hoped to extend the air service to India so as to make it possible to cover the distance from London to British India in less than seven days. However, in 1922, aircraft could not carry loads heavy enough to compete with railway transport, and, although motor cars could be used, the railway was preferred. The railway that Holt discussed seemed to him practicable as far as construction was concerned, but his scheme was not universally thought to be feasible. The idea was not new. The concept of a railway to 'Irāq, along the Euphrates, had been discussed in the past, although Wilfrid Blunt had pointed out obstacles after his first-hand acquaintance with the Syrian desert and northern Arabia. The question of building of a railway across northern Arabia had been raised in the aftermath of Butler and Aylmer's expedition in *1325*/1908, but the proposal was set aside until after the First World War when Holt made the survey with Philby. The British by this time were dominant in 'Irāq, eastern Jordan (Transjordan) and Palestine, and the establishment of a railway link between the Mediterranean and the Arabian Gulf had become of renewed interest to them. It would have been necessary for al-Jawf to be a major station on the railway, but the fact that King 'Abd al-'Azīz was not receptive to the idea caused its postponement once more. Nevertheless, British machination concerning al-Jawf and the possibility of a railway between Jordan and the Gulf continued[12] for some time before being overtaken by the development of modern communications.

F.V. WINNETT AND W.L. REED

All the travellers to al-Jawf mentioned till now used camels to reach the area and to travel to other parts of the Peninsula. With the advent of cars and aircraft, many others made journeys to Arabia, though lacking the adventurous spirit of the earlier travellers. However, one exception is the journey of Professor F.V. Winnett, a Canadian from the University of Toronto, and his American colleague, W.L. Reed, who carried out an expedition into the regions of al-Jawf, Taimā', al-'Ulā, Madā'in Ṣāliḥ, upper Wādi'l-Sirḥān and Ṭuraif in *1381*/1962 to conduct an archaeological and epigraphical survey. The author assisted them in their stay in al-Jawf, during which they visited a number of archaeological sites and photographed the antiquities. They discovered many ancient graffiti and copied a substantial number of inscriptions from the rocks, written in Minaean, Thamūdic and Nabaṭaean, adding greatly to our knowledge of ancient al-Jawf. Subsequently, these two scholars published their studies in a valuable illustrated work, *Ancient Records from North Arabia*, which describes their travels and interprets the inscriptions they located.

---

1. See Douglas Carruthers, *Arabian Adventure: To the Great Nafud in Quest of the Oryx*, London, 1935.
2. See G.E. Leachman, "A Journey in North-eastern Arabia", *The Geographical Journal* vol. 37, March 1911, pp.265-74.
3. For his biography, see H.V.F. Winstone, *Captain Shakespear: A Portrait*, London, Jonathan Cape, 1976.
4. William Henry Shakespear, Private Diary, Shakespear's Personal Papers with H.V.F. Winstone; cf. Winstone, *Captain Shakespear*, pp.173-75.
5. Winstone, *Captain Shakespear*, pp.175-82.
6. Ibid., pp.203-08, 210.

7. See Philby, "Jauf and the North Arabian Desert", pp.241-59.
8. These are presently held by the Royal Geographical Society in London.
9. Philby, "Jauf and the North Arabian Desert", pp.252-53.
10. Ibid., p.255.
11. A.L. Holt, "The Future of the North Arabian Desert", *The Geographical Journal* vol. 62, October 1923, pp.259-71.
12. See United States. Consulate (Jerusalem), *Politics in the Syrian Desert* [Report, dated 25 August 1931, Presented to the U.S. Department of State].

PART SEVEN

THE PEOPLE OF AL-JAWF PROVINCE

26
The Settlements of the People of al-Jawf Province

While studying the ancient and recent history of al-Jawf, it is appropriate to mention the names of the major tribes in the area today and the localities they principally inhabit. Because of the harsh conditions in the past, the centripetal forces were always at work and individuals stayed with the group. Accelerating economic development in recent decades has changed the way of life for a majority. As early as 1912 the late King ʻAbd al-ʻAzīz laid down the foundations of his ambitious programme to settle the roaming tribes. As a result, out of the many tribes there has emerged in the towns and villages a new, unified, co-operative community, which, notwithstanding the former divisions between one tribe and another, is living today in perfect harmony, bound together to some degree by old tribal allegiances, but for the most part by common traditions, customs, interests, religion, language and not least by an abiding sense of national identity. By the grace of God these unifying factors increasingly contribute to social, cultural and economic co-operation. They are discernible throughout the Kingdom, making for brotherhood and cooperation in a citizenry participating vigorously in the advance of Islamic and international civilization, to attain its rightful position among the comity of nations.

The tribes mentioned here, however, were not necessarily the first or the only people to settle in the area. As we have seen, both the area of Sakākā and the town of Dūmat al-Jandal have been continuously inhabited for several thousand years. In this brief account we mention only the larger groups present today. Other significant families are known, and none has been deliberately ignored. Each has its rightful place in society. We should keep in mind what God Almighty said:

> Verily the most honoured of you in the sight of God is (he who is) the most righteous of you (al-Qur'ān, 49: 13).

Or, what Muḥammad, the Prophet (P.B.U.H.), said:

> There is no preference for an Arab over a non-Arab, except on the basis of piety.

In other words, an individual should be judged by how far he follows the path of Islam in the prescribed manner and acts righteously, as stated by someone in the following words:

> Islam is my father; I have no other father.
> I take pride in Islam when others boast of Qais and Tamīm.

Similarly, one who understood the magnificent role of Islam in changing the life of the Muslim and raising him to the level of a hero has expressed this idea by comparing Salmān al-Fārisī, a non-Arab Muslim in the Prophet's (P.B.U.H.) time, with Abū Lahab, a prominent Makkan leader who belonged to one of the strongest and noblest Arab tribes. He says:

> Islam has elevated the rank of Salmān the Persian,
> And polytheism has put down Abū Lahab, the high-born.

SAKĀKĀ

Although numerous ancient inscriptions in the area around Sakākā attest to the antiquity of settled life, yet the written material does not help us in determining when or how the first permanent settlement in what is now Sakākā was established. We list below the different quarters of Sakākā and the villages associated with it, along with the names of the major clans and families occupying them.

1. al-Ḍil' quarter: inhabited by Āl Ḍuwaiḥī Ibn Mukhtār al-Quraishī al-Jabrī of the Banū Khālid.
2. al-Shu'aib quarter: inhabited by Āl Ḍuwaiḥī Ibn Mukhtār al-Quraishī al-Jabrī of the Banū Khālid.
3. Āl Juḥaish quarter: inhabited by Āl Juḥaish of the Aslam of Shammar.
4. al-'Alī quarter: inhabited by Āl 'Alī Ibn Mukhtār al-Quraishī al-Jabrī al-Khālidī. A number of other tribes also inhabit this quarter, as well as the other quarters mentioned above.
5. al-Dir'ān quarter: inhabited by Āl Dir'ān of Āl 'Alī Ibn Mukhtār al-Quraishī al-Jabrī al-Khālidī.
6. al-Kurai' quarter: inhabited by Āl Kurai' of Shamlān of 'Anaza.
7. al-Ma'āqila quarter: inhabited by the sons of Mu'aiqal bin Ziyād bin 'Ayyāsh of al-Dahmash of 'Anaza, as well as other families belonging to various tribes.
8. al-Rāshid quarter: inhabited by Āl Rāshid of al-Asā'ida of al-Rūqa

belonging to ʿUtaiba, as well as other families belonging to a number of tribes.

9. al-Nuṣair quarter: inhabited by al-Nuṣair of Marʿaḍ of al-Ruwala.
10. Āl Maṭar quarter: inhabited by the families of al-Ḥabbāb and al-Ḥamdān of al-Sirḥān and the families of ʿUbaid al-Bīr of al-Tūmān of Shammar.
11. al-Shalhūb quarter: inhabited by Āl Shalhūb of al-Masnad of al-Sirḥān, as well as many other families of various tribal affinities.

QUARTERS OF THE NEW BUILDING SCHEMES SOUTH OF SAKĀKĀ These new residential schemes have been created in response to the growth of the town of Sakākā and the increase in the number of inhabitants of the area. It is not possible to state the exact tribal origins of the inhabitants nor to give the names of the major families. They comprise all the groups in the Jawf region generally.

AL-LAQĀʾIṬ This area is inhabited by a number of subdivisions of the two tribes of Āl Ḍuwaiḥī and Āl ʿAlī Ibn Mukhtār al-Quraishī al-Jabrī al-Khālidī, and the Zamīl subdivision of Sinjāra of Shammar, and other families of various tribal affiliations.

AL-ṬUWAIR Although in the past al-Ṭuwair represented a distinct entity with its definite geographical boundaries, today it can be regarded as a south-western extension of Sakākā, and at the same time an extension of Qārā to the north-west. This is a result of rapid and widespread growth and proliferation of various services. Al-Ṭuwair is inhabited by numerous families.

QĀRĀ Until the recent rapid increase in the population of the region as a whole due to the settling of bedouin, Qārā was regarded as the biggest of the villages in the Jawf region. Latterly, Qārā has become a large town, whose residents are of diverse tribal affiliations. However the major tribes represented are: a) al-Dughmān of al-Ruwala, and b) al-Sirḥān.

DŪMAT AL-JANDAL

1. Ghaṭṭī quarter: inhabited by al-Wārid, al-Mazyid and al-Daushaq. These came from Jubba.
2. al-Jarʿāwī quarter: inhabited by al-ʿĀbid of al-Ajibba.
3. Khadhmāʾ quarter. This includes a number of quarters:
    i. Āl ʿAbd Allāh quarter: inhabited by Āl ʿAbd Allāh of al-Rāshid of al-Sirḥān, as well as several families deriving from other tribes.
    ii. Āl Hudaib and al-Habbās quarter: inhabited by Āl Hudaib of al-Rāshid of al-Sirḥān.
    iii. al-Ḥamādā quarter: inhabited by al-Ḥamādā, a subdivision of the Maṭāwaʿa of al-Sirḥān.

   iv. al-Ḥunaibīṣ quarter: inhabited by al-Ḥunaibīṣ of al-Sirḥān.
   v. al-Mar'ī quarter: inhabited by al-Mar'ī of al-Sirḥān.
   vi. 'Ilāj quarter: inhabited by a subdivision of al-Aslam of Shammar, and al-Dandan of 'Anaza.

   Khadhmā' quarter is also inhabited by a number of families from al-Ajibba as well as al-Khābūr family and al-Rummān family.

4. al-Sumaiḥān quarter: inhabited by a subdivision of al-Ḥumaiḍān of Banū Tamīm.
5. al-Ruḥaibīn quarter: inhabited by a subdivision of al-Ḥumaiḍān of Banū Tamīm and other families from a number of tribes. It is also inhabited by a subdivision of al-Dirbās of al-Rūqa, of 'Utaiba, as well as al-Farhūd of Shammar, and al-Ḥawās, who came from Ḥā'il.
6. al-Sa'īdān quarter: inhabited by Āl Sa'īdān, who came from 'Irāq.
7. al-Salmān quarter: inhabited by Āl Salmān of al-Jarbān of 'Abada of Shammar.
8. al-Sarrāḥ quarter: inhabited by Āl Sarrāḥ of al-Jarbān of 'Abada of Shammar.
9. al-Ḥabūb quarter: inhabited by Āl Ḥabūb of al-Jarbān of 'Abada of Shammar.
10. al-'Abbās quarter: inhabited by Āl 'Abbās of al-Shafī' of al-Majīd of al-'Abādila of 'Anaza, as well as by the family of al-Qaḥm of al-Dahāmisha of 'Anaza, and al-Ḥuzaim of 'Anaza, and al-Ḥarīṣ, who came from Ḥā'il.
11. al-Sūq quarter: a large quarter, which should be classified according to the following subdivisions:
   i. al-Dir' quarter: inhabited by Āl Dir' of the Banū Khālid and also by al-Mubārak and al-Ghaṣība.
   ii. Saḥīm quarter: inhabited by Āl Saḥīm of the Banū Khālid.
   iii. al-'Arjān quarter: inhabited by al-'Arjān of al-Zaqārīṭ of Shammar.
   iv. al-'Āmir quarter: inhabited by al-'Āmir and al-Mish'al, who came from Najd.
   v. al-Buḥair quarter: inhabited by al-Mubārak and al-Ghaṣība.
   vi. al-Wādī quarter: inhabited by a number of families who came from al-Rass.
   vii. al-Darāwīsh quarter: inhabited by families of al-Darāwīsh, who came from al-Shiffa in al-Qaṣīm.
   viii. Jawā quarter: inhabited by families derived from al-Dir'.
   ix. al-Buḥairāt quarter: inhabited by al-Ṣulaihim of the Banū Tamīm, al-Hadhlūl of Banū Khālid and al-Huṭaibil of the Ruwala.

   A number of families from other tribes are also present in al-Sūq quarter.

12. al-Gharb quarter: this comprises a number of subquarters:
   i. al-Qa'ayyid quarter: inhabited by Āl Qa'ayyid of al-Asā'ida of al-Rūqa of 'Utaiba and al-Mahāwish of al-Rāshid of al-Asā'ida of 'Utaiba as well as al-Sa'dūn of al-Aslam of Shammar, al-Rizq of al-'Afrān of al-Shamrūkh of Shammar, al-Rāshid of al-Sabīla of al-Abū Sa'd of Shammar, and al-Budaiwī of al-Khuzaim of Āl Shibl (who came from

'Irāq).

ii. al-Futaikha quarter: inhabited by a subdivision of al-Sa'īdān, who came from 'Irāq.

iii. al-Ma'īn quarter: inhabited by a number of families of Banū Tamīm, as well as the Ṣāyil of al-Khābūr of al-Sirḥān.

iv. al-Judai' quarter: inhabited by Āl Judai' of Banū Tamīm and al-Miqbal of al-Dirbās of 'Utaiba.

v. al-Farrās quarter: inhabited by Āl Farrās, who came from Najd.

vi. al-Zāri' quarter: inhabited by Āl Zāri', who came from al-Madīna.

vii. al-Bādī quarter: inhabited by Āl Bādī of al-'Adwān, who came from al-Balqā' in Jordan.

viii. al-'Arjān quarter: inhabited by Āl 'Arjān of Shammar.

ix. Saḥāra quarter: inhabited by al-'Afrān and families of al-Sabīla derived from Shammar.

x. al-Ḥasan quarter: inhabited by Āl Ḥasan, who came from Rawḍa Sudair.

xi. al-Sabīla quarter: inhabited by al-Sabīla of Shammar and al-Dāḥis of al-Muḥārib of al-Shamrūkh of Shammar.

xii. al-Ḥaṣīnī quarter: inhabited by al-Ḥaṣīnī of Shammar.

xiii. al-Musayyib quarter: inhabited by al-Musayyib, who trace their descent to al-Dahāmisha of 'Anaza and came from al-Qubaisa.

xiv. al-Darbī quarter: inhabited by a number of families who came from al-Rass.

xv. al-Mudhhin quarter: inhabited by al-Mudhhin of al-Sirḥān.

xvi. al-'Uḍaibāwī quarter: inhabited by a number of families of al-Sabīla of Shammar, and al-Jibāl of al-Ḥasan.

QUARTERS OF THE NEW RESIDENTIAL SCHEMES IN DŪMAT AL-JANDAL As a result of the introduction of new settlement projects in response to the growth of the town and its general and cultural expectations, the number of tribal groups and sub-groups in these residential schemes has increased correspondingly. The natural consequence of such large-scale settlement of the people from different tribes is that the residents in these schemes are completely mixed, with no tribal group having a noticeable majority.

AL-ZABĀRA The village is of agricultural significance, with its expansion based on an approved settlement plan. Most of its inhabitants are of al-Mar'aḍ of al-Ruwala.

AL-NAẒĀYIM The village is populated by al-Ma'abhal of al-Mar'aḍ of al-Ruwala.

ZALLŪM The village is inhabited by a number of branches of al-Ruwala, Shammar and other tribes.

AL-SHUWAIḤIṬIYYA The village is inhabited by al-Dughmān of al-Ruwala, and others.

ṢUWAIR A village of noted agricultural importance with its expansion deriving from a settlement plan. It is inhabited by a number of subdivisions of al-Qa'āqi'a of al-Ruwala.

HUDAIB This is a growing village of noted agricultural potential, inhabited by al-Furja of al-Ruwala.

HADBĀN This village of increasing size is inhabited by al-Furja of al-Ruwala.

AL-'AMMĀRIYYA This village is inhabited by a number of families of various tribes.

AL-SULAIMĀNIYYA This village is inhabited by al-Ḍubayyān and clans related to them of al-Dahāmisha of al-'Ammārāt of 'Anaza.

KHAW'Ā This is a village inhabited by al-Dughmān of al-Ruwala.

'ADHFĀ' This is a village inhabited by al-Shamrūkh of Shammar.

HIJRAT AL-SĀDA This settlement is occupied by a group of al-Ramāl of Shammar.

ṬABARJAL

This is the third of the towns of al-Jawf, and it is inhabited by a number of subdivisions of al-Sharārāt, descended from Sharār bin Salmān. This tribe is to be found along the course of Wādi'l-Sirḥān, and its centre is Ṭabarjal. The tribe is also to be found in a number of other towns and villages such as al-Qurayyāt, al-Nāṣifa, al-'Īsāwiyya, al-Fayyāḍ, al-Nabk Abū Qaṣr, Maiqū', Abū 'Ajram, Dūmat al-Jandal and Sakākā.

AL-NABK ABŪ QAṢR Its inhabitants are clans of tribes of the Sharārāt.

MAIQŪ' Its inhabitants are clans of tribes of the Sharārāt.

ABŪ 'AJRAM Its inhabitants are a subdivision of the Sharārāt.

ṢAFĀN A village whose expansion is based on a settlement project: it is inhabited by a subdivision of al-Nuṣair of al-Mar'aḍ of al-Ruwala.

AL-ĀDĀRI‘ Al-Aḍāri‘ is a growing town, based on an approved settlement project and inhabited by groups of al-Ṣanūkh and al-Ghuwainim of Shammar, and al-Yamna and al-Ṭawāwiya of ‘Anaza along with other groups.

AL-RADĪFA A growing village based on an approved settlement project, inhabited by a group of al-Ramāl from Shammar.

AL-RAFĪ‘A A developing village, inhabited by some groups of al-Ramāl from Shammar.

AL-MARŪT A village inhabited by a group of al-Mar‘aḍ of al-Ruwala and others; the wells of Uwaisṭāt, al-Rughaifiyyāt and al-Zuhairiyyāt are watering places for al-Dughmān and al-Mar‘aḍ of al-Ruwala, whereas the wells of al-Sha‘īra are a watering place for some subdivisions of al-Sharārāt.

AL-‘ASSĀFIYYA This and the adjacent areas are inhabited by groups from the tribes of ‘Anaza and al-Sharārāt.

AL-MURAIR This is a watering place of al-Ruwala, used mostly by al-Fuhaiqāt and al-Ḥāzim groups.

AL-HŪJ This and the adjacent watering places are inhabited by a group made up of subdivisions of the Sharārāt.

In addition to the tribal groups in the above-mentioned towns and settlements, there are some smaller tribal groups which we list under their own names:

1. A group of roaming tribesmen is now settled in the small valleys in the eastern parts of al-Jawf. Its sub-groups are al-Banāq, al-Mājid and al-Ḥuraij. According to some of their old men, they are the Ghānim families and came originally from Najd. Some of its other sub-groups are al-Badhādhila, al-Jamīl, al-Hazīm, al-‘Anātira, al-Musailim, al-Sulaimān, and al-Sa‘d. They are found in a number of areas of al-Jawf.
2. Another such group in the province of al-Jawf has the following families: al-Darwīsh, al-‘Ajlān, al-Sharha, al-‘Alī, and al-Ḥamd.
3. Other families from the clan of Khuwaitim which originally came from the Madā’in Ṣāliḥ area trace their ancestry to ‘Antar bin Shaddād al-‘Absī and are dispersed in different parts of al-Jawf. They are: al-Rubai‘ān, al-Qa‘sā, al-Muḍ‘ān, al-Ḥuḍairī, al-Shar‘ān, al-Ghalāwīn, al-Mawāṭīn, and al-Dayādiba.

27
The Traditions of the People of al-Jawf

Perhaps the most famous and still widely observed of the traditions of the people of al-Jawf is their hospitality. In fact the Arabs of the surrounding areas refer to al-Jawf as Wādi'l-Nafākh (a misnomer for Wādi'l-Intifākh or Wādi'l- Nafkha), which means 'the Valley of Flatulence'. The metaphor implies that the people of al-Jawf entertain their guests so well that they overeat.

In the old days, of course, hospitality was more highly valued than it is today, as it required the sacrifice of meagre and hard-earned possessions. Even in times of severe shortage it demanded that the host place his guest before himself and his wife and children.

The stories that follow illustrate vividly this proud tradition.

The Seller of the Horse

The region saw two years of great scarcity during which the people suffered badly. Such hunger and despair was not unusual in the Arabian Peninsula, specially before *1350*/1930-31. One way of getting something to eat was to barter dates for grain which the bedouin brought from 'Irāq, or Balqā' in Syria. One day, some grain was brought by a bedouin to the market in Dūmat al-Jandal to be exchanged for dates or to be sold. Many townsmen gathered round the grain but had neither enough money, nor dates for the barter. In the midst of this predicament, a man named Mufaḍḍī al-'Aṭiyya rode up on a horse and asked what the matter was. The people explained their plight. This greatly touched him; he could not bear that the men should return empty-handed to expectant families and children. So Mufaḍḍī turned to the bedouin who had come with the grain and asked how much he would give him for his horse. After some haggling they reached an agreement to exchange Mufaḍḍī's horse for the grain. Mufaḍḍī then distributed the grain among the people and just walked away.

The Slaughterer of the She-Camel

A similar story is that of Muḥammad al-Ṭuraif al-Zāyid, a farmer who had a single she-camel for drawing water from a well. He depended upon her for irrigating his farm and, specifically, the date palms off which his family lived. A group of some forty bedouin from al-Ẓafīr passed by. Dismounting from their camels, they joined Muḥammad as his guests while the camel drew water from the well. He let them into his reception room, and searched around for some food with which to regale them, but found nothing except dates and water – no grain nor flour nor meat. Should he slaughter his camel, his only means of irrigating the farm and earning his family's subsistence? He reached a quick decision to do so and to offer her meat to his guests, leaving the matter of his livelihood to God, meeter of all needs. The cooked meat was soon put before the guests, who exchanged glances of wonder as to where he had secured the meat from. One of their fellows was deputed to slip out and check whether the camel was still there. The man returned with the news that Muḥammad Ṭuraif had indeed slaughtered her. Thus aware of the extent of their host's generosity, the bedouin decided to leave one of their camels with Muḥammad as a gift, each wanting his camel to be the one given. Settling upon one, they left her where she was and tried to depart. Muḥammad al-Ṭuraif refused to accept the camel, chased her out and tethered her to the caravan. But the bedouin insisted on leaving her with him, threatening to kill her and leave her carcass there. To show they meant what they had said, they raised their bows and took aim at the camel. At this Muḥammad agreed to keep her.

Next day, the bedouin brought him their best camel.

Forgiveness

The events of this story began in al-Jawf in *Sha'bān 1386*/November 1966-67 at Umm Jithjāth, near Jabal al-Ṭawīl. Two men named 'Uwayyiḍ Nājī al-'Adīlāwī and Dakhīl Allāh 'Īd Ḥumayyad al-'Azāmī al-Sharārī started fighting after a dispute over money. 'Uwayyiḍ hit Dakhīl Allāh with a stick, whereupon the latter reached for his dagger and stabbed 'Uwayyiḍ in the neck, back and abdomen. 'Uwayyiḍ died on the spot, and the murderer gave himself up to the authorities, confessing his crime.

The murdered man had a son, named Fāyil, two daughters and a wife. The judge of the Sharī'a court passed a sentence of death. According to law, when the murdered man has a minor son, the implementation of such a sentence is postponed till the boy reaches the age of majority.

When the boy reached adulthood King Khālid bin 'Abd al-'Azīz gave the final sanction for the implementation of the court's decision. The Ministry of the Interior gave its permission at the end of *Shawwāl 1401*/August 1981 for the case to proceed, authorizing the son of the murdered man to take due vengeance with the executioner's sword.

On *16 of Dhu'l-Qi'da 1401*/18 September 1981, the young man was brought to "justice square" in Sakākā after the Friday prayer, and asked formal permission to take vengeance on his father's killer. A sword was passed to him. Then in front of the large crowd he stepped out from among his uncles and the council entrusted with supervising the execution, drew the sword from the scabbard, raised it to full height and began the sway downwards to the neck of the murderer, at his feet. But at the last stage of the fatal stroke, he slowed, and finally placed the blade gently on the neck. The people were amazed, and the young man spoke forth, "I forgive you for the sake of God."

The magnanimity and hospitality of the people of al-Jawf have also been the subject of verse composed by the poets of the area.

A poet proud of his area and its traditions

The composer of the lines below is either Ghālib bin Ḥaṭṭāb al-Sarrāḥ or al-

Junaidī. He chanced to go to another area as a guest. He was a prominent man in his own area, yet to his host he was just like anyone else and was treated as such. Not receiving the attention and care which he believed he deserved, and coming from an area where generosity and hospitality prevailed, he was constrained to give vent to his hurt feelings. The following couplets, from the poem he composed on that occasion, speak for themselves:

Would that in broad daylight
  I could take down the spring of Zarqā and move it to al-Jawf

To irrigate the shady palm gardens;
  Their harvest is food for guests and wayfarers.

We [the people of al-Jawf] have slaughtered many a fat sheep for guests,
  Who feast on it alone, not crowded by a second tier.

Not like the soup of the people of al-Balqā':
  They give only trotters and anklebones to their guests.

A poet well known for his courage and generosity

Lastly, we have chosen a poem by the poet Nāṣir 'Abd al-Qādir from the 'Urūj clan, who was famous for his bravery and generosity. He tells of his delight in honouring his guest, and how sweet his tiredness is in his guest's service:

More seemly in my eyes than herding camels,
  And more seemly than the scorched desert peaks,
Is the sight of camels lined up to draw water from the well.
  Sweet to my ear is the sound of water splashing from the draw-buckets as you urge the camels on
To irrigate two hundred palms I planted by my well;
  The other hundred will follow soon.
May God help me do good deeds.
  No one is certain how the wheel of fortune will turn.
I built a house in which wayfarers find hospitality;
  I built it on the meeting point of two mounds, which everyone is aware of.
Early in the morning I bring forth my shapely coffee pots,
  With a fresh brew that can be smelled from afar,
Ready for desert travellers pressing hard their mounts;
  For four nights they have been traversing [barren tracts].
They rush at my door, swift as sparrows,
  Driven by hunger, nearly starved to death.
Sweet is the grazing of camel herds on verdant pastures;
  Camel-herds truly enjoy this life.
You see milch camels grazing with the pregnant ones:
  A beautiful sight to behold but for covetous warriors lurking behind.
Many a camel-herd's skull was blown apart,
  The bullets bringing an end to his life.
The sharp spears of raiders snatch the camels away,
  Leaving the [helpless] owners to seek refuge under the [shady] shrubs.
When rains do not fall in season,
  Farmers live on the harvest [of their palm trees].
While the bedouins seek provisions from settled folks,
  They sell their camels cheap to buy food.

APPENDIX I

Recent Development in al-Jawf Province

The sources of the information and data included in this Appendix are reports, letters and telephonic messages of the private institutions and government offices, departments and agencies. This information is available in the records of the respective bodies, and anyone wishing to delve deeper into any matter discussed here may write either direct to the concerned body or to the 'Abd al-Rahman al-Sudairi Foundation, PO Box 458, Sakaka, al-Jawf, Kingdom of Saudi Arabia.

In this section, we summarize major advances made by the Jawf region in the fields of agriculture, education and health, in the provision of physical and social infrastructure, and in otherwise raising the standard of living for all, in recent times.

Since the early 1950s, the Kingdom of Saudi Arabia has experienced rapid transformation, economic and social as well as educational. The availability of greater financial resources in the 1970s helped the country to overcome some of the development constraints faced earlier, and during the two decades to the early 1990s the pace of change gained further momentum after the Kingdom adopted a system of coordinated planning for economic and social development. The Kingdom has thus been able to establish a modern economic infrastructure and achieve major improvements in the provision of public services. The present standard of living of its citizens in most ways compares favourably with that prevailing in the developed world. Like all other parts of the Kingdom, the Jawf region – whose population at the end of 1992 was estimated to be a little above 200,000 – benefited fully from the Government's resolve to promote human welfare and social justice in the country.

AGRICULTURE

Al-Jawf has been an agricultural region from ancient times, and at present the province has a special agricultural importance on account of a number of factors, including the quality of its soil and the abundance of water.

The General Directorate of Agriculture and Water was established in al-Jawf in *1379*/1959-60 to supervise the distribution of land among the citizens and develop water resources. With its headquarters at Sakaka, it has two branches, one in Dumat al-Jandal and the other in Tabarjal.

Agricultural land in al-Jawf distributed amongst the citizens between *1392* and *1412*/February 1972 and July 1991 measures a total of 568,750 dunams (1 dunam = 1,000 sq.m.). By 1994 another 500,000 dunams of land were ready for distribution. In addition, there were 3,000 older land holdings comprising 56,000 dunams.

Al-Jawf has been cultivating date palms since antiquity, and the dates of al-Jawf are famous for their quality. Recent expansion of the land under cultivation and supportive Government measures have helped to increase the number of fruit-bearing date palms by nearly threefold in recent years to some 600,000. The number of younger non-fruit-yielding palms was calculated at 300,000 in 1993.

Of the cereals, the most important crop in al-Jawf is wheat. The area under wheat cultivation in *1404*/1984 was 140,000 dunams and the amount of wheat produced was

15,000 tons. By *1412*/1991 the yield had grown to 120,000 tons from 240,000 dunams, an eightfold increase in just seven years.

Other agricultural crops of al-Jawf are barley, olives, grapes, figs, pomegranates, apples, pears, apricots, melons, and vegetables like onions, tomatoes, marrows, pumpkins, and cucumbers, all of them showing a gradual increase in the quantity produced year after year.

A factor in persuading the bedouin to settle and turn to agriculture was the subsidies offered by the Government to those who used to frequent the Wadi'l-Sirhan. These subsidies were offered in response to suffering arising from famine, in particular during the years *1377-79*/1957-60. The amirate of al-Qurayyat, then headed by the Amir 'Abd Allah bin 'Abd al-'Aziz al-Sudairi, and that of al-Jawf followed this interim solution with a submission to King Sa'ud bin 'Abd al-'Aziz of a project to settle the bedouin in Wadi'l-Sirhan.

It was proposed that land for farming and housing be distributed among them in predetermined areas where essential services would be made available, thus inducing stable agricultural settlements. The idea was not new: the late 'Abd al-'Aziz bin Ahmad al-Sudairi, when amir of al-Qurayyat, had put a similar proposal before King Sa'ud during His Majesty's visit to the region in *1373*/1953-54, and the late King had welcomed the idea.

When the Government approved the scheme, the people responded with enthusiasm. Unfortunately, those responsible for its execution did not appreciate the importance of settling the bedouin in a limited number of places. This led to the scattering of the settlers in dozens of villages and hamlets over the whole length of the Wadi'l-Sirhan from al-Qurayyat to al-Nabk Abu Qasr, with the resulting difficulty in providing adequate services. The project thus suffered an early set-back. Then in *1392*/1972, Tabarjal was designated as the most important agricultural area in the Wadi'l-Sirhan, the purpose being to make Tabarjal the metropolis of the Wadi. Those still living in the desert flocked to this new developing settlement and to its adjoining areas and entered upon farming there with vigour and determination.

A noteworthy development in the field of agriculture in al-Jawf is the establishment of a public company named JADCO (Jawf Agricultural Development Company) in *1407*/1987. In *Rabi' I 1409*/November 1989, the Company was granted by the Government 60,000 hectares of land in the great plain of Busaita, south of Tabarjal and adjoining the Wadi'l-Sirhan on its south-western side. Since then it has made great strides towards clearing and cultivating the land. The main crops obtained are wheat and barley, of which around 15,600 tons and 17,600 tons respectively were produced in 1992. Three hundred tons of olive oil were also produced in the same year. Sixty-five thousand fruit trees had by then been planted.

The Farmers' Annual Competition

To encourage the people of al-Jawf to develop their lands, the amirate of al-Jawf has organized since *1394*/1974 an annual competition of the farmers of the region. The prizes, in cash and kind, go to the three best producers of various field crops and fruits. The prizes come from the Government and from various institutions and persons interested in encouraging the growth of agriculture in the country and the region. The value of the prizes and those in kind, distributed among the farmers, has ranged annually between 350,000 and 500,000 Saudi riyals. The occasion is an annual festival for farmers – a forum for the exchange of knowledge and experience, introducing modern practice and technology, and providing material as well as moral support to the farmers.

The Agricultural Bank

Giving someone a piece of land to cultivate is not enough to set him up as a farmer. A first-time farmer, usually short of capital, needs a large amount of money for buildings, tools, machinery, and equipment. The need for further capital can arise even when a farmer is already established. To help the farmers overcome their monetary problems, the Government runs the Agricultural Bank, a sub-branch of which was opened in al-Jawf Province in the beginning of *1385*/1965. The sub-branch was upgraded to a branch in *Jumada I 1394*/May-June 1974, with enhanced managerial and monetary powers to meet the aspirations of the farmers. A sub-branch was opened in Tabarjal in *1397*/1977. Al-Qurayyat Province is also served by a sub-branch.

The Bank also offers loans for specific agricultural projects. Thus, since 1968 the Bank has lent its support to 64 agricultural and related projects in the two provinces of al-Jawf and al-Qurayyat. Among those projects, 17 have related to poultry farming, 22 to sheep production, and 11 to wheat and fodder production. By *1412*/1992 loans granted by the Bank to the farmers of al-Jawf and al-Qurayyat had totalled some 700 million riyals.

Range and Animal Development Research Centre

The Range and Animal Development Research Centre was established at Sakaka by the Ministry of Agriculture and Water in 1982 – the first centre of its kind in the Arab Middle East. The Saudi Arabian Government commissioned the Food and Agriculture Organization of the United Nations to help establish the material facilities and provide an international staff to start it off. The foremost objective of this national-level institution is to help in developing the pastures and animal wealth of the country. Thus the Centre carries out research into the deterioration of grazing lands and into impediments to animal growth in the country as a whole, but especially in the northern region.

Its beneficial effects are already evident. For instance, the Centre has issued numerous research articles and publications, mostly dealing with issues concerning the northern region. It has established a farm for research into camels and sheep rearing, where there are now 100 camels of the four strains in the Kingdom and more than 500 sheep. Another such farm has been set up in the Tabarjal area. In the Busaita area, the Centre has established a 1600-hectare station to propagate seeds of the 14 most suitable vegetation types for the grazing lands in the region.

WATER RESOURCES

The Jawf region has abundant subsurface water resources, both in the upper layers of the ground and in the deeper aquifers. At some places in the region surface water is also available.

In the past, in some parts of Dumat al-Jandal the farms were irrigated by water obtained from the manually-dug springs, whose water was carried through surface or subsurface channels; whereas in the western parts of Dumat al-Jandal and in Sakaka and other settlements irrigation depended upon water drawn up from the wells, using animal power. In *1368*/1948-9 the Jawf region had the first engine-powered water pump installed. The first artesian well in Dumat al-Jandal was sunk in *Ramadan 1373*/1954 and was named al-Musairi'a. The second was sunk in al-Sudairiyya in Sakaka on *19 Rabi' I 1390*/25 May 1970 and proved to be the first water fountain in Sakaka from which water flew up from internal pressure. There then followed a project of the Ministry of Agriculture and Water to provide water to 23 different villages and hamlets in the region, and by *1404*/1984 24 water-supply schemes towards that end had been completed. Another four water-supply schemes (for the settlements of al-'Adhfa, al-Labba and al-Sadda, Bait and al-Nazayim) have been completed in the meantime.

Water in the Jawf region, generally, is of excellent quality, and especially that of Dumat al-Jandal, as was proven by the College of Pharmacy of King Sa'ud University in Riyadh. Hence, a water bottling plant was established in Dumat al-Jandal in 1985 under the name of Al-Jawf Water Bottling Company, the water being sold under the brand name "Hilwa". The plant produces 15.4 million litres annually, with a daily capacity of 168,000 litres.

MINERAL RESOURCES

Large recoverable deposits of phosphate, valuable as a fertilizer, have been discovered in the north-western parts of the Jawf region. The deposits near Thaniyya in the Wadi'l-Sirhan area have been estimated to be the richest in the Kingdom, and the deposits in al-Jawf and other northern parts of the country are so extensive that they place Saudi Arabia – with the total identified resources of 7,800 million tonnes – fifth in the phosphate resources worldwide. Exploration is in its early stages, and mining has yet to start.

Other industrial minerals found in the Jawf Province are clay, high-magnesium dolomite, and silica-rich sand.

ELECTRIC POWER

Electric power supply in al-Jawf started in *1389*/1969-70 with a modest scheme aimed at generating and distributing 480 kilowatts. The number of customers benefiting from this scheme reached 500 in *1395*/1975. (The term "customer" is often a building having several individual apartments, owned by a single landlord, with only one power-supply meter.) An ambitious expansion project to supply the whole Jawf region with electric power then followed. The generating capacity rose to 41.6 megawatts in *1404*/1983-4. A central 5-turbine fossil-fuel steam-electric plant, together with a transmission network, was completed in *1404*/1984-5. Tabarjal, which was not linked with the main network, got its own generating unit in *Sha'ban 1403*/June 1983. The capacity of that unit was then enhanced to 23.024 megawatts.

By the end of *Shawwal 1412*/April 1992, the generating capacity of the two power stations had reached 148.024 megawatts, serving 13,380 customers – 1,220 of them being farms.

HYDROCARBON FUELS

Saudi Aramco's marketing wing responsible, among other things, for distributing hydrocarbon fuels in the domestic market, has one of its major bulk-storage depots of petrol, diesel oil and kerosene in al-Jawf Province.

EDUCATION

The principal resource for upgrading the level of human development is education. It is not surprising, therefore, that the educational advancement of its people has been the most important component of the development effort of the Kingdom of Saudi Arabia. Ever since the unification of the country under the late King 'Abd al-'Aziz Al Sa'ud, the expansion of opportunities for free education at all levels and for all elements of society has been an accelerating process.

The modern educational system of Saudi Arabia drew extensively during its initial stages on the earlier system, whose aim was to teach the humanities "with religion at the centre". The need for secular education as a supplement to the traditional subjects was, however, soon felt, and the goal of meeting that need was pursued with determination. In order to contribute maximally towards meeting the varied human-resource needs of the country, the present educational system of the country is fully diversified (within the limits imposed by the cultural setting of the society) in respect of educational opportunities.

In al-Jawf, as in other areas of the Kingdom, children used to attend the *kuttab*, the traditional school for teaching the Qur'an and basic reading and writing. Many of those taught in schools of this type later became teachers in al-Jawf themselves, including Shafaq bin Marzuq al-Rashid, ʻAbd al-ʻAziz bin Shafaq al-Dumairi, Ahmad bin Khalifa al-Mazhur, Musallim al-Brahim al-Marran, Khalif bin Musallim al-Sattam, Manawir al-Hayis, Samir ʻUmar al-Dirʻan, Shabib bin Satm al-ʻAbd Allah al-Salih, Ibrahim ʻAbid al-Brahim al-Jabab, Muhammad bin Khalid al-Washih, ʻAbd al-Rahman bin Salaiʻ al-Marzuq al-Dirʻan and *al-Shaikh* Khalaf al-Bakhit. Many young people benefited at the hands of these *shaikhs*. The last mentioned, *al-Shaikh* Khalaf, who died in *Dhu'l-Hijja 1388*/February-March 1969, taught a large number of the people of Dumat al-Jandal. He was an excellent teacher of the Qur'an and of its learning by heart and contributed a great deal towards casting his society in the mould of the culture of Islam.

Al-Jawf witnessed the introduction of the modern system of education with the establishment of a single school of 60 pupils in Sakaka in *1362*/1943. The school had only one teacher, *al-Ustadh* Ahmad Abd al-Majid, who had come from Makkat al-Mukarrama.

As a spur to education, a proposal was submitted jointly by the amirates of al-Jawf, al-Qurayyat and Tabuk to the Government of the late King ʻAbd al-ʻAziz to grant scholarships to each of the three amirates for their students, whether bedouin or settled. The Government agreed to sanction a monthly stipend for each of the students from the desert – with a view to attracting bedouin to settle and send their children to school. This step was taken in *Safar 1369*/December 1949. The young of the region took to education with zeal, and their parents – bedouin or settled – were keen to see them admitted to schools.

The Government next constructed a large number of new schools, to fulfill educational needs Kingdom-wide. Schools in the Jawf region were initially placed under the control of al-Madina Province. Later, they were brought under the direction of the Department of Education of the Eastern Province (with its headquarters in al-Dammam). The Director of Education in that province at the time was *al-Shaikh* ʻAbd al-ʻAziz al-Turki. He took some important decisions to boost the region's provision of education, in particular in the places where the bedouin had recently settled.

An office to serve as a link between the Director's office in al-Dammam and the Jawf schools was established in al-Jawf in *1377*/1957-58. This "Central Inspection Office" was gradually upgraded: in *1380*/1960-61, to the Office of Education; then some years later, to the Supervision Office, with an independent position; and finally, in *1398*/1977-78, to the Directorate of Education.

A factor in reconciling the bedouin to the benefits of formal schooling was the hardship faced during the famine years – *1377-79*/1957-60. Large numbers turned from the nomadic life to settle in the towns and villages, where the educational needs of their children were met and the facilities taken advantage of.

The following statistics show the expansion of education in al-Jawf over an 8-year period to *1412*/1992.

Boys' schools

	1403-04/1983-84		*1411-12*/1991-92	
	No. of Schools	No. of Students	No. of Schools	No. of Students
1. Elementary Schools	70	10,923	82	17,523
2. Intermediate Schools	20	2,604	31	4,968
3. Secondary Schools	7	1,287	12	2,625
4. Teacher Training Institutes	3	41	Closed	
5. Schools for Combatting Illiteracy (adults)	28	1,468	23	1,215
6. Intermediate Night Schools	3	350	3	423
7. Secondary Night Schools	2	144	2	257

The number of Saudi teachers and other school employees in the educational year *1402-04*/1983-84 was 474, whereas non-Saudi teachers numbered 705. By the academic session *1411-12*/1991-92, the number of the former had risen to 1,372 and the latter had decreased to 610.

In order to overcome the shortage of Saudi teachers in schools, an "Intermediate College for Training of Teachers" was established in al-Jawf (at Sakaka) in the academic year *1403-04*/1983-84. The number of students – who are either working teachers or fresh secondary school-certificate holders – in the College in its first year was 235. The name of the College was changed to "The College for Teachers in al-Jawf" in *1409*/1988-89, when it started offering degree-level courses. The first group of students taking these courses completed their studies in *1412*/1992, with 124 students obtaining baccalaureate and 27 a special diploma. The total number of students in the College during the academic session *1411-12*/1991-92 was 1,200. The teachers and lecturers number 82, twelve of them being Saudi.

An institute of religious studies was established in Sakaka in *1386*/1966. It is affiliated with the Imam Muhammad bin Sa'ud University and teaches at two levels, intermediate and secondary. The number of students who obtained certificates (intermediate or secondary school) from this Institute by *1404*/1984 was 200. By the academic session *1411-12*/1991-92, this number had risen to 302. The number of teachers in the Institute is 14, five of them being Saudis. During the *1411-12* session the number of students was 210.

The Ministry of Education also runs four clinics in al-Jawf Province serving the students and teachers, and other staff of the educational community.

Girls' Schools

There has been a tremendous growth in the enrolment of girls in schools since the 1970s, notwithstanding the fact that female education on a regular basis started quite late in the Kingdom.

The first school for girls in al-Jawf started in *1382*/1962-63. Parents sent their daughters in increasing numbers, and the girls, too, were very enthusiastic: a large number from the earlier crops of students from the school completed their higher studies at universities, joined institutes for women teachers, or received training in the Nursing Institute, which was opened in Sakaka in *1402*/1981-82. The majority are now working as teachers at different levels of female education.

To raise the proportion of qualified Saudi female teachers, an intermediate college for women was opened in the *1401-02*/1980-81 academic year. In the year *1402-03*/1982-83, the number of students in the college was 150. This number had risen to 683 by the academic year *1411-12*/1991-92.

The following statistics indicate the growth of female education in the region over an 8-year period to *1412*/1992.

	1403-04/1983-84		*1411-12*/1991-92	
	No. of Schools	No. of Students	No. of Schools	No. of Students
1. Elementary Schools	43	5,882	47	10,374
2. Intermediate Schools	14	2,400	19	3,260
3. Secondary Schools	6	785	7	1,634
4. Schools for Combatting Illiteracy (adults)	21	566	8	452

In *1403-04*/1983-84 there were 405 Saudi female teachers at all levels, and 315 non-Saudi teachers. By *1411-12*/1991-92 the figures were 923 and 286 respectively.

The education of women is segregated at all levels. A separate Directorate of Female Education, with a subordinate branch at Dumat al-Jandal, oversees the girls' schools and women's colleges in the region. The Directorate also runs a clinic to serve the female students, teachers and other staff of the female educational institutions.

Kindergartens

To care for the starting education of very young children, a kindergarten was established in Sakaka by the people on a cooperative basis in *1391*/1971. Beginning with 67 toddlers, the number had risen to 320 by *1403-04*/1983-84. In *Muharram 1407*/September 1986, the 'Abd al-Rahman al-Sudairi Foundation opened a kindergarten at Sakaka as part of its cultural programme for the area. In the academic year *1412-13*/1992-93, the number of children in the Foundation's kindergarten was 80, while their lady teachers numbered four. In *1409*/1988-89, a kindergarten was opened in Qara by the Jam'iyyat al-Birr al-Khairiyya, a welfare society with its headquarters at Sakaka (see below). The Society also took over the control of the kindergarten of Sakaka (the one established on a cooperative basis) in the same year. The Jam'iyyat al-Birr al-Khairiyya opened another kindergarten in Sakaka in *1411*/1990-91. The total number of children in the three kindergartens of the Jam'iyya is at present about 450, their trained female teachers and other staff numbering 37.

Three kindergartens work under the Centre for Community Development (of Dumat al-Jandal), described below. The first, established in *1398*/1977-78 is at Dumat al-Jandal, with 203 children and ten female teachers. The second, established in *1402*/1981-82, was at Tabarjal, the number of children and their lady teachers being 67 and three, respectively. The third, at al-Adari', established in *1412*/1992, has 25 children and one mistress.

The Ministry of Education launched two new kindergartens, one each at Sakaka and Dumat al-Jandal, for the children of the teaching community, during the 1992-93 academic year.

One man who played a prominent role in serving the cause of religious education and preparing a large number of young men of the Jawf Province in accordance with the tenets of Islam was *al-Shaikh* Faisal bin 'Abd al-'Aziz bin Mubarak. His arrival at Sakaka as the Qadi (judge) of al-Jawf in *1362*/1943 had a profound effect on the educational and cultural emphasis. For, besides playing his role as a judge and leading a model life, *Shaikh* Faisal devoted much of his time and energy to teaching. He did this in the Market Mosque, constructed through his initiative, with residential facilities for poor students. *Shaikh* Faisal used this mosque for calling people to God. He would sit there every day after the afternoon prayer to teach the Holy Qu'ran and its *tahfiz* (commitment to memory) to a large number of students, many of whom, after completing their courses, would emulate the *Shaikh* and teach other groups in different parts of the mosque. After the sunset prayer he would have a session in his house for teaching the Prophet's (P.B.U.H.) sayings and traditions and their explanation. From morning till noon he would adjudge legal cases and give advisory opinions on religious matters at his house. After the noon prayer he would sit in the mosque with advanced pupils and scholars to guide them in their study of books on the life of the Prophet (P.B.U.H.) and the Unity of God. As if all this was not enough, he found some time in the early morning to teach the fundamentals of the Islamic law of inheritance to children before they went to school. After the evening prayer the same students would again come to the mosque to learn from him the fundamentals of Arabic grammar.

The *Shaikh* was deeply learned in religious studies, especially in the interpretation of the Qu'ran, and in *hadith*, jurisprudence and matters relating to belief. He wrote a number of books of acknowledged merit on these topics.

The school of *Shaikh* Faisal established at the mosque continued to function after this wise, generous and pious man died in *Dhu'l-Qi'da 1376*/June 1957, leaving neither money nor even a house in any of the nine regions of the Kingdom where he had served as a judge. On his death one of the main streets of Sakaka was named Faisal Road in his memory. The mosque he had built was also named after him.

Technical education and vocational training

Technical education and vocational training in the Kingdom are the responsibility of the General Organization for Technical Education and Vocational Training, which opened its "Vocational Training Centre" at Sakaka in *Rajab 1391*/August 1971 and has since qualified thousands of students. In the beginning only four trades were offered by the Centre as the courses of study. At present the Centre has training programmes at the secondary-school level in ten different fields, which are:

1. Motor-vehicle technology
2. General electricity
3. General masonry
4. General building construction
5. (Automobile) Bodywork repair
6. Metalwork and welding
7. Refrigeration and air-conditioning
8. General machine-work
9. Basics of radio and television
10. Vocational guidance.

In addition to its regular morning programmes, the Centre offers evening programmes for government employees.

HEALTH

All public-sector medical services are free, and are funded by the Central Government, highly attentive to the health of the nation, and especially to primary health care.

The first modern clinic in al-Jawf Province started working in Sakaka in *1356*/1937. It gradually evolved into the present 310-bed al-Amir 'Abd al-Rahman bin Ahmad al-Sudairi Central Hospital. Equipped with the most modern facilities, the hospital now has 76 physicians and surgeons, 46 of them specialists in specific branches of medicine or surgery. In addition, three other government hospitals are working in the region. The first is at Dumat al-Jandal with 39 beds and 17 doctors, 10 of them specialists. The second is at Tabarjal, opened in the beginning of *1406*/1985, with 71 beds. It has 23 doctors, 13 of them specialists. The third is the 100-bed "Mental-Health Hospital" at Sakaka, established in *Safar 1404*/November-December 1983. The number of doctors in it is nine, three of them psychiatrists.

Mention should be made here of the sole private-sector hospital in al-Jawf at present. This is the 100-bed al-Muwaishir Hospital at Sakaka, established in *Dhu'l-Hijja 1410*/July 1990.

To complement the services given by the hospitals, there are 32 public sector clinics, or primary health centres, some of them in various villages in the region and some in the three towns. These clinics work under the control of the hospitals in their areas.

There are five private-sector clinics in the region, four of them in Sakaka and one in Dumat al-Jandal.

All clinics in the region are part of an integrated referral system and play a vital part not only on the curative side but also in the preventive field.

Two auxiliary institutions in the region extend help, in their respective fields, to the hospitals and clinics of the area. These are the Anti-Malaria Station, opened in *1381*/1961-62, and the Anti-Bilharziasis Station founded in *Rajab 1394*/July 1974. These stations have brought about a marked decline in the incidence of these diseases.

The position of the Health Office in al-Jawf, established in *1394*/1974, was raised to the level of a directorate in *1406*/1985-86. This directorate is responsible for all administrative affairs relating to health. In addition, there is a medical board, comprised of doctors, to attend to all matters requiring expert medical opinion or certification.

There are two medical institutes in the region to train paramedical staff. The first of them, opened in *1400*/1979-80, is for women; the second, for men, was inaugurated in *1404*/1983-84. The present trainees in each of the institutes number 111 and 183 respectively. The number of teachers in the institute for women is 17, and in that for men, 19.

MUNICIPAL AND RURAL AFFAIRS

The Government attaches great importance to the provision of municipal services to all areas of the Kingdom. In al-Jawf, the first municipality was established in Sakaka in *1376*/1956-57, whereas the second was set up in Dumat al-Jandal in *1394*/1974-75. Later on, Tabarjal too was given municipal status. Each plays its role in such fields as spatial planning, safeguarding the environment, and public hygiene.

In early days priority was given to urban centres, with rural areas lagging behind. Urban-rural disparity had next to be addressed. The provision of basic municipal and other services to groups of adjacent villages from a central location was introduced. Such a group of settlements is called a "village cluster" (*al-Mujamma' al-Qarawi*) – such as that set up in *1399*/1978-79, with its headquarters in Qara. Depending on their location, other villages fall under the municipal care of the nearest town.

Here is a listing of village groupings:

A: *Qara Village Cluster*

1. Qara
2. al-Tuwair
3. Zallum
4. Suwair
5. al-Shuwaihitiyya
6. Sulaimaniyya
7. Khaw'a
8. Hudaib
9. al-Fayyad
10. al-Nazayim
11. al-Rafi'a
12. al-Hadban
13. al-'Ammariyya
14. 'Adhfa
15. al-Murair
16. Mughaira

B: *Villages affiliated to the Municipality of Dumat al-Jandal*

1. al-Adari'
2. al-Radifa
3. Abu 'Ajram
4. Maiqu'
5. Safan
6. al-Shaqiq
7. al-'Assafiyya
8. Muwaisin
9. Thaniyya Umm Nakhila

C: *Villages affiliated to the Municipality of Tabarjal*

1. al-Nabk Abu Qasr
2. al-Nabbaj
3. Subaiha
4. al-Jarawi
5. Shighar
6. Shaiba
7. al-Fayyad al-Gharbiyya
8. Sudai'

COMMUNITY AFFAIRS

The policy of the Government of Saudi Arabia in regard to community development is to "help the people help themselves". It encourages the formation of cooperatives by which the community pools its resources for social and economic development. Hence the establishment of community-development centres in various parts of the country. In al-Jawf, Dumat al-Jandal was chosen as the place for this purpose. There are three self-help cooperative societies in the Province. The following is an account of the Centre and the three societies.

The Centre for Community Development at Dumat al-Jandal was established in *Dhu'l-Hijja 1397*/November 1977 in response to the needs of the people of Dumat al-Jandal and the nearby villages. In addition to its normal functions, the Centre runs three kindergartens, and has a family welfare section and a section devoted to encouraging gifted children. Each of its various sections works under the Ministry concerned with the respective activity, whereas the Centre itself falls under the Deputy Ministry of Social Affairs.

The Centre supervises three cooperative societies that have been formed in the Province.

The Multi-purpose Cooperative Society is an agricultural cooperative society, with its headquarters at Sakaka, established in *Rabi' I 1386*/July 1966. At present it has 1,122 members. The activities of this society are as follows:

i. Marketing and lending agricultural tools, machinery and equipment, and providing their assembly and maintenance services.
ii. Collecting and marketing agricultural produce.
iii. Marketing fertilizers, pesticides, seeds, and animal feed, and the fuels and lubricants needed for agricultural machinery.
iv. Breeding chickens for meat and eggs.
v. Supplying the date-palm saplings of the best breeds.

The Tabarjal Agricultural Society was formed in *Jumada I 1409*/December 1988. It has at present 443 members, and its share capital is 1,371,800 riyals. Its aims are similar to those of the preceding society, with its sphere of activity restricted to the Tabarjal area.

The Cooperative Society for Preventive Medicine and Treatment was established at Sakaka in *Safar 1393*/March 1973, with a share capital of 109,900 riyals, the purpose being to meet some of the health needs of the citizens. Its main objectives are to supply medicines and medical equipment as well as infant food. It runs a clinic and pharmacy at Sakaka.

WELFARE

In the Kingdom of Saudi Arabia, most of the work for public welfare is done by government departments and agencies. With its free education at all levels, free medical care, free homes for the old and the mentally handicapped, free residential nurseries for orphans, and a number of facilities for the physically handicapped, Saudi Arabia is indeed one of the first-rank welfare states in the world. However, every government has its own vision of the future of the society and its own limitations and priorities, and there is always room for those who want to work independently for the well-being of others. The two main non-governmental welfare institutions working in al-Jawf Province are the 'Abd al-Rahman al-Sudairi Foundation and the Jam'iyyat al-Birr al-Khairiyya (the Charitable Society).

The 'Abd al-Rahman al-Sudairi Foundation

The 'Abd al-Rahman al-Sudairi Foundation was established by virtue of the Royal Order No. A/442, dated *9 Ramadan 1403*/20 June 1983. The origins of the Foundation can be traced back to *1383*/1963, when the author of this work established a small public library at Sakaka for the benefit of the general public. With the passage of time, the library needs of the area grew, and the author was able, with the support of His Majesty King Fahd bin 'Abd al-'Aziz Al Sa'ud, to have a new, purpose-built edifice constructed for the Library, which would also fill the role of cultural centre for the area. Simultaneously, it was felt that running a complex of this size required a permanent source of income and a standing corporate body as its parent body. That is how the idea of the Foundation materialized. An endowment for the Foundation was established by the author. The financing of the Foundation's activities is secured by the profits from the endowment – invested partly in al-Jawf, so as to contribute to its economic growth – as well as from donations from a number of generous persons from al-Jawf and outside. The Foundation works under the voluntary direction of members of the author's family.

The principal object of the Foundation is to manage and finance the public library, Dar al-Jawf lil-'Ulum, an account of which is given below in the section on public libraries and museums. In addition, the following objectives were envisaged at the time of the Foundation's inception:

i. To contribute towards preserving the archaeological, literary and other heritage of al-Jawf Province.
ii. To support studies and disseminate information about the area.
iii. To publish a monthly periodical on topics of interest to the people of the area and the country.
iv. To build at Sakaka a mosque, a hospital and a kindergarten.
v. To organize each year – in cooperation with the amirate of al-Jawf – a festival week for al-Jawf (The Jawf week) during which a camel race, an exhibition of handmade carpets from the region and the Farmers' Annual Competition take place.

Several of these objectives have been realized: to help preserve the local heritage, a museum has been set up by the Foundation (see below); a kindergarten was established by the Foundation in *Muharram 1407*/September 1986 (see above); a periodical (entitled *al-Jawba*) was started in *Jumada I 1411*/November 1990 and is being regularly published, though on a semi-annual basis at present; the mosque (al-Rahmaniyya Mosque) has been recently completed; and lastly, "the Jawf week", initiated by the author in *1385*/1965, has been revived after remaining suspended for some years. It was last held in October 1994 under the auspices of the Foundation.

Over the years, the Foundation has been expanding the scope of its activities as needs are perceived. It has been organizing English-language classes, Arabic-language classes (for expatriates), computer-training classes for men as well as women, and Qur'anic lessons for children. In addition to the kindergarten mentioned above, it now runs three elementary schools, for boys, for girls, and for the children of the expatriate community using English as the medium.

The author anticipates the Jawf of the future receiving ever increasing benefits from the Foundation.

Jam'iyyat al-Birr al-Khairiyya

Jam'iyyat al-Birr al-Khairiyya (the Charitable Society) was established in *1405*/1984-85 by charitably-minded persons from among the people of al-Jawf. This Society, with Amir Sultan bin 'Abd al-Rahman al-Sudairi, Governor of al-Jawf, as its president, has its headquarters at Sakaka and branches at Dumat al-Jandal and Tabarjal. Its activities are directed towards the welfare of hundreds of needy families in al-Jawf Province. The Society gives them assistance in the form of cash and in kind on a recurrent basis till their circumstances improve. In addition, the Society actively contributes to the educational and cultural development of the local community. It runs three kindergartens (see above) and, with the cooperation of the local Directorate of Education, two institutions of special education for the handicapped, one for boys and the other for girls. A centre for the welfare of handicapped children is also being set up by the Society.

Youth Welfare Services

The Government sees the welfare of youth calling for more than formal education. Several Ministries contribute towards assisting the young in cultural and sporting activities. For instance, the Ministry of Education provides sporting facilities in schools and encourages boy scouting. The Ministry of Municipalities and Rural Affairs provides recreational facilities in its park. The Ministry of Labour and Social Affairs has its own programmes for the purpose, including those in the fields of arts, culture and sports. Specifically, the General Presidency for Youth Welfare is charged with this area of responsibility. The Presidency opened its Head Office for Youth Welfare in al-Jawf in *1394*/1974-75 to serve the needs of the whole northern region. There are eight clubs working in the northern areas under the supervision of that office. These are:

1. The Qal'a (Citadel) Club, Sakaka
2. The 'Uruba (Arabism) Club, Sakaka
3. The Jandal Club, Dumat al-Jandal
4. The Badana Club, 'Ar'ar
5. The Masira Club, al-Qurayyat
6. The Samud Club, Turaif
7. The Tadamun (Solidarity) Club, Rafha
8. The Intilaq (Start) Club, Qara.

Through these clubs the Office gives direction to all its sporting, educational, cultural and social programmes for youth. These clubs have played a prominent role in providing healthy outlets for the energies of the young people of the country and in developing their personalities.

The complete complex of the 'Uruba Club was built by the Presidency in *1403*/1982-83, modelled on the most modern of the clubs in the Kingdom. This complex, built at a cost of 150 million riyals, comprises playgrounds (including a football ground) and their appurtenances, the administrative offices of the Club, a gymnasium, and a swimming pool.

PUBLIC LIBRARIES AND MUSEUMS

There are at present three public libraries in al-Jawf, including Dar al-Jawf lil-'Ulum (the library in Sakaka run by the 'Abd al-Rahman al-Sudairi Foundation), described below in some detail. There is a public library in Sakaka established by the Ministry of Education in *1397*/1977. At present its book collection numbers 22,000, and there are 23 journals on the subscription list of the Library. It opens from 7.30 a.m. to 2.30 p.m and from 4.00 p.m to 9.00 p.m.

Another library is the public library in Dumat al-Jandal, named after His Royal Highness al-Amir Turki bin 'Abd al-'Aziz Al Sa'ud, who opened it in *Sha'ban 1402*/June 1982. This library is also run by the Ministry of Education and has a collection of 10,630 volumes. It acquires 18 journals on a regular basis and opens from 7.30 a.m to 2.30 p.m. and from 4.00 p.m. to 11.00 p.m. It is hoped that in the near future the third town, Tabarjal, will also acquire its own public library and that library services will be extended to the villages of the Province through a mobile public library.

Dar al-Jawf lil-'Ulum

Dar al-Jawf lil-'Ulum is the public library funded and managed by the 'Abd al-Rahman al-Sudairi Foundation. As stated earlier in the account of the Foundation, this library developed out of a small public library established by the author in 1963. Its present building, to which the Library was shifted in the beginning of 1984, was completed with the Government's financial grant sanctioned by His Majesty King Fahd bin 'Abd al-'Aziz. This two-storey building, with a 2,350 square metre floor base, is located in a beautifully landscaped 34,368 square metre compound and forms the chief constituent of the Foundation's complex. A 268-seat auditorium juts out from the middle of the front of this rectangular structure which the building essentially comprises.

Dar al-Jawf lil-'Ulum (literally, al-Jawf's House for Knowledge), with a capacity of 200,000 volumes, consists of two adjoining libraries, mirror images of each other, one for men and the other for women, the latter being the first of its kind in the Kingdom. The stock of the Library, which includes books, rare books, manuscripts (original or facsimile), photographs, stamps, films, microreproductions, etc., now exceeds 60,000 items, 12 per cent of them in languages other than Arabic. A special collection on the Arabian Peninsula, with emphasis on the local history, has been created by the Library to help scholars and researchers. At present the Library subscribes to 150 journals. Another hundred or so serial titles, including governmental reports, are received free. The Library holds complete bound files of back issues of some important periodicals. It has a dictionary card catalogue (complete computerization of the catalogue is under way), and its collections have been organized according to the *Dewey Decimal Classification* and the latest *Anglo-American Cataloguing Rules*.

To manage the Library more efficiently and to give better service to its readers, modern techniques for information storage, processing and transfer – like computers, databases, photocopies, facsimile transmission, etc. – are fully used in the Library. The Library is connected online with the KACST (King 'Abd al-'Aziz City for Science and Technology in Riyadh) reference database, which is linked to a large number of databases in the western world. This facility is of special significance, making the Library a regional resource centre and opening new opportunities. To provide library services to young readers, there is a separate children's library annexe with its own collection.

The Library opens for nine hours in two shifts on all week days except Fridays.

The Library frequently organizes lectures, seminars, conferences, meetings, and other such activities at its auditorium.

Dar al-Jawf lil-'Ulum is an active cultural force in the life of the community. To meet the varied demands made on it, it has professional staff with a high degree of technical skill and a great sense of dedication.

The reading room of Dār al-Jawf lil-'Ulūm: the Foundation's public library in Sakākā.

Hand-woven rugs from al-Jawf.

Museum of Antiquities and Folk Heritage

This museum at Dumat al-Jandal is one of the six museums established by the Department of Antiquities and Museums of the Ministry of Education in different parts of the Kingdom. Dumat al-Jandal was chosen as one of the sites in view of the archaeological importance of al-Jawf generally, and Dumat al-Jandal especially. The Museum was completed in *1412*/1992 at a cost of 19 million riyals. It comprises exhibition halls, a branch for conservation and storage of artifacts, a photography branch, a survey and drawing branch, a library, and a film-projection hall. The collection, ranging from the Stone Age to the present day, includes stone tools, pottery and pottery sherds, coins and other metallic objects, inscribed stones, and objects of daily use from folk heritage, all relating to or recovered from al-Jawf Province.

'Abd al-Rahman al-Sudairi Foundation Museum

This museum was established in 1984 in the basement of the Foundation's public library, Dar al-Jawf lil-'Ulum, at Sakaka. The basic collection came from the author's valuable personal collection of antiques, objects of folk heritage, and locally-handcrafted carpets. Augmented by gifts from other people, the collection has been steadily growing over the years and now includes coins, and stones with pre-Islamic and Arabic inscriptions. This collection is expected to be relocated in the new hotel-cum-museum (AL-NUSL) that the Foundation has established in Sakaka.

COMMUNICATIONS

Roads

Roads are an important part of the physical infrastructure, which is a prerequisite for the creation of an industrialized economy. A directorate of roads was established in the Province by the Ministry of Communications in *1400*/1979-80. In the following 12 years, 1,500 km. of unpaved roads were asphalted under the supervision of this directorate. The region is now well provided with paved roads.

The interregional roads link the Province in three directions: north-east to 'Ar'ar on the Tapline road; south-west to Tabuk by a road which divides into two at al-Qaliba, one leading west to Tabuk and the other south-south-east to Taima' and then southward to al-Madinat al-Munawwara; and to the west-north-west, via the road running through the Wadi'l-Sirhan (often called the gateway to Arabia) to al-Qurayyat and onwards to Jordan and Syria.

At present no direct southward road links al-Jawf to central Saudi Arabia, though a road is anticipated between al-Jawf and Ha'il. This will traverse the dunes of the great Nafud, following almost the same route by which the 19th-century European travellers to Arabia toiled between those two sites. The Ha'il-Jubba section of this proposed road is already functioning. When completed, the road will be one of the most important arteries in Saudi Arabia, since it will provide connection, via the shortest possible route, between the central parts of the country and its northern and north-western parts as well as Jordan and Syria.

In addition to the major roads, many smaller intra-provincial roads in al-Jawf link the villages. Then there are still smaller roads leading to important agricultural areas and farms.

The towns of the region are now served by the interregional public transport system operated by the Saudi Public Transport Company. It is now possible for anyone to travel by air-conditioned buses to other parts of the Kingdom.

Air links

The present airport of al-Jawf lies equidistant from the towns of Sakaka and Dumat al-Jandal on a vast high plain near the northern edge of al-Nafud desert. It was inaugurated in *1397*/1977 by HRH Prince Turki bin 'Abd al-'Aziz Al Sa'ud. In 1994 the number of incoming and outgoing domestic flights (of Saudia Airlines) at the "Jouf" airport was 49 per week. In *1401*/1981 62,200 passengers were handled by the airport. By *1410*/1990 this number had risen to 96,900, comparing favourably with the national average of a yearly increase of 1.49 per cent during the same period. In the same nine years the amount of cargo consigned through the airport increased from 192 tons to 474 tons yearly, the national annual average increase being 9.83 per cent.

Telephone, telegraph and telex services

The telephone service has improved substantially in the Province during recent years. There are six telephone exchanges in the region, with a capacity of 20,200 lines, the central exchange for the whole northern region being at Dumat al-Jandal, with a capacity of 1,320 trunk lines. The following breakdown for 1994 fills out the picture:

Place	*Available Lines*	*Assigned Lines*
Sakaka	11,430	9,314
Dumat al-Jandal	3,891	2,475
Tabarjal	950	946
Qara	1,946	1,475
al-Nabk Abu Qasr	973	117

There are 48 coin- or card-operated telephone booths installed in different towns and villages of the region. Car telephone service is now being used by 27 subscribers.

In addition, there are five telegraph centres in the region, one each at Sakaka, Dumat al-Jandal, Tabarjal, Thaniyya Umm Nakhila, and 'Assafiyya. Telex services are available at Sakaka, Dumat al-Jandal and Tabarjal.

BANKING SERVICES

In view of the expanding economic and commercial activity in the region and the consequent growth in the demand for banking, stocks and shares, and currency exchange services, several Saudi Arabian banks have opened their branches in the towns and villages of the Province to provide a wide range of banking services. In order of the dates of their opening, they are as follows:

1. Riyad Bank
2. Al-Rajhi Banking and Investment Corporation
3. National Commercial Bank
4. Saudi French Bank
5. Arab National Bank.

Mention should be made here of the Jawf branch of a very different kind of bank, the Saudi Credit Bank, established by the Government of Saudi Arabia for the welfare of the citizens. This branch, at Sakaka, was opened in *Rajab 1397*/June 1977 and serves the people of al-Jawf and the Province of the Northern Borders, giving loans for the purposes of marriage, house repair, and establishing a trade. In the 15 years from its inception, the branch had advanced loans worth 123.2 million riyals to 8,036 persons.

Another similar noteworthy institution is the Real Estate Development Fund, established in *1394*/1974. The Fund extends loans for the construction of houses, office buildings, and business and commercial shops, markets and complexes. It has thus contributed to the welfare and security of the citizens and the upgrading of their standards of living. By the end of *1413*/middle of 1993 the local branch of the Fund had granted loans amounting to 2,103.77 million riyals to 8,364 persons from al-Jawf Province.

The services of the Agricultural Bank in al-Jawf Province are described above (see *Agriculture*).

The Jawf Chamber of Commerce and Industry

As commercial and industrial activity grew, the local business community, in *1405*/1984-85, formed the Jawf Chamber of Commerce and Industry, with a view to promoting their common interests. Ten years on, it had 1,147 firms and individuals as members. In *1409*/1988-89, a branch of the Chamber was opened in Tabarjal, the business community of which forms a little more than 16 per cent of the total membership.

APPENDIX II

Facsimiles of the Documents Relating to the Turkish Occupation of al-Jawf, 1872-73

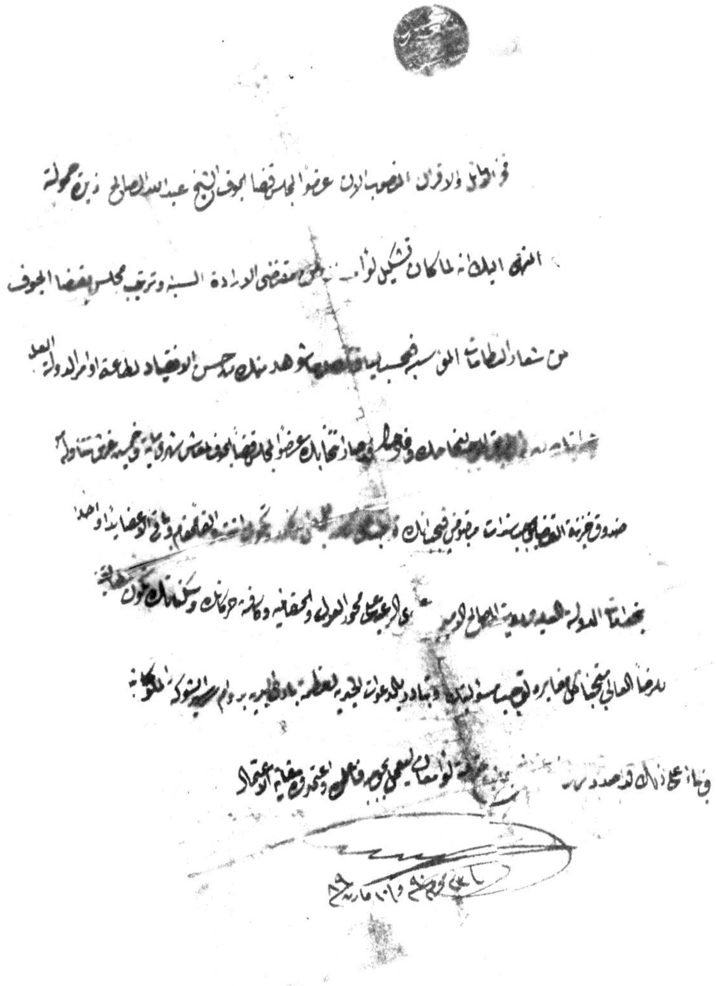

Document 1
Fragment of a letter of appointment (dated *22.1.1290*/22.3.1873) of al-Shaikh 'Abd Allāh Ṣāliḥ as member of the Administrative Council of al-Jawf.

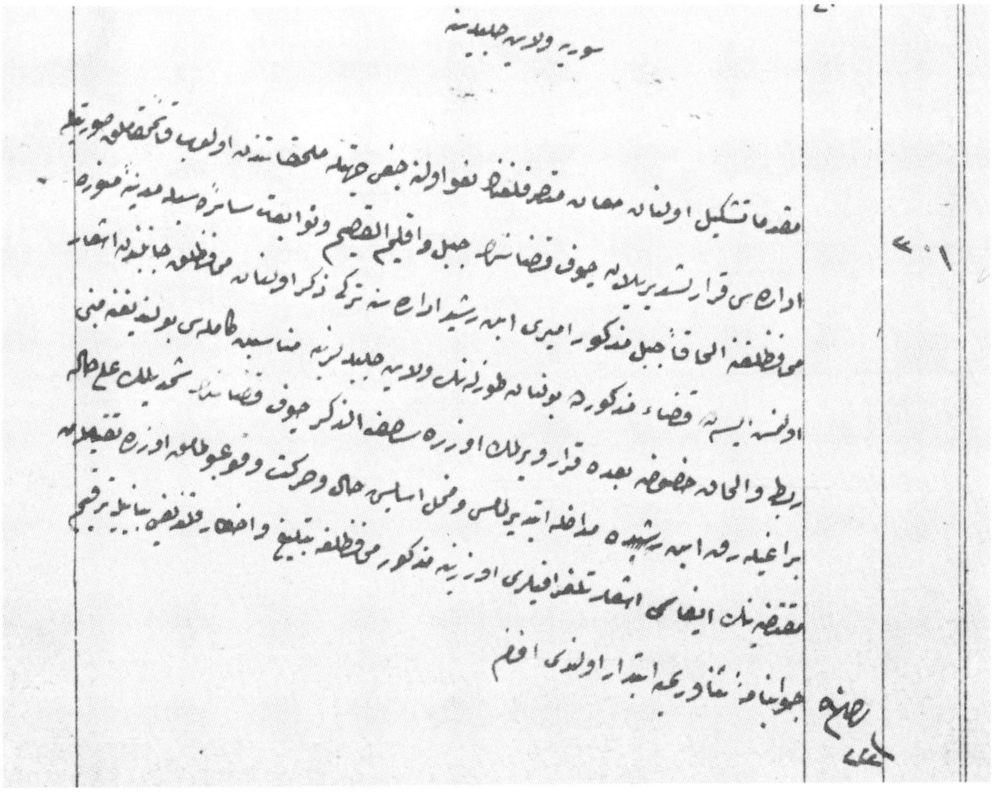

Document 2
Letter, dated *23.3.1290*/21.5.1873, to the Province of Syria.

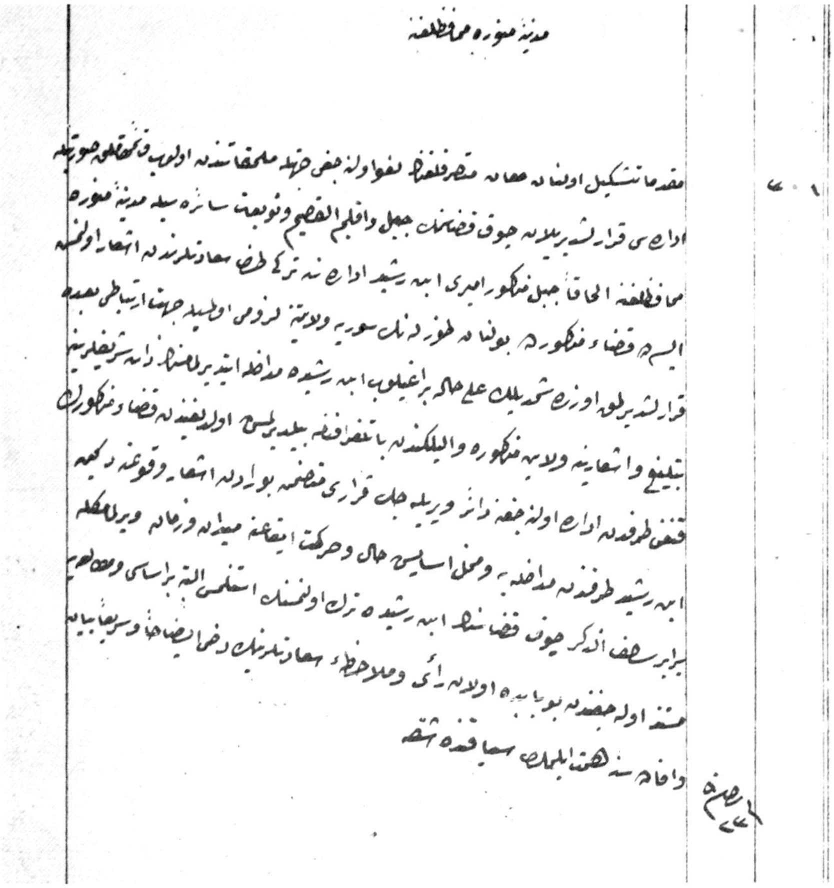

Document 3
Letter, dated *23.3.1290*/21.5.1873, to the Province of al-Madīnat al-Munawwara.

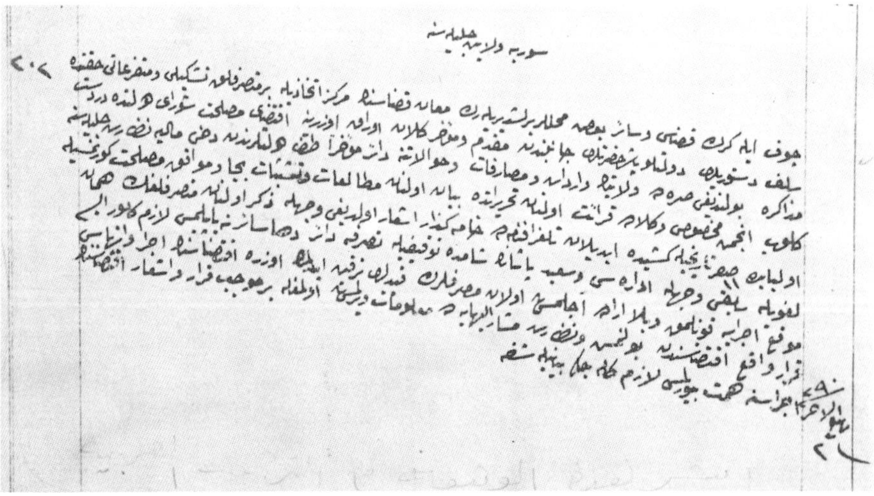

Document 4
Letter, dated *2.4.1290*/30.5.1873, to the Province of Syria.

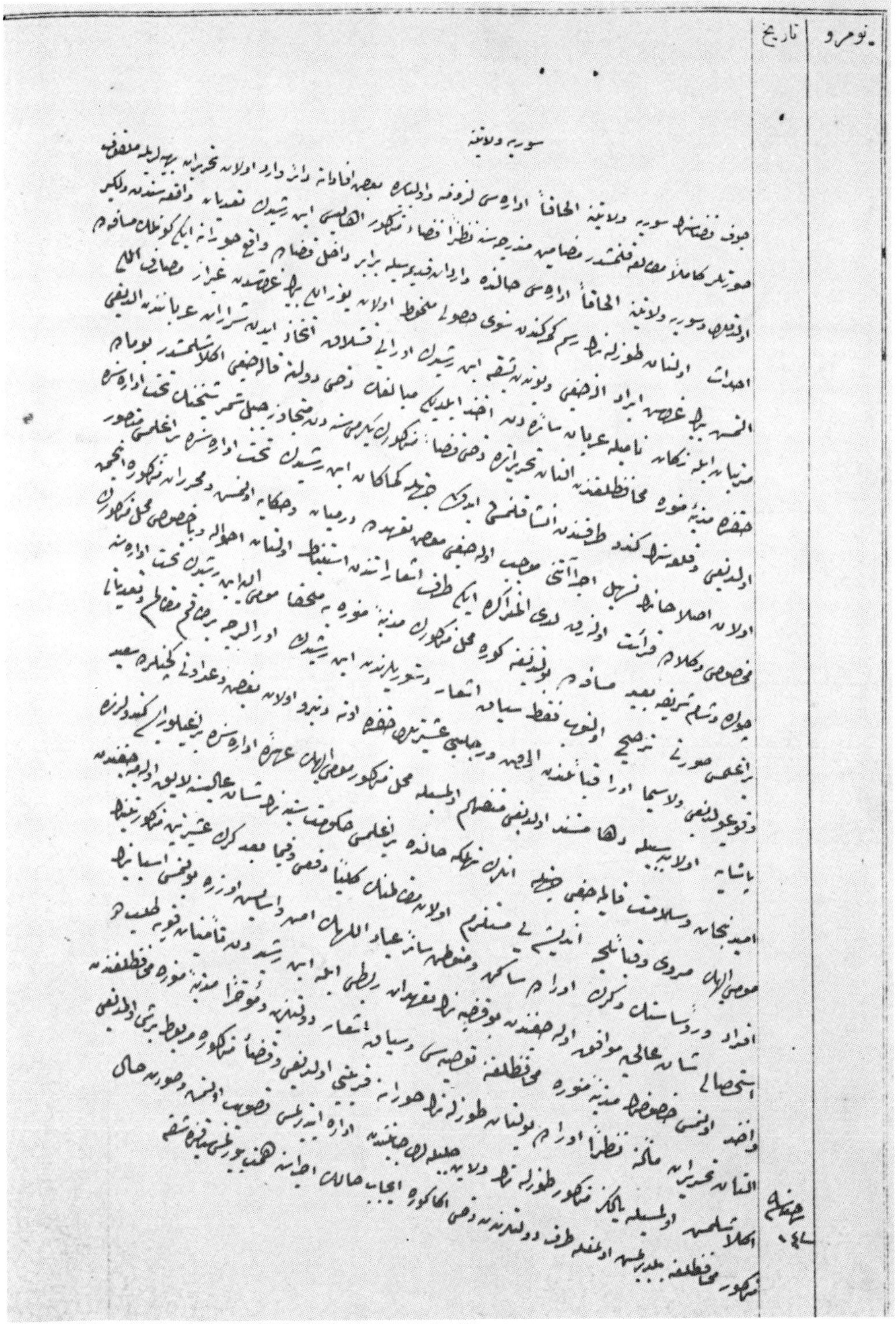
نومرو | تاریخ

سوریه ولایتنه

Document 5
Letter, dated *14.7.1290*/7.9.1873, to the Province of Syria.

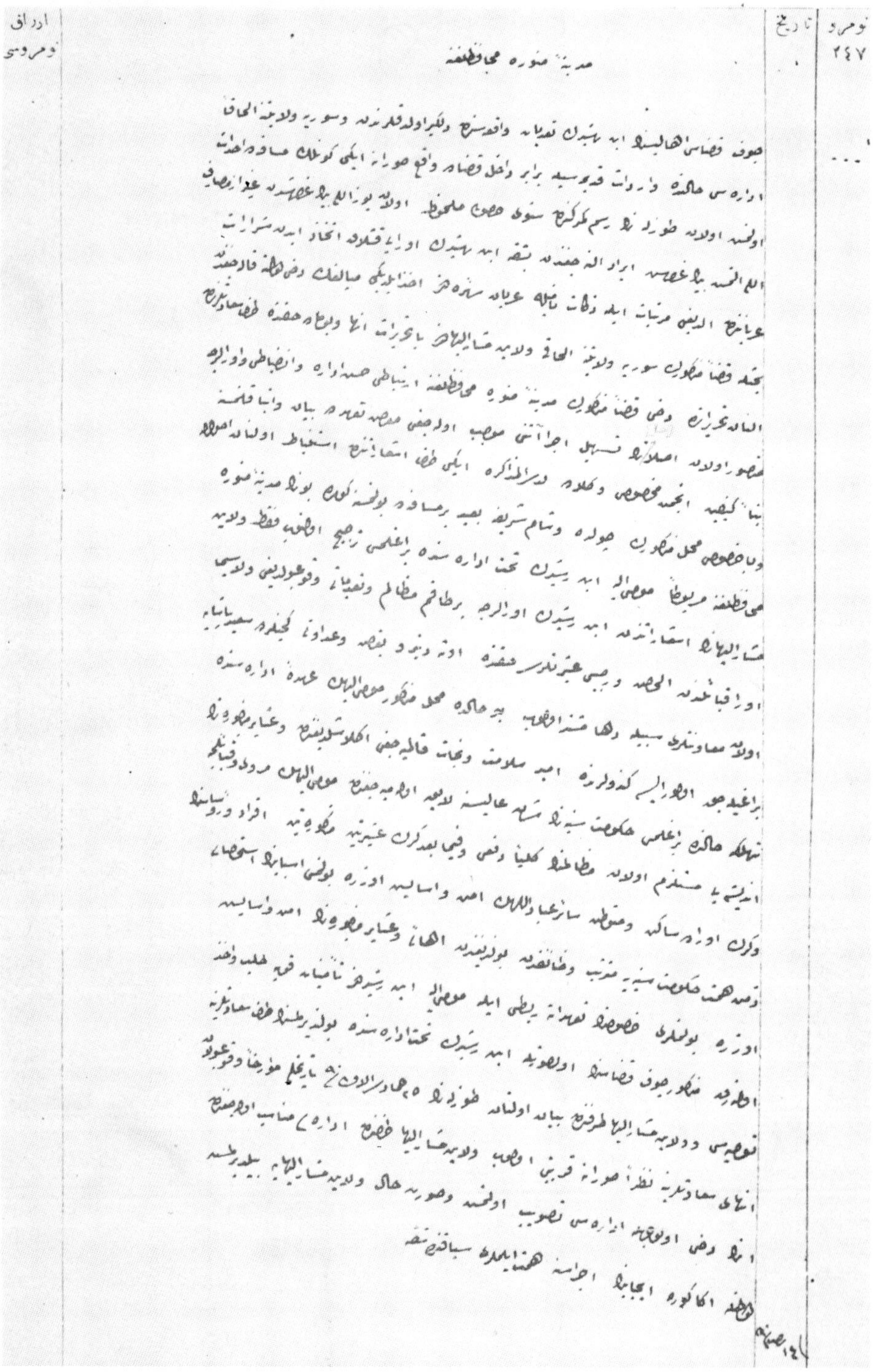

نومرو ۲۴۷

تاریخ

اوراق نومروسی

مدینهٔ منوره محافظتنه

Document 6
Letter, dated *14.7.1290*/7.9.1873, to the Province of al-Madīnat al-Munawwara.

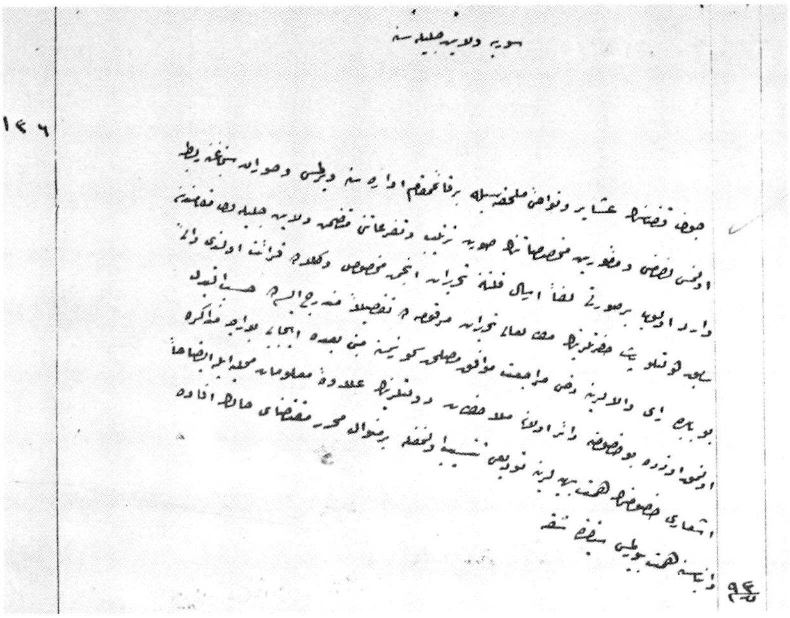

Document 7
Letter, dated *12.9.1293*/12.10.1876, to the Province of Syria.

Document 8
Letter, dated *1.12.1290*/31.1.1874, to the Province of al-Madīnat al-Munawwara.

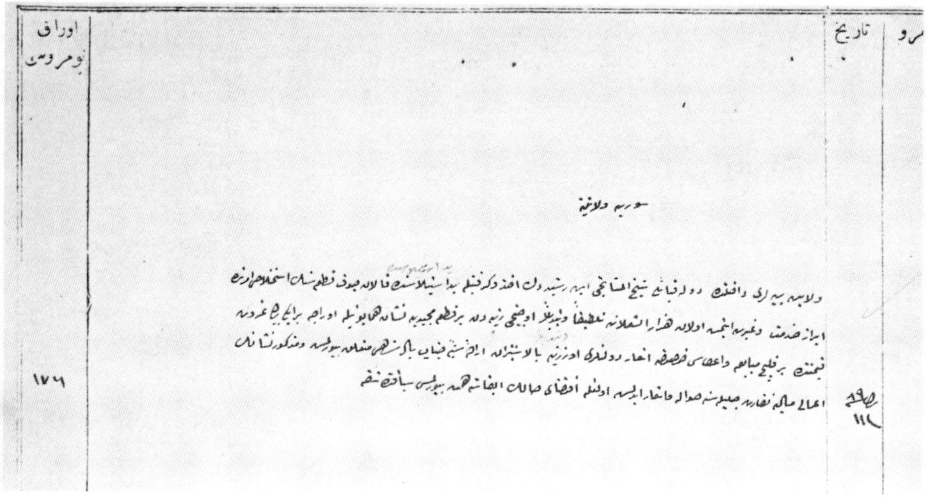

Document 9
The document relating to the reward to be given to Hazzā‘ al-Sha‘lān.

APPENDIX III

Dates of the Establishment of the Government Departments, Institutions, etc. in al-Jawf Province

Name of Body	Year of Establishment
(Bodies whose names are followed by the word "al-Jawf" are located in Sakākā.)	
1. Amirate of al-Jawf	*1341*/1922-23
2. Department of Wireless, al-Jawf	*1349*/1930-31
3. Department of Finance, al-Jawf	*1349*/1930-31
4. Department of Customs, al-Jawf	*1349*/1930-31
5. Telegraph Office, al-Jawf	*1349*/1930-31
6. Directorate of Police, al-Jawf	*1362*/1943
7. Sharī'a Court, al-Jawf	*1362*/1943
8. Passports Office, al-Jawf	*1375*/1955-56
9. Municipality of Sakākā	*1376*/1956-57
10. Centre for Social Care and Education, al-Jawf (for orphans and other underpriviliged children)	*1376*/1956-57
11. Directorate of Education, al-Jawf	*1377*/1957-58
12. Religious Trusts (Awqāf) Office, al-Jawf	*1378*/1958-59
13. Organization for the Promotion of Good and the Suppression of Evil, al-Jawf	*1378*/1958-59
14. Organization for the Promotion of Good and the Suppression of Evil, Dūmat al-Jandal	*1378*/1958-59
15. Directorate of Agriculture and Water, al-Jawf	*1379*/1959-60
16. Malaria Eradication Station, al-Jawf	*1381*/1961-62
17. Social Security Office, al-Jawf	*1382*/1962-63
18. Agricultural Bank, al-Jawf	*1384*/1964-65
19. Civil Defence, al-Jawf	*1384*/1964-65
20. Sharī'a Court, Dūmat al-Jandal	*1384*/1964-65
21. Branch of the Directorate of Agriculture and Water, Dūmat al-Jandal	*1385*/1965-66
22. Institute for Religious Sciences, al-Jawf	*1386*/1966-67
23. Directorate of Girls' Education	*1389*/1969-70
24. General Establishment for Electricity	*1390*/1970-71
25. Central Hospital, al-Jawf (Renamed in *1410*/ 1990 as Amīr 'Abd al-Raḥmān bin Aḥmad al-Sudairī Central Hospital at Sakākā)	*1391*/1971-72
26. Centre for Vocational Training, al-Jawf	*1391*/1971-72
27. Directorates of Posts; al-Jawf and Dūmat al-Jandal	*1393*/1973-74
28. Secret Service	*1393*/1973-74
29. Civil Defence, Dūmat al-Jandal	*1393*/1973-74

Name of Body	Year of Establishment
30. Post Office, al-Jawf	*1393*/1973-74
31. Directorate of Prisons, al-Jawf	*1393*/1973-74
32. Traffic Police, al-Jawf	*1393*/1973-74
33. Investigation Police, al-Jawf	*1394*/1974-75
34. Health Office, al-Jawf	*1394*/1974-75
35. Labour Office, al-Jawf	*1394*/1974-75
36. Municipality of Dūmat al-Jandal	*1394*/1974-75
37. Sharī'a Court, Ṭabarjal	*1394*/1974-75
38. Directorate of Telegrams and Telex, al-Jawf	*1395*/1975-76
39. Branch of the Ministry of Trade, al-Jawf	*1395*/1975-76
40. Directorate of Police, Ṭabarjal	*1395*/1975-76
41. Branch of the Ministry of Public Works	*1396*/1976
42. Sa'ūdī Arabian Red Crescent Society	*1396*/1976
43. Branch of the Civil Service Bureau	*1396*/1976
44. Centre for Social Care, al-Jawf (for the elderly and disabled people)	*1396*/1976
45. Agricultural Bank, Ṭabarjal	*1397*/1976-77
46. Centre for Community Development, Dūmat al-Jandal	*1397*/1976-77
47. Directorate of Posts	*1397*/1976-77
48. Emergency and Patrols Police, al-Jawf	*1397*/1976-77
49. Civil Affairs Office, al-Jawf	*1397*/1976-77
50. Directorate of Police, Dūmat al-Jandal	*1397*/1976-77
51. Sa'ūdī Credit Bank	*1397*/1976-77
52. Social Security Office, Ṭabarjal	*1397*/1976-77
53. Branch of the Directorate of Agriculture and Water, Ṭabarjal	*1398*/1977-78
54. Anti-Narcotics Department, al-Jawf	*1398*/1977-78
55. Emergency Force, al-Jawf	*1398*/1977-78
56. General Directorate for Municipal and Rural Affairs, Northern Region	*1398*/1977-78
57. General Organization for Petroleum and Minerals	*1398*/1977-78
58. Saudia Airlines Office, al-Jawf	*1398*/1977-78
59. Saudia Airlines Office, Dūmat al-Jandal	*1398*/1977-78
60. Branch of the Ministry of Justice, al-Jawf	*1399*/1978-79
61. Directorate of Sa'ūdī Telephone, al-Jawf	*1399*/1978-79
62. Department of Traffic, Ṭabarjal	*1399*/1978-79
63. Rural Council (Village Cluster), Qārā	*1399*/1978-79
64. Television Station, al-Jawf	*1399*/1978-79
65. Directorate of Roads, al-Jawf	*1400*/1979-80
66. Range and Animal Development Research Centre, al-Jawf	*1402-03*/1982
67. Branch of the Bureau of General Supervision	*1403*/1983
68. Chamber of Commerce and Industry, al-Jawf	*1405*/1984-85
69. Directorate of Health Affairs	*1406*/1985-86

APPENDIX IV

Quarters of Dūmat al-Jandal as Described by Georg Augustus Wallin

Georg Augustus Wallin, the first European traveller to visit al-Jawf, in *1261*/1845, discusses the history and other features of the town of Dūmat al-Jandal at length.[1] Among other things, he describes the different divisions – which he calls quarters or "sooks" – of the town.[2] The following is a summary of his description of each of the twelve quarters which Dūmat al-Jandal comprised at the time of his visit:

1st quarter: al-Gharb. This quarter had six subdivisions, namely ʻAshwān, Ibn Ḥaṣīnī, Ṣināʻ al-Marʻī, al-Jafriyya, ʻAin Umm Sālim, and Ibn Qaʻayyid. These subdivisions were near to each other and were situated in the north-western end of the valley. They had a population of about a hundred families, mostly from a Shammarī tribe, Ḥamūlat al-Manāṣiba. The greater part of these families lived in the Ibn Qaʻayyid (which was the principal *sūq* of this quarter), al-Jafriyya, and Ibn Ḥaṣīnī subdivisions. The residents of al-ʻAshwān were all from the Ruwala tribe originally, whereas those of the ʻAin Umm Sālim subdivision were from the Sirḥān tribe. The people living in the Ṣināʻ al-Marʻī were artisans from Syria and Arabia who had taken up residence in the town. It seemed to Wallin that the Gharb quarter was one of the more recent quarters of the town.

2nd quarter: al-Dirʻ, or Sūq Ibn al-Dirʻ. This was the oldest part of the town, with a total of about 130 families. Many houses in this *sūq* were constructed of hewn square stones like those used in the Qaṣr Mārid and the ʻUmar bin al-Khaṭṭāb mosque. It was said that the largest section of the population of this quarter had come from Shaqrā' in Najd. "Beni Der are mentioned by [Carl] Ritter (Erdk. xii. 347) as inhabitants of a valley in the Agâ chain called Hafl, who perhaps may be regarded as the ancestors of the present inhabitants of this 'sook'." Wallin suggests that they may have moved from there, taking "the most convenient, and still generally used, route over Alkasîm to the two mountains of Tay, and from thence continued their way over Gubbé up to Algawf". Certain families of a more ancient race which claimed to have originated in Jubba, described themselves as al-Qarārīṭ. Wallin supposed that the "Karârît" of al-Jawf mentioned in *al-Qāmūs* as "Kuroot" [Qurūṭ] were from the Kalb tribe. Wallin correctly recalled that the Kalb tribe used to live in this area and probably in Jubba, too, where a quarter was still known in Wallin's day as "Sook Alkilab". Wallin related that when he later visited Jubba, people informed him that the Qarārīṭ of al-Jawf still had ancient texts; however he makes it clear that he did not hear this from the people of al-Jawf.

According to Wallin there were three springs in al-Dirʻ: al-Kubrā, Bard Zubaida, and ʻAin al-Jamal.

3rd quarter: Sūq al-Saʻīdiyyīn or al-Sarrāḥ was occupied by five tribes, al-Saʻīdiyyīn, al-ʻUmar, al-ʻAbbās, al-Salmān and al-Ḥabūb, about 120 families in all. This was supposed to be the oldest quarter after al-Dirʻ.

4th quarter: al-Ruḥaibiyyūn had 70 families, said to be from the village of Ruḥaiba in Syria, which Wallin says was between Ḥawrān and Nabk. This quarter contained a spring of running water called al-'Arūs.

5th quarter: al-'Ilāj was made up of 40 families, who had originated in al-Ṭafīla.

6th quarter: Khadhmā', named after a spring in the centre of this quarter. About 60 families were living here, originally from Wādi'l-Sirḥān.

7th quarter: al-Dalhamiyya. Originally a small quarter of nearly 20 families, of the same origin as the families in al-Sarrāḥ.

In addition to the above seven quarters described by Wallin as forming a semi-circle, there were five other smaller quarters:

8th quarter: al-Qarāṭīn. This was in the western area of the valley. Two families were recorded by Wallin as residing there, allied with the people of al-Gharb.

9th quarter: al-Wādī which had eight families, allied with al-Dir'.

10th quarter: Ghuṭṭī. This had two families allied with al-Sarrāḥ.

11th quarter: al-Sa'īdān had a palm plantation owned by a single family living in Khadhmā'.

12th quarter: al-Jar'āwī. This quarter contained four families, who came from Jubba and traced their descent to al-Ramāl, one of the tribes of Shammar.

---

1. Wallin, pp.25-44.
2. Ibid., pp.27-30.

Selected Bibliography

The author and the ʻAbd al-Raḥmān al-Sudairī Foundation are grateful to the authors and publishers of the books listed below whose works have been quoted, and are particularly indebted to those marked with an asterisk for permission to make use of copyright material.

ʻAbd al-Raḥīm, ʻAbd al-Raḥīm ʻAbd al-Raḥmān. *al-Dawlat al-Saʻūdiyyat al-Ūlā, 1745-1818 C.E./1158-1233 A.H.* Cairo, Maʻhad al-Buḥūth wa'l-Dirāsāt al-ʻArabiyya, 1975.

*Adams, McC.; Parr, Peter J.; Ibrāhīm, Muhammad; and Mughannum, ʻAlī S. "Saudi Arabian Archaeological Reconnaissance 1976: The Preliminary Report on the First Phase of the Comprehensive Archaeological Survey Program." *Atlal: The Journal of Saudi Arabian Archaeology*, vol. 1, *1397*/1977, pp. 21-40 and plates 1-19.

Abū ʻAliyya, ʻAbd al-Fattāḥ Ḥasan. *al-Dawlat al-Saʻūdiyyat al-Thāniyya, 1256-1309 A.H./1840-1891 C.E.* Riyadh, Dār al-Marrīkh, *1405*/1985.

Allan, Mia. *Palgrave of Arabia: The Life of William Gifford Palgrave, 1826-88.* London, Macmillan, 1972.

al-Ansary, A.R. *Qaryat al-Fau: A Portrait of Pre-Islamic Civilization in Saudi Arabia.* London, Croom Helm, 1982.

al-Balādhurī, Aḥmad bin Yaḥyā. *Futūḥ al-Buldān.* Edited by Ṣalāḥ al-Dīn al-Munajjid. 3 pts. Cairo, Maktabat al-Nahḍat al-Miṣriyya, 1956-57.

Bell, Gertrude. *The Letters of Gertrude Bell.* Selected and edited by Lady Bell; with an introduction by Jan Morris. Harmondsworth, England, Penguin Books, 1987.

Bidwell, Robin. *Travellers in Arabia.* London, 1976.

Bindaqjī, Ḥusain Ḥamza. *Jughrāfiyyat al-Mamlakat al-ʻArabiyyat al-Saʻūdiyya.* 3rd ed. Jeddah, The Author, *1401*/1981.

Blunt, Lady Anne. *A Pilgrimage to Negd, the Cradle of the Arab Race.* 2 vols. London, John Murray, 1881. Reprint ed., London, Frank Cass, 1968.

*Bowersock, G.W. *Roman Arabia.* Cambridge, Harvard University Press, 1983.

Brent, Peter. *Far Arabia: Explorers of the Myth.* London, Weidenfeld & Nicolson, 1977.

*Butler, S.S. "Baghdad to Damascus viâ el Jauf, Northern Arabia." *The Geographical Journal*, vol. 33, May 1909, pp. 517-35.

Carruthers, Douglas. *Arabian Adventure: To the Great Nafud in Quest of the Oryx.* London, 1935.

al-Dayel, Khaled Abdulaziz. "Excavations at Dumat al-Jandal, Second Season, *1406*/1986." *Atlal: The Journal of Saudi Arabian Archaeology*, vol. 11, *1409*/1988, pp.37-46 and plates 28-42.

al-Dayel, Khaled Abdulaziz, and al-Shadukhi, Abdulaziz. "Excavations at Dumat al-Jandal *1405*/1985." *Atlal: The Journal of Saudi Arabian Archaeology*, vol. 10, *1406*/1986, pp.64-79 and plates 73-85.

Doughty, Charles M. *Travels in Arabia Deserta.* 2 vols. Cambridge, Cambridge University Press, 1881.

**Encyclopaedia of Islam*, New ed.

S.v. "ʻAlī b. Abī Ṭālib", by L. Veccia Vaglieri.

S.v. "al-ʻArab", by A. Grohmann.

S.v. "Djawf", by M. Quint.

S.v. "al-Djawf", by J. Mandaville.

S.v. "[Djazīrat] al-ʻArab", by G. Rentz.

S.v. "Dūmat al-Djandal", by L. Veccia Vaglieri.

Euting, Julius. *Tagbuch einer Reise in Inner-Arabien.* 2 vols. Leiden, Brill, 1896-1914.

Forder, Archibald. *Ventures among the Arabs in Desert, Tent, and Town*. Boston, W.N. Hartshorn, 1905.

Freeth, Zahra, and Winstone, H.V.F. *Explorers of Arabia from the Renaissance to the End of the Victorian Era*. London, Allen & Unwin, 1978.

*Guarmani, Carlo. *Northern Najd: A Journey from Jerusalem to Anaiza in Qasim*. Translated from the Italian by Lady Capel-Cure, with introduction and notes by Douglas Carruthers. London, Argonaut Press, 1938.

*Ḥamd al-Jāsir. *Fī Shimāl Gharb al-Jazīra*. Riyadh, Dār al-Yamāma, *1390*/1970.

*Ḥamd al-Jāsir. *al-Mu'jam al-Jughrāfī li-Bilād al-'Arabiyyat al-Sa'ūdiyya: Shimāl al-Mamlaka*. 3 vols. Riyadh, Dār al-Yamāma, *1397*/1977.

al-Hamdānī, al-Ḥasan bin Aḥmad bin Ya'qūb. *Ṣifat Jazīrat al-'Arab*. Edited by Muḥammad bin 'Alī al-Akwa' al-Ḥawālī. Riyadh, Dār al-Yamāma, *1394*/1974.

Haykal, Muḥammad Ḥusayn. *The Life of Muḥammad*. Translated by Ismā'īl Rāgī A. al-Fārūqī. n.p., North American Trust Publications, 1976.

*Hitti, Philip K. *History of the Arabs*. 10th ed. London, Macmillan, 1970.

Hogarth, David George. *The Penetration of Arabia*. London, 1904. Reprint ed., Beirut, 1966.

Holt, A.L. "The Future of the North Arabian Desert." *The Geographical Journal*, vol. 62, October 1923, pp. 259-71.

Huber, Charles. *Journal d'un Voyage en Arabie (1883-84)*. Paris, Société Asiatique, 1891.

Ibn al-Athīr, 'Alī bin Muḥammad. *al-Kāmil fi'l Tārīkh*. 10 vols. Beirut, Dār al-Kitāb al-'Arabī, 1983.

Ibn Bishr, 'Uthmān bin 'Abd Allāh. *'Unwān al-Majd fī Tārīkh Najd*. 2 vols. Riyadh, Maṭābi' al-Qaṣīm, *1385*/1965-66.

Ibn Ḥajar al-'Asqalānī, Aḥmad bin 'Alī. *al-Iṣāba fī Tamyīz al-Ṣaḥāba*. 4 vols. Cairo, Maṭba'at al-Sa'āda, *1328*/1910.

Ibn Ḥazm, 'Alī bin Aḥmad. *Jamharat Ansāb al-'Arab*. Edited by 'Abd al-Salām Muḥammad Hārūn. Cairo, Dār al-Ma'ārif, 1977.

Ibn Hishām, 'Abd al-Malik. *al-Sīrat al-Nabawiyya*. Edited by Muṣṭafā al-Saqqā, Ibrāhīm al-Abyārī and 'Abd al-Ḥafīẓ Shalabī. 2 vols. Cairo, Muṣṭafā al-Bābī al-Ḥalabī, 1955.

Ibn Khaldūn, 'Abd al-Raḥmān bin Muḥammad. *Tārīkh Ibn Khaldūn*. 7 vols. Būlāq, Egypt, *1284*/1867.

Ibn Qayyim al-Jawziyya, Muḥammad bin Abī Bakr. *Zād al-Ma'ād fī Hady Khair al-'Ibād*. Edited by Shu'aib al-Arna'ūṭ and 'Abd al-Qādir al-Arna'ūṭ. 5 vols. Beirut, Mu'assasat al-Risāla, 1979.

Ibn Sa'd al-Zuhrī, Muḥammad. *al-Ṭabaqāt al-Kubrā*. 9 vols. Beirut, Dār Ṣādir, 1957-58.

Ibrāhīm bin Ṣāliḥ bin 'Īsā. *Tārīkh Ba'ḍ al-Ḥawādith al-Wāqi'a fī Najd. . . .* Riyadh, Dār al-Yamāma, *1386*/1966.

*Ingraham, Michael Lloyd; Johnson, Theodore D.; Rihani, Baseem; and Shatla, Ibrahim. "Saudi Arabian Comprehensive Survey Program: c. Preliminary Report on a Reconnaissance Survey of the Northwestern Province (with a Note on a Brief Survey of the Northern Province)." *Atlal: The Journal of Saudi Arabian Archaeology*, vol. 5, *1401*/1981, pp. 59-84 and plates 65-97.

al-Jāḥiẓ, 'Amr bin Baḥr, *al-Bayān wa'l-Tabyīn*. Edited by 'Abd al-Salām Hārūn. 4 vols. in 2. Cairo, Maktabat al-Khānjī, *1395*/1975.

*Jawād 'Alī. *al-Mufaṣṣal fī Tārīkh al-'Arab qabl al-Islām*. 10 vols. Beirut, Dār al-'Ilm lil-Malāyīn, 1976-78.

Kaḥḥāla, 'Umar Riḍā. *Mu'jam Qabā'il al-'Arab al-Qadīma wa'l- Ḥadītha*. 5 vols. Beirut, Mu'assasat al-Risāla, *1402*/1982.

al-Kalbī, Hishām bin Muḥammad bin al-Sā'ib. *Kitāb al-Aṣnām*. Edited by Aḥmad Zakī Bāshā. 2nd ed. Cairo, Dār al-Kutub al-Miṣriyya, 1925.

*Khan, Majeed; al-Kabawi, Abdulrehman; and al-Zahrani, Abdulrehman. "Preliminary Report on the Second Phase of Comprehensive Rock Art and Epigraphic Survey of the

Northern Province *1405*/1985." *Atlal: The Journal of Saudi Arabian Archaeology*, vol. 10, *1406*/1986, pp. 82-93 and plates 86-93.

King, Geoffrey. *The Historical Mosques of Saudi Arabia*. London, Longman, 1986.

King, Geoffrey. "A Mosque Attributed to 'Umar b. al-Khaṭṭāb in Dūmat al-Jandal in al-Jawf, Saudi Arabia." *Journal of the Royal Asiatic Society*, 1978, pp.109-23.

Lawrence, T.E. *Seven Pillars of Wisdom: A Triumph*. London, Jonathan Cape, 1935.

Leachman, G.E. "A Journey in North-eastern Arabia." *The Geographical Journal*, vol. 37, March 1911, pp. 265-74.

Lorimer, J.G. *Gazetteer of the Persian Gulf, Oman and Central Arabia*. 2 vols. in 6. Calcutta, India, Government Printing House, 1908. Reprint ed., Farnborough, England, Gregg International, 1970.

al-Maidānī, Aḥmad bin Muḥammad al-Nīsābūrī. *Majma' al-Amthāl*. Edited by Muḥammad Muḥyi'l-Dīn 'Abd al-Ḥamīd. 2 vols. Cairo, Dār al-Fikr, 1972.

al-Maqdisī, Muḥammad bin Aḥmad. *Aḥsan al-Taqāsīm fī Ma'rifat al-Aqālīm*. 2nd. ed. Edited by M.J. De Goeje. Leiden, Brill, 1906. Reprint ed., Beirut, Maktabat al-Khayyāṭ, n.d.

al-Mārik, Fahd. *Min Shiyam al-'Arab*. 4 vols. Beirut, al-Maktabat al-Ahliyya, 1963-65.

al-Mas'ūdī, 'Alī bin al-Ḥusain bin 'Alī. *Kitāb al-Tanbīh wa'l-Ishrāf*. Edited by M.J. de Goeje. Leiden, 1894. Reprint ed., Beirut, Maktabat al-Khayyāṭ, 1965.

al-Mas'ūdī, 'Alī bin al-Ḥusain bin 'Alī. *Murūj al-Dhahab wa Ma'ādin al-Jawhar = Les Prairies d'Or*. Edited, and translated into French by C. Barbier de Meynard and Pavet de Courteille. 9 vols. Paris, Société Asiatique, 1861-77.

*al-Muaikel, Khaleel Ibrahim. "A Critical Study of the Archaeology of the Jawf Region of Saudi Arabia with Additional Material on its History and Early Islamic Epigraphy." 2 vols. Ph.D. dissertation, University of Durham, 1988.

Muntakhabāt min al-Shi'r al-Nabaṭī li Ashhar al-Shu'arā' Najd. n.p., n.d.

*Musil, Alois. *Arabia Deserta: A Topographical Itinerary*. New York, American Geographical Society of New York, 1927.

Musil, Alois. *Northern Neǧd: A Topographical Itinerary*. New York, American Geographical Society of New York, 1928.

Nasir, Sari J. *The Arabs and the English*. London, Longman, 1976.

Nolde, Baron Eduard. *Reise nach Innerarabien, Kurdistan und Armenien 1892*. Brunswick, Friedrich Vieweg, 1895.

Palgrave, William Gifford. *Narrative of a Year's Journey through Central and Eastern Arabia (1862-63)*. 3rd ed. 2 vols. London, Macmillan, 1866.

*Parr, Peter J.; Zarins, Juris; Ibrāhīm, Muhammad; Waechter, John; Garrard, Andrew; Clarke, Christopher; Bidmead, Martin; and al-Badr, Hamad. "Preliminary Report on the Second Phase of the Northern Province Survey *1397*/1977." *Atlal: The Journal of Saudi Arabian Archaeology*, vol.2, *1398*/1978, pp. 29-50 and plates 19-45.

*Philby, H.St.J.B. "Jauf and the North Arabian Desert." *The Goegraphical Journal*, vol. 62, October 1923, pp. 241-59.

Philby, H. St.J. B. *Saudi Arabia*. London, Ernest Benn, 1955.

al-Rashid, Saad A. *Darb Zubaydah: The Pilgrim Road from Kufa to Mecca*. Riyadh, Riyadh University Libraries, 1980.

*Sa'd bin 'Abd Allāh bin Junaidal. *Bilād al-Jawf, aw, Dūmat al-Jandal*. Riyadh, Dār al-Yamāma, *1401*/1981.

Sadleir, George Forster. *Diary of a Journey across Arabia (1819)*. Cambridge, England, Falcon Oleander, 1977.

Seetzen, U.J. "Beytrage zur Geographie Arabiens." *Monatliche Correspondenz zur Beförderung der Erd-und Himmels-kunde*, vol. 46, November 1808, pp. 386-88.

al-Sharīf, 'Abd al-Raḥmān Ṣādiq, *Jughrāfiyyat al-Mamlakat al-'Arabiyyat al-Sa'ūdiyya*. 2 vols. Riyadh, Dār al-Marrīkh, *1404*/1984.

Speidel, M.P. "The Roman Army in Arabia." *Aufsteig und Niedergang der romischen Welt*, no. 2.8, 1977, pp. 687-730.

al-Ṭabarī, Muḥammad Ibn Jarīr . *Tārīkh al-Rusul wa'l-Mulūk*. Edited by M.J. De Goeje and others. 4 vols. in 15. Leiden, 1879. Reprint ed., Beirut, Maktabat al-Khayyāṭ, 1965.

Troeller, Gary. *The Birth of Saudi Arabia: Britain and the Rise of the House of Sa'ud*. London, Frank Cass, 1976.

*al-'Uthaimīn, 'Abd Allāh Ṣāliḥ. *Nash'at Imārat Āl Rashīd*. Riyadh, Riyadh University Libraries, *1401*/1981.

Wallin, Georg Augustus. *Travels in Arabia (1845 and 1848)*. Cambridge, England, Falcon Oleander, 1979.

al-Wāqidī, Muḥammad bin 'Umar. *Kitāb al-Maghāzī*. Edited by Marsden Jones. 3 vols. London, Oxford University Press, 1966.

Ward, Philip. *Ha'il: Oasis City of Saudi Arabia*. Cambridge, England, Oleander Press, 1983.

*Watt, W. Montgomery. *Muḥammad: Prophet and Statesman*. New York, Oxford University Press, 1977.

*Whalen, Norman M.; Ali, Jamaludein S.; Sindi, Hassan O.; and Pease, David W. "A Lower Pleistocene Site Near Shuwayhitiyah in Northern Saudi Arabia." *Atlal: The Journal of Saudi Arabian Archaeology*, vol. 10, *1406*/1986, pp. 94-101 and plates 94-100.

*Whalen, Norman M.; Davis, Wilbon P.; and Pease, David W. "Early Pleistocene Migrations into Saudi Arabia." *Atlal: The Journal of Saudi Arabian Archaeology*, vol. 12, *1410*/1989, pp. 59-75 and plates 43-45.

Winder, R. Bayly. *Saudi Arabia in the Nineteenth Century*. London, Macmillan, 1965.

*Winnett, F.V., and Reed, W.L. *Ancient Records from North Arabia*. Toronto, University of Toronto Press, 1970.

Winstone, H.V.F. *Captain Shakespear: A Portrait*. London, Jonathan Cape, 1976.

Winstone, H.V.F. *The Illicit Adventure: The Story of Political and Military Intelligence in the Middle East from 1898 to 1926*. London, Jonathan Cape, 1982.

Wüstenfeld, Ferdinand. *Register zu den genealogischen tabellen der Arabischen stamme und familien. . . .* Osnabruck, Otto Zeller, 1853. Reprint ed., 1966, S.v. "Kalb ben Wabara".

Yāqūt al-Ḥamawī. *Mu'jam al-Buldān*. 5 vols. Beirut, Dār Ṣādir, 1955-57.

*Zarins, Juris. "The Prehistory of the Jowf-Sakaka Area." 1977. Al-Sudairī Foundation MSS.

*Zarins, Juris. "Rajājīl: A Unique Arabian Site from the Fourth Millennium B.C." *Atlal: The Journal of Saudi Arabian Archaeology*, vol. 3, *1399*/1979, pp. 73-77.

INDEX

Notes: 1. Numbers in *italics* refer to illustrations; 2. In the context of the inhabitants of the Jawf Province, the branches, clans and families of larger tribes are indexed collectively under the tribe's name where identified. Where not identified, they are collectively indexed under *clans and families*; 3. Dieties and idols are collectively indexed under this phrase. 4. Of the authors quoted or cited and named in the text, modern authorities are not indexed, nor are the narrators of the earlier authors.; 5. Al in the beginning and al- and its variants have been ignored in alphabetizing. Names beginning Banu and wadi (except for Wadi'l-Sirhan) have been inverted